# Locomotives of the
# Great Central Railway

The post-1912 era wrought some of J.G.Robinson's finest work, yielding designs that could hold their own with anything of comparable size. Without doubt, Robinson's best passenger engines were the two classes of 'Director' 4–4–0, 11E and 11F, introduced in 1913 and 1919 respectively. Here, at Guide Bridge, No.508 PRINCE OF WALES an 11F from 1922, waits with a down express.

ISBN 871608 27 9

# Locomotives of the

# Great Central Railway

*Volume Two :– 1912 to British Railways*

**by**

**E.M.Johnson**

Published by
IRWELL PRESS
3 Durley Avenue, Pinner, Middlesex, HA5 1JQ
Printed by Amadeus Press Ltd, Huddersfield

# VALOUR

IN MEMORY OF

## G. C. R. EMPLOYEES

WHO GAVE THEIR LIVES FOR THEIR COUNTRY

1914 — 1918

# Contents

*Unless otherwise stated, all photographs contained in this volume are
from the authors collection.*

# Foreword

It had been intended to conclude the first volume of this work with a review of the first of Robinson's celebrated 'Director' class locomotives. Pressure of space on Volume 1 led me away from that particular path with the result you see here: a survey of the Great Central locomotive classes built from 1913 onwards. In the initial stages of planning it became apparent that to give anything like a comprehensive coverage of what was undoubtedly Robinson's best work it would be necessary to re–design the framework in which the work was first conceived.

Several reasons quickly became manifest: the last of the second Directors came out in LNER livery, with the final 9Q (B7) engines appearing in the early years of the LNER. Other factors conspired. Even the first 9Qs did only a bare eighteen months in traffic in Great Central guise. The massive and solid–looking 9P (B3) design did legendary work on the Great Northern main line out of King's Cross from 1923–27; so to have limited the outlines to the Great Central era proper would have cramped the whole style of the work. Furthermore, the success of the Robinson Directors and 8K 2–8–0s, not to mention the 9N 4–6–2 tanks, left only one option open and that was to extend coverage beyond the boundaries set by the end of the year 1922.

With that much said, the reader should find very comprehensive coverage of the last of the G.C. loco classes. Those of us fortunate enough to remember the Directors at work post–1948 will see these Robinson stalwarts still hard at it, sometimes in a condition that was not entirely un-becoming. Thus, too, extensive coverage has also been given to the 'Scottish Directors', a sorely–neglected class if ever there was, and proof, if any were needed, of the efficacy of Robinson's engineering.

And yet, as ever, there are gaps. We are still waiting to plug the holes regarding the engines brought into the Great Central fold via the incorporation of the Lancashire, Derbyshire & East Coast and Wrexham, Mold and Connah's Quay railways. More frustrating still is the omission of much to do with Gorton Works, especially when a wealth of valuable material is waiting in the wings.

**One of the finest views of a Robinson 4–6–0 to appear in the post-Grouping period is, surely, this one of No.6165 *VALOUR* and No.5424 *CITY OF LINCOLN* roaring past Glazebrook in March 1939 with a special train conveying LNER directors and their guests to Aintree to watch the Grand National.**

*W. Potter*

# Introduction

With the introduction of the Sir Sam Fay or Class 1 4–6–0 of 1912, Robinson's development as a locomotive engineer might be observed, by an outsider, as having reached something of a high point. The previous year had seen the arrival of the magnificent 8K 2–8–0 goods locomotive that was to be multiplied so successfully for service in the First World War. The following year, 1913, would see the creation of the celebrated Directors, arguably Robinson's best passenger design.

'Sir Sam' had thus arrived, or at least had been conceived, on the Great Central locomotive scene, roughly half way through Robinson's twenty two year term of office as head of the company's locomotive department. Sandwiched between the highly successful 2–8–0 and the first of the Directors, the big 4–6–0 makes an interesting contrast between previous passenger designs and those that were to follow in its wake. Though the 'Directors' took on certain design features of the 'Sir Sams', their mechanics owed a lot to the evolution of Robinson's pioneer 4–4–0 class – the 11B/C and 11D variants.

Standing between the arrival of the Directors and the end of the Robinson era, like some grim, dark colossus, is the four year period belonging to the First World War. Aside from the grim loss of human life with its attendant misery and destruction, there lay the desperate shortage of materials and strain on manpower that were to make Robinson's life at Gorton that much harder. In March 1916 we find him complaining of the difficulty he was experiencing in keeping men at Gorton through the attraction of better wages paid to men engaged on munitions work outside. In common with most other railway workshops, production of armaments had to be accommodated alongside the production of new locomotives, which slowed down drastically, and the repair of existing engines; all at a time when train services nationally were being stretched to their limits.

That fateful summer of 1914 had seen the completion of a batch of 8K 2–8–0s, fifteen of which had been built at Gorton between January and June. Just two examples of Robinson's mixed–traffic version of the 'Sir Sam Fay' design, the Glenalmond (Class 1A), had seen the light of day before the dark clouds of war were on the horizon. Between August and December of 1914 a further eight members of the class emerged from Gorton. The close of 1914 saw the emergence of the first two of Robinson's massive 1B 2–6–4 tank, the first example in this country of an engine using this wheel arrangement. 1915 saw the last of the Glenalmonds, the un–named no.280 in January of that year. A mere eight new engines left the Gorton shops in 1915, the second series of the 1B tanks nos. 274 – 276 and nos.336 – 340. 1916, the year of Jutland, Verdun and the Somme saw locomotive production at Gorton reach its low water––mark; just four 1B tank engines were built between June and August.

The rather ungainly–looking 1B tanks had their ranks strengthened by a further six arrivals in 1917. Further examples of Robinson's very successful and sturdy 9N 4–6–2 tank design of 1911 emerged at this time – one per month from June through to October. Then in the November of that year the first passenger 4–6–0 since the end of 1913 arrived on the scene, Robinson's biggest and heaviest tender locomotive to date, the magnificent 'Lord Faringdon' or Class 9P. This massive, solid machine remained the only one of its class until June 1920 when a further five were embarked upon.

1918, the final year of conflict, dawned with the emergence of the Robinson Class 8M – the large boilered version of the already very successful 8K 2–8–0. Seven 8Ms were turned out from Gorton in that year with a further twelve to follow before Grouping. Paradoxically, the First World War had entered its final bitter year when, in the first three months, Gorton's only wartime R.O.D. 2–8–0s appeared. Just one more new locomotive managed to

appear in that year, yet another permutation of the 4–6–0 theme – the Class 8N. This was something of a hybrid design, using the enlarged boiler of the 8M 2–8–0 together with this engine's cylinders and motion and substituting 5′ 8″ driving wheels (1″ bigger than the previous mixed traffic design, the 'Glenalmond.'. Two further examples of the 8N were turned out in the first half of 1921.

Observation of Locomotive, Carriage & Wagon Committee Minutes during these dire times give us a little more insight into the situation:

*14th April 1916: Robinson ... 'more difficulty being experienced in obtaining material...'*
*26th May 1916: 'Very little progress made in getting material. Consideration as to use of scrap timber (normally sold as firewood) for making rail keys. A suitable key–making machine may be purchased.'*
*27th October 1916: Robinson explains troubles with men at Gorton affecting munitions work and locomotive work.*
*9th March 1917: 'There has been a large increase in engine failures during 4 weeks ended February 24th.'*
*20th April 1917: Mr.Thom (R.A.Thom, Gorton Works Manager) interrogated at length with regard to the previous item; his report was accepted.*
*25th May 1917: The Chairman stresses the necessity of 'not letting repairs to rolling stock get into more arrears.' Enquiries regarding wagon repairs done by an outside firm.*
*26th October 1917: The supply of hydraulic power at Gorton has become quite inadequate . Serious delays are taking place with the output of flanged plates and men are working nights and weekends. It will be necessary to install one additional set of 3–throw horizontal hydraulic pressure pumps. Authorization given to tender for same.*

At the same time as the previous problems at Gorton it was also reported:

*'Problems have arisen with the motor–driven blower for supplying blast air for the smithy, forge and drop hammer shops. The smithy has shut down, once for eight days, and again for twenty hours.' Robinson requested a duplicate electric blower to be supplied, 'so that continuous work can take place, avoiding great dissatisfaction amongst the men when we have to send them home for a period.'*
*23rd November 1917: The above improvements were authorized and authority given to Robinson to accept the most favourable tender submitted.*
*8th March 1918: Attention drawn to several engine failures in express trains reported to Traffic Committee. Robinson reports trouble with tubes – difficulty of getting tubes to put in engines.*

The Armistice terminating this 'War To End All Wars' was signed on November 11th 1918. No previous event had had such cataclysmic effects on life throughout Britain. In four dark years the social, industrial and economic structure of the country had altered beyond imagining. For the railways, inflation, a depleted workforce and a system that had been stretched to the core lay before the companies. Eleven days into peacetime brought the following missive from the locomotive, carriage and wagon committee; an item that sounded somehow familiar:-

*'With present staff and accommodation it is quite impossible to keep pace with firebox renewals. Upon Mr.Robinson's recommendation, authority given for 20 new boilers and fireboxes complete but without mountings.'*

Ten 'Directors' were built to Class 11E and turned out from Gorton between August and December 1913. No.430 *PURDON VICCARS* was the second of the batch, delivered on September 27th. The locomotive is seen here outside Manchester's London Rd station facing towards Ardwick. William Purdon Viccars had been a director of the Great Central from 1900 to 1906 and was Deputy Chairman from 1906 to 1918. A Leicestershire man and son of a one-time Mayor of the city, he lived at Anstey Pastures, Leicester. Other railway interests included being a director of the Cheshire Lines Committee and the Humber Commercial Railway and Dock Company. He died in 1918 at the age of 72 years, and was succeeded as Deputy Chairman

by Walter Burgh Gair. Looking at the locomotive the condition of which is, typically, immaculate. Every external surface gleams with a mirror-like finish even down to the visible polished steel of the internal motion. Hours and hours of work expended by men who must have had a total faith and pride in what they were doing. Rarely commented on are the five (four on left side) boiler washout plugs, covered by brass caps, on the firebox wall above the handrail. Above these are the two (three on left side) 'blisters' that covered inspection caps (introduced around 1911) through which could be examined the internal surfaces of the firebox, stays and plates.

# Class 11E Directors

Of all the locomotive types to run on British railways, the 4–4–0 was the longest – lived and spawned the most variants. For the Great Central this was the type inherited from Charles Sacré, developed and improved by Parker and Pollitt and which drew the first of the company's expresses into the capital in those early years. It took the genius of Robinson to refine and distil the breed. Never quite at ease with the 4–6–0, it was with the 4–4–0 configuration that some of his finest work lay. This was to manifest itself in the 6′ 9″ engines universally known as the 'Directors' – so named after the distinguished gentlemen who served on the managing board of the company.

The success of the class led to further engines being built after the First War, between 1919 and the end of the company's existence in 1922 – the so–called 'Improved Directors'. Their success obviously impressed Gresley, who, as C.M.E. of the newly–formed LNER group, authorised construction of a further 24 for service in Scotland. Though the differences between the three main batches are (with one exception) relatively minor, we shall view them as three separate types.

Empirical work done with the 11B Class had enabled Robinson to evaluate firebox length in relation to tube length. It must have come as a considerable disappointment that the Sir Sam Fay design had

thrown up so many weaknesses and so quickly. Yet the last 'Sir Sam' had yet to appear before the first Director emerged from Gorton – in the late summer of 1913. With a broad outline very similar to the Class 1, the Directors were something of a 'lookalike' to their 4–6–0 progenitors. Differences there were and lessons had been learnt. Firstly, the enormous 'Sir Sam' boiler had been scaled down to improve its steam raising capacity, the maximum diameter of 5′ 6″ had been slimmed down by 3″ to 5′ 3″; most importantly, the barrel length had been reduced from an incredible 17′ 3″ to 12′ 3″. Firebox length was retained at 8′ 6″ but, owing to a more generous amount of room available on the 4–4–0 with its wider spaced axles, an improved ashpan layout could be provided with no restrictions on the access of air and consequent freedom from choking ash.

Though the new boiler was a complete success some 'fine tuning' took place after the appearance of the 1B 2–6–4 tank engine. This locomotive used a boiler of similar outline to the first Director but with an altered tube layout, the small tubes being reduced from 175 of 1⅞″ outside diameter to 157 and the superheater heating surface reduced by the fitting of elements with shorter loops. This produced one single boiler (designated G.C. Standard No. 5 which was subsequently fitted to both the original Directors and the suc-

ceeding engines (Class 11F).

In respect of superheater element protection, three separate devices were carried in the engines' lifetime: the class was built with Robinson's improved steam jet draught retarder. This device, which operated in conjunction with the blower, blew steam via nozzles along the superheater flues, neutralizing the draught provided by the blower and thus keeping the elements at a relatively low temperature. Robinson had filed a patent for the original version of this apparatus in 1911. Though the devices seemed effective enough in theory, the reality was different. Reports exist of boiler flues becoming choked with soot as a result of the device and flames licking back from the firebox to the footplate with over-zealous use of the apparatus. Doubtless because of these difficulties, the draught retarders were replaced by the combined blower and steam circulating valve which passed a small amount of steam through the elements themselves with the blower on. In conjunction with this apparatus, the superheater header discharge valve was fitted to the left-hand side of the smokebox. The purpose of this valve, which was operated by a rod passed through the boiler handrail, was to discharge steam from the elements when the engine was stationary, and so prevent any movement. Admirable as these devices were, they were over-complicated for the purpose

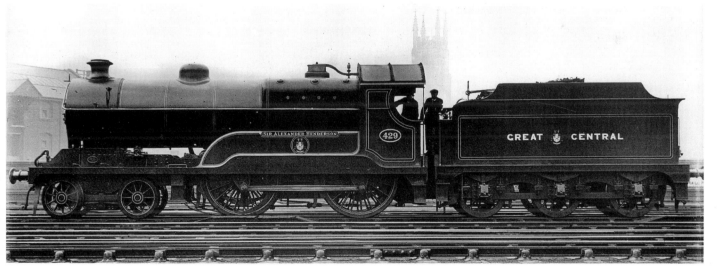

No.429 *SIR ALEXANDER HENDERSON* emerged from Gorton works on Saturday, August 16th 1913. Named to honour the company Chairman, the locomotive cost the Great Central £2937. The vagaries of naming enable us to identify the locomotive within a period 1913 to 1917. Mechanical lubrication, fitted to these engines when built, is carried and the steam jet draught retarder remains in place: the pipe for the steam supply can be seen projecting from the top left-hand side of the smokebox. Our location is just outside Manchester London Road station, evidenced by the Great Central's grain warehouse on the left and St.Andrew's church, Ancoats whose soot-blackened form dominated the railway here until modern times. Sir Alexander Henderson was a director of the Great Central from 1897 to 1899 whereupon he became Chairman in succession to the legendary Sir Edward Watkin. Henderson remained in this post throughout the company's history up to 1922. In 1916 he became a Peer taking the title Baron Faringdon. The corresponding 'Lord Faringdon' was then used to christen the pioneer 9P Class 4–6–0 which was built in 1917. The name 'Sir Douglas Haig' (after the British C-in-C) was then bestowed on No.429. Just to complicate the naming process, Sir Douglas was made an earl in 1919. 429 then took the name Prince Henry in honour of the fourth child of King George V and Queen Mary. Executive, soldier and prince; 429 had had chequered titles throughout its forty one year life. And with this royal title, then numbered into British Railways stock as 62658, she was withdrawn in August 1955.

they served and were replaced in early LNER days by Gresley's simple snifting valve, which relied simply on the admission of air to the elements when steam was shut off.

Had the Sir Sam Fay design been more of a success it begs the question as to whether or not the Directors would still have been built. Research proves the answer to be a fairly concrete 'yes' – hinted at first in a report presented by Robinson to the Locomotive, Carriage & Wagon Committee on October 1st 1912:

> *Gentlemen, as the work for the engines under construction in the 1912 programme is completed in the Forge and Smithy and other material in an advanced condition elsewhere in the shops, it will be necessary to decide as quickly as possible the programme for the year 1913, more especially having regard to the state of trade and the great difficulty in obtaining materials. In order to keep our shops supplied, I have found it necessary to put in hand forging and casting for ten passenger engines of the 'Sir Alexander' [sic] Class. We are badly in want of passenger tender engines to enable existing passenger engines to be stopped for extensive repairs and as this class of engine fitted with a superheater and larger cylinders will be able to do practically as much work as the big 'Atlantic' type engine not superheated and at a cost of about £500 per engine less to construct\*, it is obvious it will be an advantage to the company to carry this out..........*

Notice the reference to the 'Sir Alexander' Class (11B), none of which were built (save for rebuilds) after 1904 and the perennial request for further motive power resources.

*\* The first Atlantics cost £3750 each to build.*

As will be seen, the Directors employed the same cylinders and motion as the so-called 'Sir Alexanders' providing some necessary ground work in the shops for the new class. Detail design work in the form of drawings also suggest the notion of a new passenger class afoot in the latter half of 1912 viz:

29/8/1912 – axle box keeps 11E.
1/10/1912 – 4–4–0 express passenger engine.
12/10/1912 – 4–4–0 proposed passenger engine.
25/11/1912 – 11E driving spring link brackets.
19/11/1912 – 11E bogie axles.
3/1/1913 – smokebox 11E.
6/1/1913 – 11E platform details and handrails.

All the aforementioned suggest a logical development from the earlier 11B design and certainly not the 'rush job' in the wake of the first few months of the 'Sir Sams' that some sources have suggested.

Development work done with the 11B and its resultant transition into the C and D

class variants had given Robinson a sound front end design for his 4–4–0: a cylinder block with 19″ bore and 26″ stroke cylinders fed by piston valves of 10″ diameter. In the complicated story of the 11B class, mention was made of the piston valve cylinders fitted to No. 1026. Because the original motion was retained on the initial 11Bs (to avoid the expense of designing and producing fresh sets of valve gear) outside admission of steam to the valves was required. A principal advantage of the piston valve is its normal use of inside admission of steam. That is to say that steam is fed to the cylinder inside of the two pistons that make up the valve. Exhaust, at a lower pressure, results on the outside of the valve which does away with the need for high pressure glands on the piston valve rod. To keep costs down on the Directors and, bearing in mind the speed with which the design appeared, the cylinder block developed from the 11B design was used with its attendant outside admission piston valves. This made the two classes the only G.C.engines to use this type of valve. Incidentally Robinson was in good company with his outside admission piston valves; they were used on the rebuilt Bulleid Southern Railway Pacifics in B.R.days to produce one of the finest free running engines in the country.

Our photographs show the large and amply–proportioned qualities off to advantage. The likeness to the 'Sir Sam Fay' design is immediately apparent with the 'family' features such as cab, boiler mountings, smokebox front and tender all recognisable. Artist Robinson undoubtedly was, but his contribution to sound engineering principles and practice – the use of empiri-

cal methods, standardisation of components and solid, four–square construction and inherent robustness were now manifest. A noteworthy departure from the 'Sir Sam' design was the use of a 'boxed–in' footplate or platform valance covering the coupled wheels. Strangely enough, this deep valance does not appear to have been fitted to the first engine when built, appearing as an afterthought and then applied to subsequent members of the class. Removed from the engines in their post–Grouping life, this device gave an air of discretion to the Directors' lower quarters, though no doubt loco crews cursed the thing when it came to 'oiling up'.

The boiler, pressed to 180lb. p.s.i. as on the 'Sir Sam Fay', was pitched slightly lower than the latter – at 8′ 9″ – there being no necessity to clear the tops of the rocking levers operating the piston valves. As with the 4–6–0, superheating was built in to the Directors from new using Robinson's own system. Wakefield mechanical lubricators were fitted to the engines when built; subsequently Robinson is reported to have been dissatisfied with these and substituted, instead, his own 'Intensifore' system with sight-feeds in the cab. Cylinder lubrication was augmented by the use of brass-cased tallow cups which can be identified along the bottom of the smokebox.

A nicety of style, and a familiar Robinson device, was the reduction in width of the running plate or 'platform' (from 8′ 9″ to 8′ 0″) ahead of the leading coupled wheels, a touch also applied to the subsequent 'Directors'.

The Directors were turned out in the Great Central passenger livery with the then well established rich 'Brunswick'

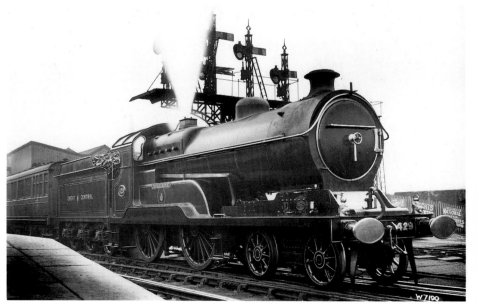

**No.429 in its third, and final, guise: *PRINCE HENRY*, at the head of an up express at Guide Bridge in typically gleaming Great Central condition.**

Walter Burgh Gair was a director of the Great Central from 1906 to 1922 and succeeded Purdon Viccars in 1918 as Deputy Chairman until Grouping. A financier, Gair was Managing Director of Barings, the bankers and went on to become a director of the LNER. No.433, the engine named after him, was the fifth locomotive of the 11E class, emerging from Gorton Works in October 1913. We go to Manchester London Road for this view of an immaculately turned out No.433 waiting, with safety valves blowing off, for the 'right away' with an up express. A detail revealed by close scrutiny of the original picture is the short cover over the reversing rod. Only this engine, along with *SIR CLEMENT ROYDS (q.v.)* and *PRINCE GEORGE* appear to have had this short cover, and only for a short period. The later (longer) cover shrouded the bolted joint in the reversing rod and it can only be assumed that aesthetic considerations prevailed upon Robinson to provide something that covered the unsightly blemish. Great Central signalling enthusiasts can take in the gallows signal. Close scrutiny of the picture will reveal the pneumatic operating apparatus, introduced here by the company in 1909.

In a slightly later period we have moved just outside the station to take in an opposite-hand picture of No.433. The locomotive carries the superheater header discharge valve on the side of the smokebox. This device, along with Robinson's combined blower and steam circulating valve was fitted to the engines from around 1919 in lieu of the steam jet draught retarder incorporated from new. Robinson's own Intensifore lubrication is in use on the engine, the original Wakefield mechanical system having been displaced in the years after 1916. *WALTER BURGH GAIR* was withdrawn in August 1953 as British Railways No.62654.

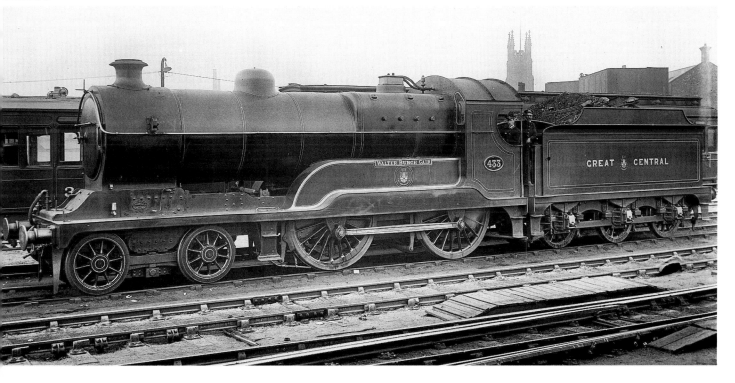

*PURDON VICCARS* on view at Gorton in the late 1920s, wearing the first LNER style of numbering and lettering (though without the original ampersand and full stops), painted in the overall black colour scheme lined out in red. The chimney is the Doncaster style of 'flowerpot' but retaining the original dome cover. Nicely groomed with paintwork gleaming, the polished metalwork on the smokebox, a sine qua non of the Robinson era, is missing.

At Manchester Central No.431 *EDWIN A.BEAZLEY* waits on one of the centre roads. Directors were a very familiar sight here, consolidated by the GC's partnership with the Great Northern and the Midland in the triumvirate that was the Cheshire Lines Committee. Edwin.A.Beazley was a director of the GC from 1900 through to Grouping and subsequently became a director of the LNER. Alone of all the Directors whose names graced their company's locomotives, Mr.Beazley chose a simple 'A' instead of a full name; a rather singular personal preference.

The same engine on view at Gorton shed in the immediate post-Grouping years. No.431 is still in Great Central condition mechanically, but appears in LNER apple green with the simplified cabside lining and Great Central cast numberplate. The framing under the footplate appears as black, lined red. 7½″ letters in gold, shaded red and black, appear on the tender side with ampersand and full stops between. The fitting on the smokebox side is part of the later superheater element protection apparatus, the header discharge valve.

Something of a hybrid condition is presented by this view of 5431. Wearing LNER green livery, second version (no ampersand and full stops) and with cut-away valances, the header discharge valve has given way to the side snifting valve arrangement and the original graceful chimney has been replaced by the 'flowerpot'.

*Collection of Brian Hilton*

**In this Gorton picture, dated May 29th 1938, No.5432 *SIR EDWARD FRASER* appears ex-works in nicely varnished, all-over black, lined red. By the looks of things, the buffer beam and smokebox front have yet to be finished off. The third type of chimney approximating to Robinson's own has been fitted, together with the lower, flatter pattern of dome cover which had begun to appear in the 1930s. The longer pattern of ash ejector is now carried, along with a sight screen to the cabside.**

**All the Directors, re-classified after Grouping from 11E to D10, became the property of British Railways. Though long ousted from their First Division duties of express work on the London Extension, the class maintained a significant presence, especially on the lines of the former C.L.C. On June 5th 1954 *SIR EDWARD FRASER* now numbered 62653 approaches Knutsford with a 7-coach stopping train from Chester to Manchester Central. In this, the final condition of the class, boiler mountings are as seen in the previous view, with snifting valve just visible behind the chimney. A smokebox renewal has given rise to snaphead rivetting around the wrapper and the top lamp iron has been lowered to sit on the smokebox door, a consideration brought about by safety requirements relating to the Manchester – Sheffield electrification. Twin handles have replaced the Robinson spoked wheel that was such a hallmark of the Great Central era. BR lined black livery completes what is otherwise a pleasing vintage scene.**

*B.K.B.Green*

green providing the main body colour. This was lined with a single black and two white lines, appearing as a panel on the cab side and tender tank and on the boiler lagging bands. Main frames above the platform, along with the valance of both loco and tender, footsteps and buffer casings were of a claret colour (referred to in some specifications as 'Crimson Lake'). The valancing was double–lined vermillion, the lines being carried over across the deep section over the coupled wheels. The splasher panel in the same Brunswick green (in contrast to the Atlantics) was bordered by a polished brass beading, the latter lined black edged with white, the company crest with the motto 'Forward' enclosed in a roundel in the centre. Careful observation of the cab and tender sides will reveal a contrasting black border to the panel. Wheel centres were painted in the same glorious green body colour with white lining; wheel tyres were finished in plain black.

As with all other Robinson classes in the LNER era, the Directors underwent changes in appearance and mechanical detail that altered their personality somewhat. Principal amongst these were the cutting away of the valance under the footplate, the loss of the green livery (an LNER economy measure inaugurated in 1928) and the substitution of the elegant Robinson chimney for a 'Flowerpot' design along with a flatter dome cover to bring the class within the LNER composite loading gauge. Fortunately, the class were not disfigured for too long by the substitute chimneys, for a third pattern, resembling the Robinson model, was substituted in the 1930s. Another visual alteration was the appearance of oil feed piping along side the boiler casing, a result of the change from the Intensifore system to the Wakefield Eureka pattern of lubricator on eight of the ten engines. (Nos. 5435 and 5436 were fitted with sight–feed lubricators of the Detroit pattern).

All but No. 5431, 'Edwin.A.Beazley' were fitted with piston valve rings of the Knorr multiple ring design between 1933 and 1935. These maintained greater steam tightness than the broad rings fitted previously and were applied to other LNER piston valve locomotives also. A further development in the same vein was the application of the Trofinoff Automatic by–pass piston valve. The 'Directors' were by no means the first engines to be given these valves, the Metropolitan Railway 0–6–4 tank engine 'Lord Aberconway' having this distinction. Designated T.A.B. for short, the valves could move to the outside of the steam chests when steam was shut off – as when coasting down a long gradient, the object being to promote freer running by avoiding compression of air in the

Another naming peculiarity applied to the 11Es concerned No.434 *THE EARL OF KERRY*. This gentleman, an Irish M.P., did not include the parliamentary prefix 'The Rt.Hon.' and suffix 'M.P.' either side of his title, giving credence to the theory that the directors in question had some say in exactly how their names appeared. Perhaps the transient nature of politics had something to do with it! Manchester London Rd is again the venue for our picture; this time we have a broadside view, not an entirely common standpoint from which to observe a locomotive. From the selected angle, however, the Wakefield mechanical lubricator can be spotted on the left-hand framing. This puts the picture firmly in the 1913 – 1916 time span: the original picture shows a North-Eastern bow-ended coach behind the tender, indicative of a cross-country working.

For a change of viewpoint, we step backwards to look at No.435 *SIR CLEMENT ROYDS* on shed at Neasden in its early days, and presenting an 'as built' view of the 11E class. Original condition is suggested by the presence of mechanical lubrication via the 'Wakefield' lubricator. The pipe projecting from the top of the smokebox and running behind the boiler handrail is from the pyrometer with which the class was equipped from new. Recording the steam temperature in the superheater header, the pyrometers were discontinued from around 1916 and were not used on the subsequent (11F) engines. The commodious Robinson cab is seen to advantage, the standard feature of steel angle and 'T' bracing for the roof is clearly identifiable. 435 was amongst the longest-lived of the original Directors, lasting until 1955. Numbered as British Railways 62656 she was withdrawn in the January of that year. Succumbing in the August was No.62658 *PRINCE GEORGE* with 62653 *SIR EDWARD FRASER* as the last casualty, departing in the October.

A 'crow' on the whistle is sounded by No.435 alongside platform 5 at Manchester Central on empty coaching stock duties. Oddly enough, some forty years later the class would return to this stamping ground of their youth to perform these very same duties immediately prior to their demise. Compare this picture to our other views and note the short cover over the reversing rod. *(q.v. No.433)*.

It was not until 1932 that the first Directors found their way off their parent system and on to the lines of their erstwhile competitors; so it is pleasing to find a photograph of an 11E on something of a 'foreign' working. On this occasion *SIR CLEMENT ROYDS* in lined black livery is running through Wood Green with an up excursion train composed of seven vehicles. Great Western stock is prominent at the front of the train, with two unidentified coaches at the rear, the last item is a van, possibly a horsebox.

By the beginning of 1954 only half of the original Directors were left in traffic. Humdrum duties are now the order of the day for *SIR CLEMENT ROYDS* as it moves empty coaching stock, from a St.Pancras express, out of Manchester Central and along to Cornbrook carraige sidings in March 1954. Despite its menial task, the engine, now numbered 62656 of class D10, is smartly turned out, with clean paintwork, bright lining and polished numberplate; one might even say a distinct improvement on some 1930s LNER views! Nevertheless, the picture provides an excellent example of these engines in their final condition. The snaphead rivetting around the smokebox wrapper has been commented on before, and notice the same fixings have been applied to the buffer plank, something not seen in GC days. Twin handles have replaced the Robinson spoked wheel on the smokebox door and the top lamp iron has been dropped below the handrail. Still, all the proud GC character and majesty is manifest yet, albeit to last for just another nine months.

*B.K.B.Green*

A splendid scene at Guide Bridge in later Great Central days (header discharge valve and Intensifore lubrication on the locomotive) as No.436 *SIR BERKELEY SHEFFIELD* enters the station from the east with a down Manchester express. The 10-coach train is made up of two party saloons behind the tender with 8 clerestories forming the remainder of the stock. Sir Berkeley Sheffield himself was a director of the GC from 1909 to 1922 so his tenure is contemporary with our photograph. The gentleman's full title was 'Sir Berkeley G.D.Sheffield Bart.', his address in 1920 was given as Normanby Park, Scunthorpe, Lincolnshire. Built in November 1913, No.436 was one of the first Directors to be withdrawn. Along with 430 it went for scrap in March 1953.

As LNER No.5436 *SIR BERKELEY SHEFFIELD* leaves York with a York – Bournemouth express in 1930s. The second pattern of chimney is carried and the tall dome cover is still retained. The photograph illustrates the arrangement of twin snifting valves either side of the smokebox, a feature carried only by three engines of this class, 5431 & 5437 being the others.

*C.Ord*

No.437 *CHARLES STUART-WORTLEY* at Stalybridge with a train of empty coaching stock. Built in November 1913 No.437 was renamed *PRINCE GEORGE* c.1920 in honour of the youngest surviving child of King George V and Queen Mary. The picture dictates a fairly early view due to the presence of the Wakefield mechanical lubricator on the mainframe and the steam jet draught retarder appearing on the smokebox side. Charles Stuart-Wortley was a director of the Great Central from its inception in 1897 to its demise in 1922. An M.P., he was created Baron Stuart of Wortley in 1916 and his title was later transferred to 9P 4–6–0 No.1168. A notable music lover, his wife, Alice, was a devoted companion of the composer Sir Edward Elgar. Letters recently studied reveal that Alice Stuart-Wortley, whom the composer called 'Windflower', inspired the beautiful themes of Elgar's violin concerto. Facts far removed from locomotives it is true, but the love of music and railways is very often intertwined!

A study in style and elegance: the renamed No.437 *PRINCE GEORGE* waits at the west end of Guide Bridge station with a down express.

cylinders. 5431 was the first engine to be fitted with these valves; 5429, 5430, 5432 and 5435 were subsequently equipped in 1937/38. The T.A.B. valves had also been used on Robinson's first 4–4–0 design (D10) with reported success. A reliable source speaks well of these valves describing them as a big improvement on the Robinson outside admission piston valve: much freer coasting, with some economy in coal and water.

Ash ejectors of the long pipe pattern replaced the original short version – the device was removed from around 1940 onwards. Sight screens were fitted to the cab sides between 1933 and 1937, a small modification which must have added to the convenience and comfort of the engine crews. The Gresham steam assistance for the sanding gear, which supplied only the front coupled wheels, was removed in the early 1930s. Gravity sanding for reverse running had been provided from new and sandboxes were fitted in front of the tender bulkhead (q.v.)

In common with standard Great Central locomotive practice, steam brakes were used for the engine and tender with vacuum ejector (supplied by the Vacuum Brake Company) for braking the train.

## ALLOCATION AND WORK

Deployment of the 'Directors' on the London – Manchester trains indicated the strength and success of the class. On introduction they had ousted the 'Sir Sams' from the trains and had quickly built up a reputation as a very free running and powerful engine. Speeds of up to 90 m.p.h. were recorded by the engines in their early days. The 'Directors' held their position on the London – Manchester service until the introduction of the B17s in the 1930s.

On introduction, nine out of ten of the Directors were stationed at Neasden where they had replaced Atlantics. One, No. 438, was based at Gorton and was posted briefly to York. No. 434 'The Earl of Kerry' was transferred to Gorton in 1918 for one year. With the arrival in 1919–1920 of the first of the 'Improved Directors' (Class 11F) some displacement of the earlier machines took place. This resulted in Nos. 434 and 435 being sent to Sheffield with 436 and 438 making a brief appearance at Woodford. At Grouping the bulk of the class were based at Gorton, three engines (429, 432 and 437) remaining on the strength at Neasden.

By the time all the 11Fs were in traffic the rest of the original Directors were displaced from Neasden and moved away to Gorton and Annesley respectively. Stopping trains were worked from the latter shed, although this was only a brief aberration – in 1924 all ten locomotives were at Gorton for a short period. Later that year, however, Nos. 430 & 431 were transferred to Neasden.

Some forays away from the former Great Central main line took place in the 1920s. 437 was used on the Sheffield Pullman in July 1924 and spent a week at King's Cross shed working stopping trains from London over the G.N. main line as far afield as Huntingdon and Peterborough. The short–lived Pullman service was extended to Manchester (Central) for five months from April 1925 and was handled by Directors, Nos. 435 & 437 being recorded as booked engines. This service ran non–stop from King's Cross to Sheffield via Retford – 161·2 miles in 177 minutes, an average speed of 54·6 m.p.h.

Transfers proper away from the former Great Central system began at the end of 1932. No. 5431 was sent to Leeds (Copley Hill) in October that year, was swapped for Gorton's No. 5434 and was joined by No. 5432; the two remained in the Yorkshire

The haze surrounding No.438 reminds us of the attendant smoke, dirt and grit that surrounded our steam locomotive depots. *WORSLEY TAYLOR* is on shed at Gorton in the Great Central's latter years. It is difficult to visualise nowadays in a somewhat de-industrialised Manchester just exactly how much heavy industry surrounded the place in those far-off days. My father came to Manchester from Liverpool in the difficult days of the 1920s to join the city's police force. As a 'rookie' police constable he did a spell of duty in the Gorton district delivering notices of jury service to various households in the area. I well remember his account of a pall of smoke that he had seen hanging, smog-like in the distance. He queried this with a lady and asked her: *"whatever is that place over there?"* *"That, lad, is Gorton Tank!"* came the reply, uttered apparently with a mixture of pride and supressed indignation that a Mancunian was seemingly ignorant of such matters. Henry Wilson

Parliamentary Bills and had acted for the MS&L in their trials and tribulations with the Metropolitan Railway in the 1890s. He pulled off something of a coup when, in 1870 at the age of 23, he married Sir Edward Watkin's only daughter. Worsley-Taylor was made a Baronet in 1917 – his address at that time is given as Moreton Hall, Whalley, Lancashire. He was Conservative M.P. for Blackpool from 1900 – 1906 and was a K.C. He died in 1924. This left-hand view of 438 should be compared with that of No.435 at Neasden. Progress has now resulted in the removal of the Wakefield mechanical lubricator and substitution by the 'Intensifore' system; this is augmented by the two oil cups, one for the cylinders and a smaller one for the valve chests. The steam jet draught retarder has been removed and the later header discharge valve substituted between the boiler and smokebox handrails. On the original photograph a small rivetted patch is visible where the pipe to

What might be termed a 'borderline' case is provided by this view of *PRINCE GEORGE* about to depart from Guide Bridge with an up express in 1924. No.437 received its LNER number (5437) in the November of that year and ran with the 'c' suffix to the Great Central number in the meantime. Interestingly, the company initials are without the ampersand and full stops, though the LNER green has been applied. The cabside has LNER simplified lining, a black border edged white, the GC cast brass numberplate has been retained, providing a most interesting specimen for a livery study. Mechanically, the valance below the footplate has yet to be cut away and Ross 'pop' safety valves have replaced Robinson's four-column cased valves of the Ramsbottom pattern; the change-over taking place around Grouping. An ash ejector of the short pattern is fitted, these appeared on the locomotives after building. As a footnote, the locomotive in the background is No.427 *CITY OF LONDON* bearing what appears to be a stopping passenger train headcode.

A Director in his prime. An immediate success, the 11Es were put into traffic on the London – Manchester trains, duties they handled with consummate ease. In original condition, No.438 *WORSLEY TAYLOR* lifts a five-coach express out of Marylebone and heads for the North.

*Collection of Brian Hilton*

A fascinating panorama of Gorton loco yard in the immediate post-Grouping period. *WORSLEY TAYLOR* is depicted in a broadside view against a backcloth consisting of the coal-crushing plant for the colloidal fuels and the coaling stage. Looking 'ex-works', the locomotive appears in LNER green, lined black and white, with the first version of the shaded lettering (ampersand and full stops), 'c' suffix to the number and retention of the Great Central cast brass numberplate. Careful scrutiny of the original photograph suggests a darker green or, possibly, even black for the coupling rod valance, raised mainframe section and tender frame. Liveries in this period, as already described, were apt to border on the experimental and there is, regretably, no hard evidence to confirm these suppositions.

**In the last year of its life, *WORSLEY TAYLOR*, now as 62659, joins forces with Ivatt 2–6–2T No.41235 as it heads out of Knutsford towards Plumley with a Manchester – Chester stopping train. June 5th 1954.**

*B.K.B.Green*

city until the end of 1938.

Thus, in the mid–1930s Leeds had two engines, Gorton and Neasden had three each with two based at Sheffield. By now the Directors were being ousted from the London–Manchester trains by the newer B17s, a class that appear to have been less than popular with the former Great Central locomen. The new influx of motive power caused a migration of the 11Es (now re–classed as LNER D10) from Gorton and Neasden to Sheffield. From here workings to York, Hull, Retford, Lincoln and Nottingham took place with Scarborough and Newcastle appearing on rosters for excursion traffic.

By the outbreak of World War II all ten engines were the property of Sheffield (Darnall), though this did not last long – 5429 & 5431 went to Mexborough in early 1940 to work cross country trains to Hull and Grimsby from Sheffield. A change in

duty was recorded when Directors were seen on goods trains in the early war years, sitings as far flung as Newcastle and even Edinburgh being logged.

Apart from brief transfers to Doncaster and Langwith from the end of 1941 to early 1943, all the 11Es remained at Sheffield for the duration of the War.

The War over, Directors crossed the Pennines to Liverpool (Brunswick), 5435 spending two months there from May 1946. At the end of the LNER period the last migration of the class began when transfers to sheds of the Cheshire Lines took place. Seven locos went from Sheffield; three to Brunswick, three to Northwich and one, 'Purdon Viccars', to Trafford Park, Manchester. Finally, in October 1949, the last three engines were moved west from Sheffield: 'Walter Burgh Gair', 'Sir Berkeley Sheffield' (inappropriately!) and 'Worsley Taylor'.

At the end of 1948 the L.M.R. had taken control of engine working on the former Cheshire Lines railway and Great Central engines were ousted from supremacy on a system they had dominated throughout.

Our pictures show Directors at work on Manchester – Chester stopping trains. The railway through the Cheshire countryside had provided a happy hunting ground for many Great Central classes over the years. Station pilot turns at Manchester Central were also on their agenda around this time and the sight of these handsome, yet begrimed veterans simmering away on stand–by lingers in my early memory. A far cry, maybe, from their original duties but it is on these workings that myself and so many present day enthusiasts will best remember them.

## SUMMARY OF CLASS 11E 4–4–0 (LNER D11)

| NUMBER | BUILDER | DATE BUILT | NAME | WITHDRAWN |
|--------|---------|------------|------|-----------|
| 429 | Gorton | August 1913 | PRINCE HENRY | February 1954 |
| 430 | – ' – | September 1913 | PURDON VICCARS | March 1953 |
| 431 | – ' – | October 1913 | EDWIN.A.BEAZLEY | May 1954 |
| 432 | – ' – | October 1913 | SIR EDWARD FRASER | October 1955 |
| 433 | – ' – | October 1913 | WALTER BURGH GAIR | August 1953 |
| 434 | – ' – | November 1913 | THE EARL OF KERRY | August 1953 |
| 435 | – ' – | November 1913 | SIR CLEMENT ROYDS | January 1955 |
| 436 | – ' – | November 1913 | SIR BERKELEY SHEFFIELD | March 1953 |
| 437 | – ' – | November 1913 | PRINCE GEORGE | August 1955 |
| 438 | – ' – | December 1913 | WORSLEY TAYLOR | November 1954 |

NOTES:-

a) No.429 was named Sir Alexander Henderson until 1917 and then Sir Douglas Haig until around 1920.

b) No.437 was named Charles Stuart Wortley until around 1920.

c) In LNER days 5429 and 5435 exchanged tenders with 6165 and 6168 of class B3 (9P).

No.275 at Guide Bridge in front of one of the well-known 'Manvers Main' coal wagons. The huge, rather ungainly, bulk of the engine gave rise to the nickname 'Crabs' ante-dating the application of this title to the Hughes 2–6–0s of the London Midland & Scottish Rly. This locomotive was a Gorton engine from the time of its delivery in 1915 until transfer to Mexborough in 1940. At Gorton, 275 had spent much of its life trundling between Guide Bridge and Ashton Moss, a part of the town of Ashton-under-Lyne and the site of extensive transfer sidings for the exchange of trans-Pennine freight.

# Class 1B 2–6–4 Tank

At the end of 1914, the year that had seen the start of the First World War, the first two of the giant and ungainly 2–6–4 tank engines of Class 1B were rolled out of the Gorton erecting shops.

Essentially a workmanlike brute of a locomotive, the 1B had none of the balance, poise and almost suavity of its earlier large compatriot of opposite wheel arrangement, the 9N 4–6–2 tank of 1911.

Whereas the 9N tank had been a purely Robinson–conceived design, the 1B was not essentially of Robinson's making, having been modelled to some extent on an 0–6–4 tank design belonging to the erstwhile Lancashire, Derbyshire & East Coast Railway, a concern that had been absorbed by the Great Central in 1907. The L.D.& E.C.R. D class 0–6–4T was built by Kitson's of Leeds and displayed several of that company's features, though at least one outside influence is reported as having been brought to bear on the design. R.A.Thom who had been Locomotive Superintendent on the L.D.& E.C.R. at the time of the Great Central's takeover had been appointed as Assistant Works Manager at Gorton and the appearance of his hand in the 2–6–4 tank design is one possibility in its genesis.

But whatever outlines these locomotives alluded to, their mechanics were almost pure Robinson. The boiler (G.C.R. Standard No.5) was similar to that carried by the first Directors (11E), though the small tubes were reduced from 175 to 157 and superheater elements with shorter loops were introduced. Element protection was by means of Robinson's improved steam jet draught retarder. Boiler pressure was, as with the 'Director', 180lb p.s.i. providing steam for two 21" bore inside cylinders of the type fitted to 'Sir Sam Fay' and 'Glenalmond' (though of ½" smaller diameter). As with these two 4–6–0 classes, the 10" piston valves were on top of the cylinders and were driven by rocking shafts but, in contrary practice, were of the outside admission variety, as used on the 11D 4–4–0 and the 11E Director. In the manner of the 'Glenalmonds' and the later batches of 9N tanks, the boilers carried a top feed.

Though the outlines of this 97 ton leviathan were dissimilar from the Robinson 9N tank some design parallels above platform level ensued. The application of top feed has been mentioned and to maximise water capacity the 1B's side tanks were, in the manner of the 9N, made wider than the cab. A 3,000 gallon water capacity brought the tank width out to 9' 1" whereas the cab width was only 8' 3". To avoid an excessive rear overhang when the locomotives were negotiating sharply curved pointwork the rear buffer plank was made narrower than the front one, the valance below the platform plating being inset to match underneath the centre of the bunker.

The Kitson L.D.& E.C.R. 0–6–4T had used the Allan straight link motion beloved of the LNWR, though its use had been abandoned by them from around 1897. Robinson was a committed Stephenson's link motion man and, logically, applied this well–tried and highly successful valve motion to the 1B tank. The size of coupled wheel, 5' 1", unusual for a Robinson tank engine, had, nevertheless, been successfully applied to the 9J 0–6–0 ('Pom-Pom') and had been used on several Parker and Pollitt goods and tank designs. The rear bogie, a definite Great Central novelty, was to the Lancashire & Derbyshire Kitson design, retaining the 3' 0" diameter wheels with characteristic large centre bosses. Largely unseen from photographs, a 16–plate spring was mounted over each axlebox on the inside of the bogie frames. Brakes were provided for the bogie wheels, a single cylinder being mounted on each side of the frames, between the two wheels. The piston rods were coupled to short brake levers which in turn actuated the brake hangers, cross–connections were provided between the two brake beams ensuring the necessary co–action.

Provision was also made for these brakes to be hand operated. The front pony truck, seen on the neighbouring G.N. Gresley H2 (K1) 2–6–0, was another feature new to Robinson's engines and worthy of some detail description. A steel casting was used for the centre of the truck, extending between plate frames of ⅞" steel. A flat boss, 9¼" in diameter fitted into the cup of a swing bolster, also made out of cast steel. The bolster was hung from the truck frames by four 'three–point' hangers spaced 1' 11¼" apart. This design had the stated advantage of avoiding the tilting of the bolster inherent in an inclined swing link design. A 'V' wrought iron forging at the rear of the truck provided for a radius of 4' 11" from the front of the locomotive. A spring consisting of 9 plates controlled vertical axlebox movement, the plate spring was further assisted by a coil spring on each side of the stays. A radius pin, 2½" diameter was held in a wrought iron plate–stay extending between the engine frames above the truck. The total side–play of the truck was 6½".

The 1B 2–6–4 tank had been designed for heavy haulage of coal from the Nottinghamshire and Derbyshire coalfields as far as Immingham Docks. Nos.272 and 273, which had been put into traffic in December 1914, were allocated initially to Annesley. At this time the Great War was raging, with a corresponding effect on the export of coal. This meant that the duties for which the engines had been designed had shrunk dramatically and their more or less immediate redeployment was inevitable. Notwithstanding this, a further eight examples were completed between February and December 1915.

Pressure at Gorton for the manufacture of munitions for the war effort caused post-

**One of the few pictures taken showing the 1B tanks engaged on the work they were built for: an unidentified member of the class in new condition heads a loaded coal train at Bulwell Common.**

*T.G.Hepburn/W.A.Brown collection*

ponement of a projected batch of ten examples that were to have followed. On February 2nd. 1916, however, Robinson reported to the Locomotive, Carriage & Wagon Committee: "... and as we are now having fewer demands for munition work, all the machinery in our Works which has been so occupied for some time is now available for our own purposes, I am able to undertake the preparation of parts for the construction of new locomotives. As regards the ten just mentioned [the ten postponed tanks] all the material is on the ground and in varying stages of progress, and I have given instructions for these Engines to be completed as quickly as possible." Robinson went on to ask the Committee to authorise the building, not only of the ten tanks (which he got) but also the construction of ten Directors and ten further 4–6–2 tanks (9N).

Despite his missive Robinson only got half of his batch of 4–6–2 tanks, and these did not arrive until 1917. The rest of the Directors did not begin to appear on the scene until 1919, and it was not until 1922 that the remainder were completed. Putting the case for further examples of the 1B class Robinson added: "The Tank Mineral Engines are necessary to enable us to stop heavy class engines for repairing as a great number will shortly have to be taken in hand."

The 1B tanks survived intact through the years of the LNER altered little in the visual sense, save only for the replacement of boiler mountings (see photographs). Mechanical changes were minimal; principally, one at least is known to have received smaller cylinders of 20″ bore to reduce the load on the driving axle and several other engines are known to have been fitted with new cylinders post–1943. As was the case with all superheated Great Central locomotives in LNER days, the Robinson arrangement of blower and steam circulating valve were replaced by the simpler and equally effective Gresley snifting valve situated behind the chimney (although one engine, No. 341, had one valve on each side of the chimney). Anti–vacuum valves fitted to the cylinders (see 'Glenalmond' class Vol.I) were also removed, their function being taken over by the Gresley snifters.

Earlier class members had been fitted with Wakefield mechanical lubricators and later engines, the 1917 batch of six, with Robinson's patent 'Intensifore' system with sight feeds. The Wakefield apparatus was removed from the earlier batch and the 'Intensifore' system substituted. In later LNER days, from June 1939, a volte face was made with, again, the use of Wakefield pattern lubricators for all twenty of the class. Top feed to the boiler, a device

beloved of Robinson on his later engines, was removed by the LNER as was the twin water scoop fitted to the class from new, along with the brakes on the trailing truck.

Away from the Midlands to North East coal haulage for which they were intended, wartime duties for the 1Bs extended to cross–Pennine goods traffic. In 1919 the bulk of the class (11 engines) were stationed at Annesley with a small number at Woodford. From Annesley the class worked pick–up or 'Pilot' goods trips as well as some local colliery workings; occasional forays onto passenger trains between Mansfield and Nottingham were also noted. No. 367 was stationed at Leicester and did little more than work the pick–up goods to Loughborough and back. Other work there consisted of shed shunting, pushing wagons of coal up the coal 'steep'. Occasional trips to Nottingham on slow passenger trains were also made.

In 1920 Nos. 340 & 366 were employed in piloting heavy goods trains up to Dunford Bridge. At least one engine, No. 336, was engaged on freight duties in the Manchester area at around this time. Prior to Grouping, 1B tanks were noted at Woodford and Neasden being engaged on goods workings between these points. At the end of 1922 a majority of locomotives were at Annesley, Neasden and Woodford with Langwith and Gorton having 2 and 1 mem-

**A broadside view of a 1B tank, this time No.272 at Gorton shed with our little friend from Volume I, the Class 5 0–6–0 saddletank variously known as 'Little Dick' or 'Fat Dan' which Robinson had rebuilt in 1903 to form a crane engine. On the 1B, the projection of its tank side over the cab shows clearly as does the caged-in bunker top. The sloped coal rails, in the manner of other Robinson tank designs, caused problems when mechanical coaling plants were introduced in the 1930s. In a bid to alleviate coal spillage the sloped arrangement was altered in two stages: firstly by removing the top two coal rails and finally, by removing the sloped arrangement altogether to leave three vertical rails (q.v.).**

*Collection of G.H.Platt*

One of a series of official Great Central engine views showing No.272 in 'shop grey' with full lining and used by the company to illustrate a leather-bound diagram book giving full dimensions etc. of the locomotive fleet. Though an entirely anonymous view in terms of surrounding detail (all of which was painted out on the diagram illustrations) the picture has been included for the amount of crisp detail it reveals and, in particular, the superbly-applied lining. The 1B tanks were turned out in standard Great Central goods livery of black with red and white lining as witnessed in our previous picture of the same engine. Black lines on the photograph here were transposed to red edged white when the class went into traffic. Photographic evidence shows the Great Central crest to have been placed on the front cab panel, in contrast to the arrangement seen here which reflected earlier livery practice seen on the 4–4–2 and 4–6–2 tank series. Notice too, the various underframe details: bogie brakes with one double-acting cylinder between both wheels and the application of sanding (gravity only) to all the coupled wheels; such ample sanding provision seemingly failed to counteract the design's tendency to slip.

*Collection of Brian Hilton*

One of the later series of 1B tanks, No.342 of 1916, the year of the all-time low of Great Central engine building. This broadside view at Gorton in 'shop grey' presents a stark contrast to the previous fully-lined ex-works view, the privations of wartime now eschewing any such frivolities. Notice the Wakefield pattern lubricator, fitted to all the 1914-16 engines and, the combined blower and steam circulating valve for the superheater elements prominent on the left-hand side of the smokebox.

A 1B tank out on the line: from the raised viewpoint of Chorlton Junction signalbox, on the Manchester Central – Derby line, No.336 takes the route up towards Fairfield with a mixed freight train c.1920.

*G.M.Shoults*

A nice study of a 1B in action in Great Central days and revealing the staggered nature of the running plate or 'platform' of the class. Guide Bridge is the setting as No.275 blows off whilst propelling a horsebox through the platforms.

*W.A.Brown collection*

The first of our post-Grouping pictures shows the workings of the 1B tanks over the loop line to Wembley stadium. During Wembley events these engines were often seen sweeping round this line at Neasden North Junction, their speeds causing concern. Percy Banyard recalled the late Locomotive Inspector Charlie Skinner saying: *Those Neasden laddies are no doubt good chaps, but I shall have to take up with them regarding their speeds*! Here, No.5342, in plain black LNER livery, puts up a plentiful smokescreen as it heads towards Marylebone with a train of bogie corridor stock.

*A.L.P.Reavil, W.A.Brown collection*

5342 at Neasden in early LNER days still displaying the Robinson chimney but with snifting valve behind.

*W.A.Brown collection*

Further into the LNER period and the outline of the 1B engines begins to change. No.273, the second member of the class, from December 1914, carries the hideous 'flowerpot' chimney with Gresley-pattern snifting valve behind, a lower pattern of dome cover and Ross 'pop' safety valves. The star and crescent on the smokebox door appear to be local embellishments.

*W.L.Good*

Great Central No.370 became LNER 9069 in 1946. In September 1949 the locomotive was photographed at Gorton shed with the simple form of British Railways lettering and plain all-over black livery. Notice now the reversion to Wakefield mechanical lubrication and the use of snap-head rivets on the new smokebox, a feature seemingly abhorred by Robinson. Bogie brakes have been removed and the chimney is of a new pattern, not dissimilar from the Robinson model and, certainly, a more pleasing effort than the LNER 'flowerpot.'

In the late 1940s the (by then) L3 tanks broke new ground when an allocation was made to Northwich shed on the Cheshire Lines system. On May 10th 1949 No.69052 (GC 274) is seen arriving at Hartford North with a freight from the ICI plant at Winnington (Northwich). The standard Great Central wheel and handle for fastening the smokebox door has now given way to the twin-handled arrangement.

*P.M.Alexander/Author's collection*

On the same day at Hartford grimy 69062 presents a rear aspect showing well the narrower rear buffer plank and smaller 'British Railways' lettering on the tank sides, compare with 69069. Also visible are the bars fixed over the rear cab windows when the coal rails were altered in the 1930s.

*P.M.Alexander/Author's collection*

No.69052 stands in Northwich station on October 1st 1953 at the head of a local freight working. Taken from rail-level, this picture gives some impression of the immense size of the 1B engine.

*Harold Freeth/W.A.Brown collection*

bers of the class respectively. Engines at Neasden and Woodford were employed on coal trains with Neasden crews and guards lodging at Woodford.

In early 1923 six 1Bs were sent to Immingham where they worked on dock shunting and pilot work, duties that lasted well into the Second War. 1929 saw redeployment for a number of the class with Mexborough acquiring a contingent for the purpose of banking coal trains from Wath concentration yard to Dunford Bridge; here a number remained until the end of the LNER era. This year also saw four transfers to March, the first time any deployment away from the Great Central system had taken place. Engines at March worked 'Trippers' to Peterborough East, Standridge sidings.

In the early 1930s two 1B tanks, now classified L1, were moved from Immingham to the new shed at Frodingham for duties in the new yards in the area connected with the expansion of steel–making. Other movements of the class around this time included transfers from Woodford to Neasden to assist in the running of Specials from Marylebone to Wembley Stadium. Duties further afield saw members of the class hauling light milk trains from Banbury to Marylebone and back.

At the outbreak of the Second War in 1939 allocations of 1B tanks were as follows: Frodingham 2, Gorton 1, Immingham 5, Mexborough 8, Neasden 4. In 1940 No. 5275 was moved from Gorton, after a stay there of 25 years, to Mexborough. In 1942 three 1Bs were sent from Mexborough to Sheffield for assistance with coal trains between Worksop and Dunford Bridge; they were returned to their parent shed in 1944. When the War ended Woodford used the 2–6–4 tanks on Quainton Road and Princes Risborough pick–up goods workings. The class broke new ground in 1943 when two engines were transferred to Northwich on the CLC system. This area abounds in chemical plants belonging to I.C.I. and work was found for two engines – Nos. 5274 and 5343 – hauling and banking goods and tank traffic between Hartford and Winnington Park and Winnington and Northwich, all essentially short haul work. With brief interruptions, both engines remained at Northwich until withdrawal in 1954 and 1951.

After 1945 the bulk of the engines (then reclassed 'L3' to allow Thompson's new 2–6–4 tank to take the 'L1' title) were stationed at Neasden with some later forays to Woodford to participate in local pick–up freight work to Quainton Road and a solitary overnight trip to High Wycombe. Towards the end of the LNER era, in 1947, No. 9064 (ex G.C. No. 345) moved north from Neasden to New England to work power station traffic from Peterborough to Little Barford near St.Neots.

The final duties of any note had been goods over the former Metropolitan line from Neasden shed. One engine, No. 69060 (G.C.341), had the rather dubious honour of acting as a stationary boiler at the Stratford Carriage works. Another, No. 69052 (G.C.274), eked out an existence in the same role at Gorton Works until its withdrawal in August 1954.

Though these 'Crabs' had a fairly long innings, they do not seem to have been without their shortcomings. Poor adhesion and lack of brake power seem to have been inherent problems. Percy Banyard, the late doyen of Great Central locomen who drove and fired every one of the class during his fifty–one year career, recalled being stuck for around 45 minutes inside Catesby tunnel with one of them. One driver, a

**Seen the following year, on March 6th 1954, 69052 simmers alongside the water column adjacent to Northwich sidings. These engine servicing roads could be found all over the country where extensive goods sidings existed. Quite often a small coalstage would be provided too, so that engines could stay 'on the job' all day or longer. Visiting engines would also take advantage of the facilities, especially if a turntable was available, before returning home.**

*B.K.B.Green*

Away from the noise and clamour of the industrial north to the leafy pastures of Buckinghamshire; we take a last look at the Robinson 2–6–4 tank engines in action with this shot of No.69060 (GC 341) at Wendover on the former Metropolitan & G.C. Joint line working the Quainton Road pick-up. 69060 was withdrawn in June 1954 and proceeded into ignominy (see text).

Most definitely not the work the 1B tank was built for! A last look at No.69052 on November 14th 1954 when the engine, three months after withdrawal, was engaged as a stationary boiler alongside the wagon works at Gorton. Despite its pathetic state there are still, nevertheless, some points of interest to be gleaned: the smokebox and door show particularly well-the former being of the snap-head riveted pattern, the Wakefield lubricator shows well along with the all-important oil box on the front of the sidetank. Notice, too, the dome cover has been removed leaving the dome proper to show for the obvious purpose of steam collection. Railwaymen are never without a sense of humour and the chalked message on the cabside proves the point – *Mason's Chalet – Teas etc* reads the inscription. Underneath the running number the words: *do not scrap* appear alongside the 'X' – presumably the wagon works needed No.69052 a little bit longer than the running department! The boiler survived to be used by D11 class No.62667 from December 1956 to August 1960.

*B.K.B.Green*

**No.69064 (GC 345) was one of the last of the twenty of the 1B class to be withdrawn, in January 1955. Three months later she languishes on the scrap line at Gorton Works on April 24th, the fateful 'X' on the cabside denoting imminent cutting-up.**

*B.K.B.Green*

Gorton man who rejoiced in the nickname of 'Sailor Jack', is reported to have suggested to Mr. (W.J.P.) Maclure that the side tanks would be better employed filled with sand!

So passed away the 1B 2–6–4 tank, a design of rather uncertain parentage and something of an 'ugly duckling' in the realm of Robinson's locomotives. Not a celebrated locomotive by any means, big and powerful in appearance but not, perhaps, living up to the expectations that had been placed upon it.

The Robinson 1B 2–6–4 tank engine became extinct in July 1955 with the withdrawal of B.R. No. 69069 (G.C.no. 370 of May 1917). Appropriately enough, this was the last of the twenty engines to appear in traffic.

## SUMMARY OF CLASS 1B 2–6–4 TANK ENGINE

| NUMBER | BUILDER | DATE BUILT | WITHDRAWN |
|---|---|---|---|
| 272 | Gorton | December 1914 | March 1955 |
| 273 | – ' – | December 1914 | May 1951 |
| 274 | – ' – | February 1915 | August 1951 |
| 275 | – ' – | March 1915 | July 1950* |
| 276 | – ' – | April 1915 | August 1949 |
| 336 | – ' – | April 1915 | July 1951 |
| 337 | – ' – | May 1915 | January 1951* |
| 338 | – ' – | June 1915 | October 1949* |
| 339 | – ' – | November 1915 | August 1949* |
| 340 | – ' – | December 1915 | August 1949* |
| 341 | – ' – | June 1916 | June 1954 |
| 342 | – ' – | June 1916 | February 1953 |
| 343 | – ' – | June 1916 | May 1951 |
| 344 | – ' – | August 1916 | July 1947 |
| 345 | – ' – | January 1917 | January 1955 |
| 366 | – ' – | February 1917 | May 1954 |
| 367 | – ' – | March 1917 | April 1950* |
| 368 | – ' – | March 1917 | February 1951* |
| 369 | – ' – | April 1917 | June 1950* |
| 370 | – ' – | May 1917 | July 1955 |

NOTES:–

*a) All re-numbered by the LNER by the addition of 5000 to their former numbers. Note should especially be made however to engines that carried LNER painted numerals and their GC oval plates (viz. no.5273), also to the fact that LNER re-numbering was carried out over quite a long period, two members of the 1B class (276 & 367) not receiving their post-1923 numbers until October 1926.*

*b) Under the LNER's 1946 re-numbering scheme the (then L3) class were numbered en bloc from 9050 (ex GC no.272) to 9069 (ex GC no.370). British Railways added 60000 to these numbers but note that engines against which an ast appears did not carry their BR designation. One engine, 9063, was withdrawn before Nationalisation.*

ROD No.2048 was built by North British Loco. in June 1919 and is seen here at Guide Bridge whilst on hire to the Great Central. Apart from the company name on the tender, the engine typifies the ROD locomotive as supplied for war work in France: screw jacks on footplate, ribbed buffers with side-chains prominent, rectangular numberplate, Ross 'pop' safety valves and Westinghouse pump with air reservoir underneath the cab. The condition of the pump casing gives rise to the view that a slight amount of 'persuasion' has been necessary to restore normal service! These later engines relied on Westinghouse brakes for both the locomotive and train and were equipped with two brake cylinders, one under each side of the cab. This and the attendant air reservoir can be readily discerned in the picture. Sent back to the W.D. in August 1921 and stored at Morecambe, 2048 was bought by the LNER in February 1927 and arrived at Gorton works on the 22nd October of that year to be made ready for traffic. Rebuilt to Class O4/3, it became No.6615 from February 1928, 3849 from 14th December 1946 and as 63849 was sold out of service to the War Department in 1952, becoming WD 041.

# R O D 2–8–0

The genesis and development of the original Robinson 2–8–0 (Great Central Class 8K) was covered in Volume I along with its transposition to the well–known and widely travelled locomotive first built in 1917 for the Ministry of Munitions (MM) in World War 1.

So far afield did the ROD version travel, and for so long was it part of the British and overseas steam scene, that, had Robinson built no other locomotives, his place in the higher ranks of steam locomotive designers would still have been assured.

To briefly re–cap: four contractors plus the Great Central themselves, though only in a minor capacity, were selected to build the locomotives. The standard Robinson 2–8–0 design was taken and put into production with only slight detail differences. These were:

*(a)* Substitution of copper sheet by steel for the inner firebox plates and stays. This cut the cost of construction, conserved a valuable wartime commodity and saved around 1 ton on the weight of the locomotive. Though foreign to British practice, the use of steel fireboxes was widespread abroad, particularly in America.

*(b)* The omission of water pick–up apparatus on the tender.

*(c)* Substitution of vacuum braking by air brakes. The Westinghouse pumps were mounted on the right–hand side of smokebox. The later engines, those ordered as and from North British order No. L.703 of 1918, relied on the Westinghouse brake for engine, tender and train; previous engines had also been equipped with the steam brake for the locomotive.

*(d)* Ross 'pop' safety valves in lieu of the Ramsbottom enclosed pattern fitted to the 8K.

Other minor changes included altered axles for the slightly different continental gauge (+5mm for a gauge of 1.44m) paralleled by a fractional difference in wheel tyre profile and substitution of the Great Central oval–headed buffers by round ones with ribbed stocks along with side chains. Small rectangular numberplates were placed on the cabsides, along with a similar plate on the back of the tender. The majority of the ROD engines were equipped with Wakefield mechanical lubricators, but Robinson's Intensifore system, developed in the War, was used on some of the later locomotives.

Though officially entitled 'Ministry of Munitions', the pseudonym ROD was quickly applied due, doubtless, to the fact that the letters ROD (The Railway Operating Division of the Royal Engineers) were applied to the tender sides, along with the running number, when the engines were off–loaded in France. Locomotives were shipped with coupling and connecting rods removed and stacked in the tender, and (for loading gauge compliance) minus outer chimney casing. Re–assembly was in the ROD's own workshops at Audruicq, between Calais and St.Omer, and the engines were, it seems, put straight into traffic with no special period for running–in.

Thus settled down, the RODs went to work handling troop trains and loads of military supplies; civilian trains were also hauled, typically between Calais and St.Omer with the locomotives mostly driven and fired by ROD crews.

The pioneer North British engine, ROD No. 1801, was turned out in grey, lined black and white for photographic purposes. The remainder were outshopped in plain black which extended, very unusually, to the buffer beams, eschewing the familiar vermillion. Shipped over to France minus outer chimney, with coupling and connecting rods loaded into the tender, the engines must have presented a strange sight. Two screw jacks were mounted on the front running plate, thought to be necessary for re–railing, given the condition of the track over which the engines would be operating.

Disposal of the ROD engines after the War is complicated and can really only be satisfactorily dealt with via a table (q.v.). Briefly, the post–War use of the engines falls into two broad categories: engines under hire whilst still the property of the Government, bearing in mind that State control of the railways lasted until mid––August 1921, and their subsequent use after the locomotives had been sold off by the Government.

A great deal of wrangling took place regarding the price asked by the Government for the former ROD engines. Inflation (not an entirely modern phenomenon) had soared during World War I with a consequent effect upon prices. The first N.B.Loco order worked out at £6,030 per engine. By the onset of the fourth order in 1918 the negotiated price had risen to £8,400 with labour and materials calculated as on May 4th 1918. A proviso was also made for any increases attributable to Government action. Provision was allowed for 25% of any savings made below the adjusted price to be repayable to the Ministry.

Without question, the ROD 2–8–0s acquitted themselves well in their wartime duties. Though Robinson had some reservations about his 8Ks being stable at speeds over about 20 m.p.h., the class were recorded at speeds up to twice that level with no apparent difficulty.

With hostilities finally over, the locomotives returned home from across the Channel. Temporary accommodation was provided at a variety of locations in the south of England: chief amongst these was at Tattenham Corner (near Epsom) where a massive dump of engines was formed with up to 150 incumbents deposited at

**The Great Central built only three ROD engines and, paradoxically, none of them entered traffic as such, becoming part of the company's own stock. This is No.5, the second of the trio, on view at Ardwick in Great Central days. Two immediate features remain to identify this as an ex-ROD loco: the metal straps on the smokebox where the Westinghouse pump was attached and the two re-railing jacks on the front of the running plate. No.5 became LNER 5005 in April 1926. As British Railways No.63627 it was one of the engines sold to the War Department in 1952 for service in the Middle East.**

times. Other locations for storage were at Brockenhurst, Dinton and Winchester. Something akin to the famous Disney 'Fantasia' cartoon scene, where the beleaguered sorcerer's apprentice is almost drowned by an unstoppable torrent of water poured liberally from buckets carried by broken broom handles, now presented itself, with locomotives still being turned out in earnest. These were mainly from the North British Company's works in Glasgow, with a few thrown in for good measure from Robert Stephenson. Though some found their way into traffic right away, others congregated at sites such as Gretna and (appropriately enough) Immingham.

The Great Central, who had initially planned to build 25 ROD engines, agreed to purchase three 2–8–0s completed in the first quarter of 1919. So began a process of disposal which was to take eight years. The asking price was £6,066 each. Nominally ROD Nos. 2005–7 the engines became G.C. Nos. 1,5 & 8. From this point on prices began to escalate. In April 1919 the company had its eye on ten 2–8–0s standing at Immingham and suggested a price of £8,000 apiece. Notwithstanding that this was some 25% more than had been paid already, the Government were not in a co–operative mood. Things appeared to have reached ludicrous heights when, in November the following year, the G.C. enquired as to the price of the 93 2–8–0s it had on hire; this time the price had risen to £12,000 per locomotive!

As the initial sales of the RODs were beginning, the Government, in the form of the Ministry of Munitions, began to arrange for the hire of locomotives that had not seen service in France. Companies which took up the offer of loans (numbers in brackets) were: the Caledonian (50) Great Central (93), Great Western (84), Lancashire & Yorkshire (28), London & North-Western (151), London & South-Western (17) and the North Eastern Railway (35). As engines returned from their wartime tasks even more motive power was made available for hire. This widened yet again the scope of the much–travelled Robinson machine, with the Great Eastern (42) and the South Eastern & Chatham (6) getting in on the act and all the previous hirers bar the North Eastern taking more engines on loan.

All the hirers retained the engines' Westinghouse brake equipment together with jacks and side–chains. Appearing in the very plain black livery of the ROD, only the LNWR and the GWR applied temporary running numbers to their acquisitions. The L&SWR did begin to apply their own numbers but did not continue the process.

That not all the companies who hired

RODs ultimately bought them is no reflection on the 8K design. Not all railways had a need for a large freight engine and the fact that it was built to a fairly generous loading gauge was also a limiting factor. Engines used on the Great Eastern, for instance, had to have their chimneys removed when they went into Stratford Works for repair. The LNWR barred the RODs from their main line south of Stafford because of problems in fouling platforms. On the Lancashire and Yorkshire Railway tests were made with one engine (number not recorded) on a crossover at Bolton station. The locomotive was driven at an increasing pace until it fouled the platform coping; hereafter, the L&Y decided to dispose of its holding. The 2–8–0, with a width over outside cylinders of 8' 10½", was 2½" over the standard L&Y loading gauge.

In the summer of 1919 sales of RODs began apace. Twenty of the new 2–8–0s were disposed of, ten apiece, to the LNWR (from the Immingham dump) and the Great Western. The asking price was an average £10,300 each, although it is recorded that some £100 – £200 expenditure was needed for each engine to remedy the corrosion that had occurred after standing outside on the locomotive 'dump'.

An interesting sidelight on the ROD saga is worth including at this point in the history of the type. An entry in the Gorton drawing register shows drawing work done at Gorton on May 30th 1919 for alteration of some engines to 5' 0" gauge. Obviously, some export was in mind and the Baltic state of Estonia has been mentioned in connection with this mooted conversion.

The engines sold to the LNWR eventually numbered 30 in all, another 20 having been bought in September 1919. They were numbered in the Capital list in random fashion between 12 and 2268. Later that year the company began to hire further RODs until there were 181 of them at work on the system. At this point all the original thirty were renumbered in the series 2800 – 2829 and the hired engines given numbers in continuation of this series. The renumbering of the first 30 did not follow any apparent order, neither did the renumbering above 2829 – although the sequence did show some indication of the order in which the hired engines were delivered. Of those hired, Nos. 2830 – 2940 went direct to the LNW. Nos. 2950 – 2970 had seen previous service on the L&Y, who had put their coat of arms on the side of the cab. Nos. 2971 – 2976 had been in service on the SE&CR and 2977 and 2978 had been on the LSWR. Nos. 2950 – 2978 were all sent to the LNWR in 1920; the final two, which became 2979 and 2980, had arrived in January 1921.

The company retained the Westing-

house brake equipment which it found satisfactory. As no vacuum equipment was supplied, the engines could only be used for loose coupled freight workings. Such duties seem to have been recorded on the main line north of Crewe, with Stafford as the limit in a southerly direction.

Nos. 2830 – 2980 were recalled by the Government in August 1921. The 30 that remained were again re–numbered in the series 1315 – 2451 and these all passed to the LMS who re–numbered them in 1928 in the 9600 series and then in 1930 to 9458 – 9476 to make room for G3 0–8–0s.

The use of engines on loan to various companies came to an end in the autumn of 1921 when the Government began to call in the hired stock. Large congregations of ex–ROD locomotives appeared, principally at Birkenhead, Gretna and Sandycroft (situated between Chester and Rhyl). Here the engines languished in a condition that must have been reminiscent of those at Barry decades later. This situation lasted until 1924 when the George Cohen & Armstrong Whitworth Disposal Corporation was given the job by the Government of getting rid of the steadily deteriorating stock. Large scale disposals began in 1923 with (not surprisingly) the LNER among the first customers. Three batches were bought – one at the outset (in 1923), another in 1924 and the third in 1927, a total of 273 locomotives. With latter day prices down to around £350 – £400 per locomotive the LNER were getting heavy freight engines for a fraction of the building costs of new ones.

Westinghouse equipment was removed along with steam heating gear and, as elsewhere, a copper firebox wrapper replaced the inner steel one. The locomotives were split largely between the former Great Central, North Eastern and Scottish areas. For service in Scotland cut–down cabs and boiler mountings were needed (in like manner to the Scottish Directors). The former ROD engines were classified O4/3, those with cut–down cabs O4/2 while the original G.C. (ex 8K) were given the classification O4/1. Further rebuilding of these engines took place in later years and a summary table has been included at the end of this feature in order to elucidate this. Here, though, the story gets complicated and, as remarked upon in Volume I, is worthy of a book in its own right.

Because of Robinson's Great Western tutelage interplay between his engines and those of the Great Central is always fascinating. At this point we recall that the GWR had purchased 20 RODs in 1919 and a further 80 in 1925. Familiarity with the ROD type had come through previous hirings and the company no doubt recognised that, at a mere £1,500 apiece, the engines were something of a 'snip'. They were

En route ä la guerre de 1914–18. A rare view of two ROD 2–8–0s during the sea voyage to France with military personnel posing for the camera. Shipped without their chimneys, the engines presented an even more austere appearance than usual. Notice the wagon tarpaulin labelled SE&CR and the stacks of rail in the foreground, some of which is pre-assembled into crossing 'vees'.

*Collection of Paul Dalton*

ROD No.1748 stands at Darlington with the WD operating number still appearing on the tender sides and bufferbeam. 1748 became successively LNER No.6502 and 3733. Never rebuilt, the engine was withdrawn in January 1961 as British Railways 63733.

*V.R.Webster collection*

**Apart from the LNER, the biggest purchasers of the ROD 2–8–0s were the Great Western who availed themselves of 100 of these magnificent machines between 1919 and 1925. Unfortunately neither the running number or the location can be identified in this classic Great Western scene. Watched by a pair of gangers the ROD works hard at the head of a very typical mixed freight, possibly near Cheltenham. Immediately obvious are the 'Great Westernised' features with chimney, top-feed, dome, smokebox door handles and safety valve cover all conforming to Swindon pattern. GW-type rectangular numberplates and the faintly-visible 'Great Western' legend on the tender complete the picture.**

taken into stock in July 1925 as Lot 240 and took numbers in the series 3020 – 3099. Nineteen of the bought engines had been in traffic previously as loans; eighteen of these regained their temporary GWR numbers. In the autumn of 1925 the Great Western took their ex–RODs out of traffic en bloc; thirty were given major repairs with the addition of copper inner fireboxes and GWR boiler mountings, acquiring the Great Western green livery in the process. Numbers in the series 3020 – 3049 were allocated and the repaired locos were designated Lot 241. Though not lasting as long as some of their ex–Great Central counterparts, some these engines survived until 1958.

The remaining fifty GWR RODs were patched up and left in traffic with their original steel inner fireboxes and black livery. Allocated running numbers 3050 – 3099, withdrawals began in 1927 and they were extinct by 1931. To complicate matters further it is necessary to record that in 1926, when the class was split, six of those engines downgraded were given numbers in the 3020 – 3049 series and six of these

received numbers from the 3050 – 3099 series. A useful bank of spares was retained from the withdrawn locomotives and some of the former Great Central pattern tenders found their way behind Aberdare 2–6–0s and later, to Collett's standard goods – the 2251 class 0–6–0. A few others, ignominiously, saw service as sludge tanks.

The Great Western classified the ex--ROD engines in power class D with a route availability code of blue. Though fitted with ATC equipment in 1931, the engines were unable to make full use of the innovation owing to their lack of vacuum brake. A warning plate was fitted inside the cabs notifying drivers of this shortcoming. Later detail modifications included new smokebox doors along with the removal of the piston tail–rod covers and GWR pattern pistons. Unlike the LNER who went in for some re–boilering of their examples, no new boiler design emanated from Swindon, a plan hatched in 1938 to equip the foreigners with the No.1 Standard boiler coming to nothing.

These Great Western ex–RODs saw service over most points of the company's

compass with most of the major running divisions housing examples from time to time. Of the twenty bought in 1919 (Nos. 3000 – 3019) sixteen became British Railways' property with a power classification of 7F. Of those engines from the re–shuffling of 1925, twenty–five entered BR service, the last examples going in 1958.

A final footnote to this story came about in November 1940 when the LNER loaned thirty 2–8–0s to the GWR for periods of just over two years. These were not all in original condition, one was an O5 rebuild and seven were new O4/7 rebuilds. Clearly, the GWR knew a good locomotive when it saw one!

In 1927 the LMS had bought another 75 RODs. By this time the price for the surplus locomotives had reached rock–bottom with these last examples going for the proverbial 'song' at £340 each. Only 20 entered service with the company however and the main reason behind the purchase appears to have been an acute shortage of tenders for Western Division locomotives. Observations have been made that the 2–8–0's restricted route availability precluded their

Appearing as LMS No.9638 this locomotive had a chequered history and a veritable plethora of numbers to suit. Beginning life as ROD No.2092, she emerged from the Atlas Works of North British Loco. in 1919. Bought by the LNWR the same year she was numbered first as 1694, then 2817 and thirdly as 2109. Under LMS auspices the engine became 9638 as seen here, on shed and without coupling or connecting rods. Allocated the number 9470, which was never carried, withdrawal was in 1931. The combination of LNWR buffers and chimney on a Great Central design is, to say the least, fascinating!

*W. Potter*

No.9616 was another of the batch of locomotives which the LNWR purchased in 1919. Originally numbered 1787 when new from North British Loco in that year the engine became successively LNWR 1747, 2820 and then 2400. Under ownership of the LMS, as pictured here, the engine was given the number 9616 before attaining yet another identity – as No.9455. A relatively early casualty by steam locomotive standards, this multi-numbered specimen was withdrawn for scrap in August, 1932. Worth a second glance is the Westinghouse pump, together with the retention of tail-rods and the 'not to be moved' disc hanging from the top of the tender.

(above) A number of the GW RODs survived until modern times giving spotters new to the loco identification game something of a puzzle to work out. Seen soon after leaving the Severn Tunnel with an up coal train is No.3038 which began life as ROD No.1644 and was delivered from Robert Stephenson's Darlington works in 1919. She acquired the number 3028 when on loan to the GWR and swapped numbers with 3085 in 1925. Becoming No.3038 she lasted in B.R. days until 1956.

*T.E.Williams/Author's collection*

(opposite) Robinson must have made a considerable sum of money from his various superheating devices, having been shrewd enough to patent every one as he developed them. From the RODs alone he received £60 per engine (a huge amount by today's standards) with an accompanying £10 for each one carrying the 'Intensifore' lubricator. Some idea of the widespread use made of his very successful superheaters is gleaned from this advertisement which appeared in the *Railway Gazette* in September 1921. The Superheater Corporation had taken over the manufacture and patent rights of Robinson's superheater and the use of an ROD 2–8–0 No.1801 in this contemporary advertisement provides a fascinating little snippet.

*Collection of Paul Dalton*

widespread use over LMS metals. Engines put into traffic had their steel firebox wrappers and stays replaced by copper ones, though they had done some running with the existing steel boxes. These repairs incurred expenditure of some £16,000. Tender repairs averaged out at around £400 per tender with fifty–five tenders going back into traffic behind Prince of Wales and Claughton 4–6–0s and George V 4–4–0s. Some Claughtons found their way onto the Midland Division where, with their newly-acquired red livery and Great Central pattern tenders, they looked strange birds indeed. Spares from about a dozen dismantled RODs were kept in hand for the existing stock of engines, a further twelve were scrapped by the LMS and a further batch of thirty were sold off to Messrs. Armstrong Whitworth. Initially classified 5F, the RODs were eventually re–cast as 7F.

Further forays abroad were then made by those locomotives which had been repaired by Armstrong Whitworth. Thirteen were sold to the Chinese Engineering & Mining Company and another nine to the Shanghai, Hanchow and Ningpo Railway. All these were reconditioned in the manner of the LMS locomotives, although new tenders were required. These had bodies with rounded corners and were without the well in the water tank. This left eight engines still in the hands of the company. No records appear to exist of these RODs being sold and it seems likely that the engines were cut up at the company's Scotswood Works in Newcastle.

In the interim period, in 1925, Armstrong Whitworth had purchased 25 RODs from the dump at Gretna. One (ex–ROD No. 1615), was specially overhauled as 'point of sale' material for the company. It was sold to the J & A. Brown Mining Company who own collieries in New South Wales, Australia. In Brown's ownership it ran as No. 21 and earned its keep until the early 1970s. The remaining 24, like the later purchases, were sold to Chinese concerns i.e: Shanghai–Nanking Railway, 12; Kailan Mining Company, 6. This left 6

remaining RODs which are also believed to have been sent to China. The Chinese locomotives retained their Westinghouse brake equipment and were fitted with American–style couplers and cowcatchers. Reported instances of these emigrants surviving in traffic until the the 1940s have been made but, given the nature of the situation, this cannot be confirmed. Sliding windows were fitted to the cabs and canvas screens were fixed between the engine and tender to keep out dust and draughts. Altogether a fascinating conversion; it would be very interesting indeed to know if any photographs survive of these converted RODs.

J.& A. Brown had previously purchased twelve ROD engines in 1923 and numbered them, in rather random fashion, between 12 and 24. Three of these appear to have been shipped out to Australia that year, while the ten others (nine of the 1923 batch plus No. 1615 from Armstrong Whitworth) were not sent out until mid–1927. Browns had their own ship, the SS Minmi, which made its maiden voyage with the locomotives on board. The engines, in a partially dismantled state, were off–loaded at Newcastle, with tenders following at Hexham. In 1990 the Editor of the magazine 'Steam Railway', undertook a remarkable journey to Dorrigo in New South Wales where he was able to photograph the last two of Brown's 2–8–0s, No. 2003, one of the Great Central's 1919 batch and No. 1984, a North British engine of 1918. Though the engines are not in running order they *exist* and are maintained in reasonable condition (at least visually) in a warm climate.

Another purchaser was a company by the name of Arnhold, purchasing agents for China also, who bought two engines in 1923. The pair, ROD numbers 1711 and 1808 were believed to be have been sent to Australia but, unfortunately, no information has come to light regarding their work, locations or scrapping dates.

Despite the very widespread sale of the RODs both in the U.K. and overseas, just one engine failed to sell at all. This was

ROD No. 2137, one of the North British batch, it was scrapped at Gretna in 1927.

With the return to England complete and the hire and disposal arrangements of the RODs all settled, it might be thought that the peregrinations of this much–travelled class were over; far from it! In 1941/42 sixty–one former RODs were 'called–up' for war service in Egypt, Persia, Iraq, Syria and Palestine along with thirty–one former Great Central 8Ks. Included in the latter were six engines that had previously been classed as 8M, Robinson's large–boilered version of the 8K. All ninety–two engines were re–numbered by the War Department in the series 700 – 791. Subsequently, all except Nos. 726 & 740 were re–numbered by the addition of 9000. Towards the end of 1944 Nos. 9727, 9728, 9729, 9741, 9744, 9745, 9748, 9777, 9778, 9779, 9783, 9786, 9788–91 were re–numbered again by the addition of 7000. These engines have been recorded as working on the Palestine Railways and the Haifa–Beirut–Tripoli Railway. Others from this series worked in Egypt and were re–numbered in like manner. No. 740 was lost at sea and the whereabouts of No. 726 does not appear to be recorded.

Written briefly back into LNER stock in 1942 and then out again in 1943, almost all of these 2–8–0s were converted to oil—firing and were re–painted in a light grey colour, one could hardly have called it 'livery.' In 1945, as the war in Europe ended, some of these engines in WD service were moved from traffic in Palestine and loaned to the Iraqi railway system. In 1947 two of these (former ROD Nos. 2087 & 2098) were sold to the Iraqi State Railways together with another four which had originated on the Great Central. Unlike their previous expatriate workmates none of these locomotives returned to the U.K.

The last act in this scenario of overseas travel came in 1952 when the War Department purchased a final five O4 2–8–0s from British Railways. The engines were sent to Suez where they remained until the Government relinquished the military base there in 1956. These final five were:–

A vintage view of an ex-ROD 2–8–0 which is sure to delight GWR enthusiasts! The location is Banbury with No.3025 working hard at the head of a mixed goods train. GW signals, clerestory coach and a truly 'Great Westernised' locomotive all conspire to create a classic effect. Originally numbered 3022 by the GWR, 3025 began life as ROD No.1698 when new from Robert Stephenson in 1918. The engine lasted well into BR days, being withdrawn in 1954.

63580 (GCR 8K No.69 – 3rd loco made)
63627 (ex ROD No.2006 – Gorton 1919)
63778 (GCR 8K No.1215 – N.B.L. 1912)
63809 (GCR 8K No.1222 – N.B.L. 1912)
63849 (ex ROD No.2048 – N.B.L. 1919)

At this late time there seems little to add to the Robinson 8K/ROD 2–8–0 saga as such. Very successful, widely travelled and highly regarded, they remain, for many locomen and enthusiasts, the British Railway heavy freight locomotive *par excellence*. And on this we will rest our case.

As will be observed from the table, engines were being turned out well after the end of the War. While this may seem strange, it must be remembered that contracts had been signed as late as October 25th 1918, just under one month before the November 11th Armistice.

Originally classified O4 by the LNER the former war service machines were almost indistinguishable from their ex-GC counterparts. Close inspection of this ex-North British engine shows the lack of tender water scoop gear, the characteristic 'ship's wheel', missing from the side of the tender bulkhead. Resplendent in lined black livery 6305 (ex-ROD 1991) looks ready for a lifetime's work. The engine was rebuilt to O4/7 (with the shortened O2-type boiler with round topped firebox and original cab). Withdrawal was in November, 1965.

## SUMMARY OF CONSTRUCTION OF ROD 2–8–0 LOCOMOTIVES

| BUILDER | WORKS NUMBERS | DELIVERED | R.O.D. NUMBERS | TOTAL |
|---------|---------------|-----------|----------------|-------|
| Kitson | 5183 – 5194 | 1918 | 1601 – 1612 | 12 |
| – ' – | 5199 – 5218 | 1918 | 1613 – 1632 | 20 |
| R.S.Co | 3695 – 3714 | 1917 | 1651 – 1670 | 20 |
| – ' – | 3715 – 3730 | 1917/18 | 1671 – 1686 | 16 |
| – ' – | 3731 – 3736 | 1918 | 1647 – 1688* | 6 |
| – ' – | 3737 – 3748 | 1918 | 1689 – 1700 | 12 |
| – ' – | 3749 – 3754 | 1919 | 1633/42 – 1646 | 6 |
| – ' – | 3755 – 3776 | 1919 | 1635/36/38/40/41.1733 – 1749 | 22 |
| N.W.Co | 1244 – 1267 | 1917/18 | 1701 – 1724 | 24 |
| – ' – | 1281 – 1288 | 1918 | 1725 – 1732 | 8 |
| N.B.L | 21768 – 21808 | 1917 | 1801 – 1841 | 41 |
| – ' – | 21819 – 21868 | 1917 | 1842 – 1891 | 50 |
| – ' – | 21869 – 21918 | 1918 | 1892 – 1941 | 50 |
| – ' – | 22000 – 22029 | 1918/19 | 1942 – 1971 | 30 |
| – ' – | 22030 – 22059 | 1918/19 | 1972 – 2001 | 30 |
| – ' – | 22080 – 22093 | 1919 | 1787 – 1800 | 14 |
| – ' – | 22104 – 22115 | 1919 | 2008/15 – 2020 | 12 |
| – ' – | 22116 – 22127 | 1919 | 2021 – 2031/33 | 12 |
| – ' – | 22128 – 22142 | 1919 | 2034 – 2044/2046 – 2048 | 14 |
| – ' – | 22143 – 22177 | 1919 | 2051 – 2084/86/87 | 36 |
| – ' – | 22178 – 22227 | 1919 | 2088 – 2137 | 50 |
| – ' – | 22228 – 22257 | 1919 | 2138 – 2167 | 30 |
| G.C.R | n/a | 1918/19 | 2002 – 2007 | 6 |

NOTES:–

R.S.Co: Robert Stephenson & Co. – Darlington Works.

N.W.Co: Nasmyth Wilson & Co. – Patricroft Works, Manchester.

N.B.L: North British Locomotive Co. – various works in Glasgow: Queens Park, Hyde Park and Atlas Works.

G.C.R: Great Central Rly, Gorton Works.

* Randon numbers.

† 3 of GC batch taken into stock as GC locos.

Totals: Kitsons **32**; Stephensons **82**; Nasmyths **32**; North British **369**; G.C.R **6**.

Total built to Ministry of Munitions orders = 521 locomotives.

Class O4/7 was the final Gresley rebuild of the Robinson 2–8–0s. Work began in 1938 and although most engines had been dealt with by 1944, it was not until the end of 1947 that all conversions were complete; altogether forty-one engines were dealt with. In these rebuilds the boiler barrel (known as Diagram 15D) was shortened by a further 11⅞″ compared with that applied to class O4/5

The GC cab was retained, although the angle irons on the roof were replaced by flat strips as used on class O4/2. In this very atmospheric picture No.63761, a former North British 8K of 1912, slogs past Guide Bridge East Junction signalbox, en route to Yorkshire, with a train of coal empties. As LNER No.6209 rebuilding to O4/7 had been carried out in June 1940, the engine was withdrawn in

# GCR 8K 2–8–0 Rebuild

In Volume one I made the point that the rebuilds of Robinson's 2–8–0s, along with the associated RODs, would require almost a book in their own right. That is still the case but, having travelled so far, it is worth attempting the impossible, constrained as I am by limits on space. The simplest thing to do in order to clarify the situation is to produce a basic table with what might be called 'identifying features'. The LNER locomotive classification system was very simple and entirely logical; the same could not be said for the G.C.R!

Plans to rebuild former Robinson 2–8–0s, if one excludes the cutting down of boiler mountings and cabs and fitting of new fireboxes, began in 1927 when proposals were submitted from Gorton to fit a new wide firebox boiler, possibly with a round top, and a grate area of 33 sq.ft. These proposals were not taken any further, and it was two years later, in 1929, that rebuilding proper began.

Gresley had never favoured the Belpaire firebox and had taken on board the Great Northern practice of using round topped fireboxes, coupled variously to parallel and taper boilers. In consequence, almost all the 2–8–0 rebuilds under his re-

gime followed the round top firebox theme, fitted, in the case of goods engines, to parallel barrels. Edward Thompson followed in Gresley's wake (though he was certainly not a Gresley disciple!) with his own B1 boiler and new cylinders.

One notable exception to the almost universal parallel boiler theme were the seventeen former 8M 2–8–0s. Robinson had rebuilt two of these machines before Grouping (Nos. 412 & 413) with 8K boilers and the rest followed on from 1926 through to 1943. Originally, the large 8M cab was retained but, from 1939 to 1943, these cabs were cut down to bring the class within the composite LNER loading gauge because of wartime work. Variously rebuilt, the Robinson 8M had had an interesting number of guises: as originally conceived with the 5' 6" boiler, then as an 'alternative fuel' locomotive (two engines), rebuilt with the 8K boiler and large cab retained, and rebuilt again by altering the cab profile. Five went to the Middle East where their 'alternative fuel' was oil, and Arabic numbers were applied. Finally, two engines were yet again rebuilt in 1955/56 by conversion to Thompson's Class O4/8 with round topped (100A–B1 pattern) boiler and cab.

Thompson had broken the mould almost completely when, in 1944, he introduced his Class O1 2–8–0; an outline of which had been mooted as far back as 1941. The original plan was to almost totally rebuild the O4 design with a diagram 100A boiler (as fitted to the B1 4–6–0), B1–pattern cylinders and Walschaerts motion, shortened mainframes and an L1 pony truck, new cab and Group Standard 4,200 gallon tender. In the event, to minimise construction costs, the Robinson pony truck was retained together with the wheels, original length frames and the Great Central type of tender.

A total of fifty–eight Robinson 2–8–0s, forty one former RODs and seventeen ex-Great Central engines, were rebuilt to form the new class. The former Gresley Great Northern 2–8–0 was now taking a back seat, in terms of classification, as Class O3. Thompson had intended this newly formed engine to become the LNER standard 2–8–0 and to replace virtually all the company's existing heavy freight locos. This did not happen and several examples of classes intended for extinction survived the rebuilds – J38, O4 and Q6.

## SUMMARY OF LNER CLASSIFICATION OF FORMER ROBINSON 2–8–0 ENGINES

| LNER CLASS | DESCRIPTION | IDENTIFYING FEATURES | NO. IN CLASS |
|---|---|---|---|
| O1 | Thompson rebuilds of Robinson 8K & ROD engines 1944–49. | Outside valve gear. Two side windows to cab. Round topped firebox. | 58 |
| O4/1 | Former GC 8K engine. Boiler mountings cut down 1929 onwards. | Single cut-out in cab side. Belpaire firebox. | 130 |
| O4/2 | One GC 8K (No.1185) and 16 ex-ROD locos. Cut-down boiler mountings to 12' 8⁵⁄₁₆" to suit NBR loading gauge. | Whistle lowered to firebox top. Cab roof angle irons replaced by flat strip. No waterscoop on tenders. | 17 |
| O4/3 | Former ROD engines (previously O4 but diagram not issued) with boiler mounting over 13' 0". | Whistle remains on cab roof. No waterscoop on tender. | 273 |
| O4/4 | Former ROD engines (ex LNER Nos.6287 & 6371) rebuilt 1929 with GN-pattern O2 round topped boiler. | Roundtop boiler 5' 6" diameter smokebox on saddle. Side windows to cab. | 2 |
| O4/5 | Similar rebuilds to above 4/1939 to 5/1939. | As O4/4, but GC cab retained. | 9 |
| O4/6 | Rebuilds of Robinson large-boiler (8M) engine with O4 pattern boiler. | Larger cab retained initially, but cut down 1939-43. Screw reverse in front of cab, right hand side. | 19 |
| O4/7 | Rebuilds with shorter-pattern O2-type boiler with round top. | GC-type smokebox retained. Side-windows to cab. | 41 |
| O4/8 | Thompson rebuilds with B1 type (100A) boiler 1944-1958. Included two engines from Class O4/6. | Sloping sides to smokebox saddle. Gresley chimney. Side-windows to cab. | 99 |

Sub-class O4/2 comprised seventeen engines (one ex-GCR 8K and sixteen ex-ROD machines) which acquired cut-down cabs to bring them to a maximum height of 12′ 8⁵⁄₁₆″ to fit within the NBR loading gauge. Conversions were carried out over the period 1924 – 29 and necessitated the removal of the cab roof angle iron and its replacement by flat strips. Shorter pattern chimneys 1′ 3″ high were fitted, together with flat-topped dome covers and short-pattern safety valves. Also altered was the whistle which appeared on the firebox top. No.6544 is at the head of an up freight train passing through the beautiful and remote countryside at Glenfarg, south of Perth and north of Kinross and Loch Leven. 6544 started life as ROD No.1606 and was built by Robert Stephenson in 1918. She was rebuilt to class O4/8 with round topped firebox as late as March 1958. Withdrawal was in May 1964 as British Railways 63647.

*G.H.Soole/Author's collection*

The first four members of Class O4/5 appeared in 1932 and eventually comprised nine engines. Fitted with a shortened type O2 boiler, they retained the original length frame and GC cab. Our example began life as North British built 8K No.1207 delivered in 1912. As 6207 the loco was rebuilt to the new class in June 1932. These 1932 rebuilds kept their original rear sandboxes, the later engines acquired new ones behind the rear coupled wheels in the manner of the other Gresley 2–8–0 rebuilds. Taken on August 31st 1947 the picture shows the erstwhile No.6207 (briefly renumbered 3554 in the 1946 sheme) as 3745 standing in Gorton Works yard after an overhaul. As British Railways No.63745 the engine was withdrawn in April 1959.

*C.H.S.Owen*

With Class O4/4 the familiar Robinson 8K/ROD 2–8–0 outline disappears and the round topped boilers favoured by Gresley make their debut. There were just two members of Class O4/4, LNER Nos.6371 and 6287, both former ROD engines. The rebuilding, in 1929, was fairly radical: larger boiler (5′ 6″ dia. of the type fitted to Class O2) with round topped firebox, mainframes extended by 6″ at the rear. This lengthening called for the provision of a new sandbox and a new pattern of splasher, strangely reminiscent of the earlier Robinson heavy freight engine, the Class 8A (Q4) 0–8–0. A cab with a single side window was provided, whilst at the front of the locomotive a cast smokebox saddle appeared with a Gresley chimney on top of the ensemble. A rather work-stained No.6287 appears at Frodingham shed, the scene of a massive reconstruction programme by the LNER in 1931/32. In August 1947 this engine was rebuilt again to Class O4/8; withdrawal was in May 1965.

By far the largest group of O4 variations was class O4/3 which comprised 273 of the ex-ROD locomotives which the LNER had purchased. Brought within the composite loading gauge (to 12′ 10¾″) by fitting shorter chimneys and flat topped dome covers, there was little to distinguish these from their Great Central antecedants save for lack of vacuum brake and water pick-up. No.63742 is caught here on former GC territory passing Mottram Yard on April 21st 1951 with a train of up empties. Catenary supports are erected in readiness for the Manchester – Sheffield – Wath electrification which would oust steam on this historic route. Despite this, the former ROD No.1816 has a life yet of over ten years. Rebuilding to Class O4/8 was undertaken in 1956, withdrawal was in 1963.

*B.K.B.Green*

Class O4/6 comprised the nineteen engines originally built as Class 8M. As mentioned in that section, rebuilding with the smaller (8K) boiler had begun before Grouping with the retention of the commodious 8M cab. The cab was cut down from May 1939 onwards to widen the route availability of the class in the likely event of war. Here at Doncaster on September 28th 1958 is former GC No.15 (5015 from Neepsend – 8M section) displaying its final version of cab roof as cut down in June 1940. 63917 was withdrawn in June 1962.

*W.A.Brown*

The last of the O4 sub-divisions was O4/8. Coming onstream in 1944 this class materialised as part of Edward Thompson's plan to standardise the LNER heavy freight locomotive. Altogether ninety-nine locomotives, a mixture of original Great Central 8K, ROD and one 8M 2–8–0, were worked on to form the amalgam. No.63893, a NB Loco.Co. ROD of 1919, steams along the former GC main line near Godley at the head of a mixed freight train on April 10th 1954, the second wagon appears to be carrying the base of a water tank. The Thompson parentage of the class shows well, B1 cab, boiler, smokebox and saddle all in prominent view.

*B.K.B.Green*

63906 was one of the 8Ms built with the single side window cab (formerly GC No.417). Taken at Mexborough shed on August 20th 1963 this view shows the altered pattern of front spectacles, not dissimilar from the last of the B7s. Hardy and useful these engines were; No.63906 was taken out of service in January 1965 and was outlived by only one other compatriot, former GC No.11 (BR 63913) which was withdrawn six months later.

*W.A.Brown*

Giving us a very good rearward look at the rebuilds is this picture of 63907, another Mexborough view, taken on October 12th 1963. The hooks under the cab roof would have been for anchoring a tarpaulin for tender-first running. Notice the prominent rear sandbox and extended housing over the reversing rod. Only these features now marked out the former G.C. No.418 from its 8K ancestors, some of these having acquired cut-down roofs as part of Class O4/2. 63907 was withdrawn in May 1964.

*W.A.Brown*

The first Thompson O1 2–8–0, No.6595 emerged in February 1944. Originally one of the ROD 1918 batch, it was eventually purchased by the LNER in 1927. Later renumberings saw it become 3795 and under BR, as 63795 it was withdrawn in October 1963.

*A. Swain collection*

With the arrival of class O1 in 1944 the Robinson 2–8–0 met its ultimate rebuilding: the marriage of Robinson frames, wheels, tender and front pony truck with the Thompson B1 (100A) boiler cab, cylinders and Walschaerts valve gear. Running concurrently with the rebuilding of other Robinson 2–8–0s to O4/8, conversion took place from 1944-49 with the last seven rebuilds emerging under the auspisces of British Railways. 63590 first saw the light of day as Great Central No.1243, a North British engine of December 1912. Classified originally as O4/1, rebuilding to O1 took place in December 1944. 63590 was amongst the last of the O1 conversions to be withdrawn, being taken out of service in July 1965. It is fitting that this final picture should have been taken at Gorton, in October 1949, birthplace of so many Robinson locomotives. Fitting too, that it shows something of the hard slog and grind that was inescapably so much part of the steam era.

Robinson's Class 9P 4–6–0 made its debut in 1917 with the solitary No.1169 *LORD FARINGDON*. Five further examples appeared in 1920, of which this fine specimen, No.1167 *LLOYD GEORGE*, was one. Seen at the west end of Guide Bridge station with a down express, No.1167 seems the very essence of stateliness, with an appearance and condition that was legendary amongst the pre-1923 companies. In an age when much rail travel has been reduced to the common level of the ubiquitous 'Sprinter' we can only marvel at such magnificence.

*P.F.Cooke/Authors collection*

# Class 9P 4–6–0/9P Caprotti Rebuilds

Robinson's last express passenger 4–6–0 type first appeared as a solitary example in the November of 1917. Named 'Lord Faringdon', after the Great Central's Chairman Sir Alexander Henderson who had been elevated to the House of Lords, this locomotive broke new ground for its designer in possessing four cylinders and provided yet another permutation of the 4–6–0 scheme. By using four cylinders and divided drive, Robinson was able to circumnavigate at least one of the problems that had beset the 'Sir Sam' design, namely the restrictions imposed on axlebox journal size inherent with two large inside cylinders. To feed the four 16″ × 26″ cylinders of the new engine the same boiler as that first used on the 'Sam' design was applied i.e: a maximum outside diameter of 5′ 6″, 139 2¼″ tubes coupled with 24 5¼″ flues carrying a 24 element superheater. The same grate area was adopted, viz: 26 square feet and a working pressure of 180lb. psi. was retained. Coupled wheels of the standard 6″ 9″ diameter were used, a size Robinson seems to have settled on as suitable for express working.

It has been suggested that 'Lord Faringdon' was developed in secret at Gorton during the First War and that Robinson assembled various components and materials in something of a clandestine fashion. Though the Locomotive Committee minutes are mute on this point the scarcity of materials alone in this period make such a suggestion unlikely given the repeated problems such shortages had brought about (see Introduction).

If Robinson had been inspired by the Caledonian's 'Cardean' for his 'Sir Sam Fay' then, maybe, the London & North-Western's 'Claughton' had been the guiding light behind 'Lord Faringdon.' In time-honoured Great Central fashion Stephenson valve gear was used to drive the new 4–6–0's piston valves. A brief reflection on contemporary locomotive engineering reminds us that Great Western practice had been to retain the Stephenson gear only for 2 cylinder layouts and Walschaerts valve gear allied to rocking shafts had been used for all 4 cylinder work, always with divided drive. On the London & North Western, too, Bowen–Cooke had abandoned Joy's gear and used the Walschaerts arrangement for his Claughton; but on LNW 4–6–0 the outside motion was coupled to rocking shafts, discreetly hidden, for the inside cylinders, with all four cylinders driving on the front coupled axle.

An approach that conformed to none of these conventions was adopted by Robinson for the motion layout of his new express engine. The Stephenson gear was retained and drove the two sets of valves on each side of the locomotive via rocking shafts. This arrangement caused each valve spindle to move in the same direction, at the same time feeding steam to pistons which were travelling in horizontally opposing planes – the cranks relative to the two adjacent cylinders being set at 180 degrees to one another. To perform what would otherwise have been an impossible task Robinson provided the two outside cylinders with outside admission valves and the inside pair with inside admission. In order to avoid excessively long connecting rods for the outside cylinders a longer than normal piston rod was adopted. This in turn was supported via a forward mounted

*EARL BEATTY* – the second of the 9P 4–6–0s in the process of erection at Gorton Works in the early Summer of 1920. The massive 'U' shaped bracket supporting the piston rod and crosshead are prominent behind the outside cylinders. Modellers may be interested in the profile of the mainframes – notice the irregular contours of the steel plate used, giving maximum depth over the critical areas around the coupled wheel horn slots which will eventually house the axleboxes. The boiler and firebox have been lagged and the dome cover is loosely in place. Leaning against the firebox is a short ladder, the perspective of the picture tending to exaggerate the massiveness of the locomotive. A fitter's wheelbarrow attends the sundry collection of ironmongery, all awaiting the great moment when No.1164 will be lifted onto her wheels. A feature of Robinson engines was the lack of a cast smokebox saddle, a thing widely used in latter day steam construction. The Robinson smokebox wrapper was fastened in the rear to the smokebox tube plate, the wrapper plate then being rivetted to the top of the mainframes. Notice the smokebox has been marked, but not yet drilled, for the ash ejector, handrail knobs and brake ejector pipe respectively. To the right of the picture can be seen a centre lathe, its headstock and associated line shafting from the overhead drive completely exposed. Enough, these days, to give the Health and Safety Inspectorate apoplexy!

*W.H.Whitworth/courtesy of W.A.Brown*

sleeve held on a substantial cast 'U' bracket, the sides of which held the two slidebars in which the crosshead moved. The two inside cylinders with a common single steam chest took the form of a one-piece casting bolted between the frames in line with their outside counterparts and drove the front coupled axle. In both cases the piston valve chambers for the 8″ valves were offset towards the centre of the engine giving the outside cylinders an inward inclination, something akin to the Great Western 2 cylinder 4–6–0s.

'Lord Faringdon' remained the solitary example of the 9P class until June 1920 when the first of a further five engines appeared at monthly intervals, the last of the class, No. 1168, 'Lord Stuart of Wortley' emerging from Gorton in the October of that year. Two of the later engines, Nos. 1164 and 1166 shared the Lord Faringdon pattern of cab side with the single cut-out window, itself a copy of the cab side fitted to 'Sir Sam Fay' and the first batch of Directors. Oddly enough the second of the later engines, No. 1165 'Valour' – named to honour the memory of Great Central employees killed in the First World War – had the two-window cab side with rear extension as fitted to (amongst others) the later Directors. Having reverted to the original shape of cab side for No. 1166, Robinson went back to the second pattern for the last two locomotives, No. 1167 'Lloyd George' and No. 1168 'Lord Stuart of Wortley.' 'Lord Faringdon' had been built with Ramsbottom pattern safety valves of the enclosed type, Ross 'pop' valves being substituted later and used on all five of the second batch from new. The 1920 engines were equipped with a boiler of the same type as the third version of the Sir Sam Fay boiler with 116 2¼″ tubes and a 28 element superheater. This boiler (G.C.Standard No.7) also appears in the Great Central loco diagram book with a revised date of 20th March 1923. The first LNER diagram, however, showed No. 1169 as being equipped with a boiler of the second type carried by the Sir Sam Fay i.e. 139 small tubes and a 24 element superheater. Another detail alteration concerned the alignment of the blastpipe. 'Lord Faringdon' was built with the blastpipe top level with the boiler centreline; the 1920 series had lower pipes with a correspondingly longer petticoat pipe – 1169 was later altered to the same pattern as the later engines. Robinson's ash ejector was fitted to the smokeboxes of all the class from new. In Great Central days this was of the short pattern, replaced in the LNER era by the longer version which confined ash movement away from the smokebox tubeplate, see illustrations.

Robinson's final version of superheater element protection, his combined blower and steam circulating valve was used on

'Lord Faringdon.' In conjunction with this device, the header discharge valve, mounted on the left side of the smokebox, saw to the discharge of steam remaining in the superheater header when the engine was stationary – thus preventing any unintentional movement. As with all other Robinson classes so equipped, these devices were removed after Grouping and replaced by the simpler Gresley snifting valve.

A pyrometer for measuring the temperature of the superheated steam in the header was fitted to the class when built. This device, though, seems to have fallen out of favour rather quickly and was removed in the early post–Grouping period.

Livery for this flagship locomotive was the standard Great Central passenger green embellished with black and white lining. This was complemented by claret or 'crimson lake', lined vermillion, for the coupled wheel splasher, mainframes above the footplate, cylinder clothing, motion bracket, footsteps and guard irons. As with the Atlantics the claret colour was extended to the tender valance, frames, footsteps and guard irons also. Buffer beams or 'planks' were painted vermillion edged white with an outer black border. Wheel centres were painted the same glorious green as the locomotive with white lining. Axle centres were black, lined round with a white circle. In the immediate post-Grouping period, however, a difference in painting style appears to have evolved, particularly in respect of the large, single coupled wheel splasher. A picture of 'Lord Faringdon' around this time shows the splasher clearly painted green, the black border lined white being unmistakable. The same scheme appears to be extended to the cylinder covers, motion bracket and footsteps as well. The livery style is made all the more interesting by the fact that the engine carries 'Great Central' and its original number plate. In LNER days the class, happily, escaped the funereal black of the post–1928 economies and retained the company's passenger green until the inevitable wartime decree of black, applied from around 1941. The only post–war engine to have the green reapplied was the much–rebuilt No. 6166 (q.v.).

Standard Great Central tenders with 4000 gallons water and 6 tons coal capacity were coupled to the 9P class. These tenders exhibited one distinctive feature in that they were fitted with Iracier pattern bearings. These bearings which carried the 6″ diameter by 11″ long axlebox journals had distinctive elliptical covers with both GCR and the Iracier company's name (Patent Axlebox and Foundry Company) and place of manufacture (Wolverhampton) cast on them. In early post Grouping days all six tenders were substituted by the final design of Great Central tender with self-trimming coal space provided for the 1922

series of Directors. These tenders were distinguished by a somewhat wider body with a correspondingly diminished flair between the tank side and the upper coal plate (q.v.) Two 9Ps (1164 & 1166) retained their borrowed tenders until the end of their lives but the other four eventually reverted to the original pattern of tender – between 1927 and 1933.

Under the LNER loco classification the 9P 4–6–0s became class B3, the whole of the Great Central 4–6–0 classes becoming one single 'B' series from B1 (G.C. 8C of 1903) to B9 (G.C. 8G of 1906). This simple lineage lasted until Edward Thompson upset the applecart; his mixed traffic 4–6–0 appeared at the end of 1942 and the Great Central's B1 then pushed down the line to become B18.

Whereas the bulk of Great Central locomotives retained much of their pre-Grouping identity in LNER days, with the possible exception of the Fish engines of class 8 (B5) which acquired higher pitched boilers from as early as 1923, the 9Ps were subject to a degree of rebuilding which altered their appearance considerably. This took the form of the fitting of Caprotti valve gear and was applied to four of the sextet as follows:–

| NUMBER | | CAPROTTI GEAR FITTED |
|---|---|---|
| 6168 | — | September 1929 |
| 6166 | — | December 1929 |
| 6167 | — | June 1938 |
| 6164 | — | June 1939 |

NOTE: The Caprotti rebuilds of class B3 were classified B3/2. A further sub-division of the class came in October 1943 with the complete rebuilding of No. 6166 to become, effectively, a 6' 9″ version of Thompson's new B1. This solitary rebuild was given the designation B3/3.

Gresley appeared to be fascinated by the possibilities of poppet valves for locomotive work and had first applied such valves (of the Lentz variety) to an ex Great Eastern J20 0–6–0, No. 8280, in 1925.

Applications to one of the B12 4–6–0s and to a number of his D49 4–4–0s (Lentz gear again) from 1928/29 onwards must have convinced him of the system's efficacy, a good deal of development work being done with the system culminating in its application to the *magnum opus* of 1934 – 'Cock o' the North.'

The purpose of the Caprotti valve gear was obviously to counteract the high coal consumption to which (by now) the B3 class were said to be prone. Robinson had been an adherent of short travel valve gear which undoubtedly had a bearing on the coal consumption of the 9Ps. In this respect the engines were almost certainly no worse than many of their contemporaries and had shown themselves to be masters of

*LORD FARINGDON* basks in glorious sunshine while waiting to leave Guide Bridge with an up express. The pioneer engine carries the full Great Central passenger livery of dark green with black and white lining, contrasted beautifully by the use of claret, lined vermilion. The Ross 'pop' safety valves were a substitute, from around 1919, for the previously favoured Ramsbottom cased variety. Notice the looped pipe from the top of the smokebox forming the connection to the pyrometer.

No.1169 broadside-on at Gorton shed in the early post-Grouping period. Such views, by no means commonplace, give a good impression of the bulk and outline of the 9P class. Though the engine appears in the standard Great Central passenger green, applied to all the class from new, the rich main green body colour has also been applied to the splasher panel, footplate edging, cylinder clothing and motion bracket. This appears as a substitute for the claret,lined vermilion, described in the introductory text. The pyrometer appears now to have been abandoned.

*LORD FARINGDON* bursts under St. Werburgh's Road bridge and takes the Great Central line up to Fairfield at Chorlton Junction in August 1920. The prototype of the class is in charge of the 12.25 pm Manchester Central to Marylebone express made up, on this occasion, to seven coaches.

*G.M.Shoults*

A closer look at *VALOUR* on shed in Great Central days with a posse of jolly locomen on board. The original photograph gives a glimpse of the oil tank fitted on the tender when the engine ran for some two months as an oil-burner in the 1921 coal strike. The fitting on the side of the smokebox is Robinson's superheater header discharge valve used in conjunction with his combined blower and steam circulating valve. This apparatus was Robinson's ultimate answer to superheater element protection. The looped pipe towards the rear of the smokebox is the pyrometer connection from the superheater header.

*Collection of G.H.Platt*

Great Central No.1164 *EARL BEATTY* was the second of the 9P 4–6–0s to appear, emerging from Gorton in June 1920, well after the end of the First War that had seen the birth of the class. Apart from the fitting of Ross 'Pop' safety valves (1169 had been turned out with the conventional Ramsbottom variety) the two locomotives were identical. Somersault signals on their lattice posts and 12-wheeled clerestory stock point towards a view along the Great Northern main line and we are presented with a fine view of 1164 storming along in fine style past Greenwood signal box, at the south end of Hadley Wood Tunnel, with a down express. Oil pipes for the Detroit lubricator and long-pattern ash ejector are features of the locomotive; the tender carries the earlier arrangement of LNER livery style with number on the tank side. London's urban sprawl was then beginning to encroach on this, still rural area; the field by the lineside carries a hoarding advertising the sale of freehold building plots.

A.F.Bound's distinctive lattice-post pneumatically operated semaphores give a clear 'right away' to No.1169 as departure is awaited at Guide Bridge with an up express. Along with Nos.1165 and 1167, *LORD FARINGDON* was converted to oil-firing in 1921 on the Robinson 'Unolco' system to combat fuel shortages in the miners' strikes of that year. Unlike the *SIR SAM FAY* conversions, however, the change-over was of a brief nature, actual conversion lasting only some two months. Here the massive oil tank looks distinctly out of place on top of the tender, coming within what must have been the very limits of the generous GC loading gauge. Nestling between the front and middle tender axleboxes is Robinson's 'Reliostop' train control device. As far as is known this system was not carried by any other engines of the 9P class and was removed from No.1169 in 1922, a year after this photograph was taken.

*Collection of W.A.Brown*

A scene at Guide Bridge showing the celebrated No.1165 in original condition awaiting departure with an up train. *VALOUR* was the third of the 9Ps to arrive, in the July of 1920. Built with the side-window cab, coupled to an extended roof, that had made its debut on the second series of 'Directors' in 1919, 1165 became the Great Central's war memorial engine. A shield-shaped nameplate fixed to the splasher panel read: IN MEMORY OF G.C.R. EMPLOYEES WHO GAVE THEIR LIVES FOR THEIR COUNTRY 1914 – 1918. This larger nameplate displaced the works plate which became transferred, on this one locomotive only, to the top of the cylinder clothing. This slightly unusual view shows something of the cab detail as well as the shape and lettering of the Iracier tender axleboxes.

their task when correctly handled. To pursue a little further the valve gear travel topic: given Robinson's Swindon schooling it seems a trifle strange that he never pursued this particular line of engineering thought. He was certainly not a man who was afraid of innovation and, equally, had never shown himself adverse to trying out his pet ideas. Gresley, likewise, clung to short travel valves and, again, it was Swindon who pointed him in their direction – an avenue that revolutionised the performance of his engines.

A rotary drive to the valves which were mounted vertically – two to each end of the four cylinders, was adopted. Cut–off was infinitely variable in marked contrast to the Lentz system which restricted cut–off in forward gear to five positions only. A reported decrease in coal consumption of up to 19% with the new valve gear was noted at the time. Neasden was the main staging post for the first two rebuilds from where an average mileage of some 50,000 was notched up, with reported reliability.

Despite the improvements that the Caprotti gear had brought about, it was not until 1938 (see table) that any more of the class were converted to poppet operation. Caprotti gear was used again for the final two conversions, a difference being the use of steam (as opposed to springs in the 1929 conversions) to return the valves to their seats after each opening. A steam supply for this operation was taken from the left side of the dome. Official figures set the 1938 rebuilding at £2,211.2/- per locomotive.

The weight of the Caprotti locomotives increased by 3 cwt. with the maximum axle load decreasing to 19 tons, 19 cwt. The final Caprotti conversion, No. 6164 'Earl Beatty,' was completed in June 1939, the intervention of the Second War precluding any further work in this direction.

## REBUILDING OF NO. 6166

The fitting of Caprotti valve gear was not the end of the story of the rebuilding of the B3 class. In October 1943 6166 'Earl Haig' – one of the two 1929 rebuilds – was taken in hand by Edward Thompson and completely rebuilt to resemble one of his new standard 4–6–0s – the B1 class which had first appeared at the end of 1942. Rebuilding can be a dubious term in the realm of locomotive engineering; certainly, little remained of the original 6166 save for driving wheels, bogie (placed 11″ further back) and the rear part of the mainframes. To the front of these was welded a new steel section complete with B1 cylinders and associated motion parts. Surmounting this was a B1 boiler (100A pattern) and cab. The Great Central tender survived (not the original with Iracier bearings) and, strangely enough but appropriately, a dome cover of Gorton pattern was provided, giving the rebuild a hint of its parentage. A subtle difference in appearance to the B1 came in the provision of tiny splashers, needed to cover the tops of the bigger driving wheels – 6′ 9″ diameter on the rebuild compared with 6′ 2″ on Thompson's new engine. Lost on rebuilding too, was 6166's name, making this the second of the class to became anonymous. At 71 tons, 3 cwt, the rebuild was 7 tons, 15 cwt. lighter than the original No. 1164.

Under Thompson's scheme the former Great Central 9Q (B7) and Gresley B17 4–6–0s were also to be rebuilt with two cylinders into the new Standard format. No member of the B7 class was rebuilt in the event, making the B3 4–6–0s the only Robinson engines that lost much of their pre–1923 identity. Rebuilding does not appear to have gone down too well with the new No. 6166, instances of cracked frames being recorded on several occasions, though it should be said that such defects are more common than many enthusiasts may realise and are not a result of poor design *per se*.

## ALLOCATION & WORK

'Lord Faringdon' spent the initial stages of its career at Gorton in the hands of W.Chapman, one of the shed's top–link drivers. Great Central locomotive alloca-

In this first of a trio of contrasting views showing *VALOUR* in her days on the Great Northern section, the engine has backed on to the turntable at Kings Cross station locomotive yard. This scene shows the engine in its pure Great Central state livery-wise but coupled to the wide bodied tender with self-trimming coal bunker. Short pattern ash ejector is still carried and no snifting valve has yet appeared.

Cubitt's famous train shed roof dominates the skyline as *VALOUR*, still wearing all her Great Central finery, makes a determined sure-footed start out of King's Cross terminus with a lengthy express.

*H. Gordon Tidey*

Taken at Kings Cross Top Shed in early LNER days this second picture shows the first version of the LNER re-numbering applied to this locomotive in January 1924. The new number appears both on the front buffer beam and below the L N E R lettering on the tender. On the cabside the oval outline of the parent company's numberplate can be discerned, this has been replaced by a diminutive oval plate carrying the initials of the new owners. The untidy conglomeration of pipework alongside the boiler and firebox is oil feed piping for the Detroit lubrication system fitted in lieu of the Robinson 'Intensifore' system. A Gresley-pattern sniffing valve for superheater element protection is fitted on the side of the smokebox, this fitting was later re-fitted behind the chimney. The tender, as in the previous picture, is the later wide-bodied pattern with conventional axleboxes.

The Class 9Ps, LNER B3, wore a green livery for most of their lives, at least up until 1941 when the ubiquitous wartime black appeared. 6165 received her LNER apple green livery in 1925; in this condition she poses for the photographer in the centre road at Nottingham Victoria in 1931. Notice, again, the pipework for the Detroit lubrication system and the re-appearance of the original tender. The engine number has now been transferred from the tender side to cabside. As a result of its association with fallen comrades from the First War, *VALOUR* became something of a celebrity amongst former GC locomotives in LNER days. Each Armistice Day, beginning on Thursday, November 11th 1920, the celebrated engine carried a wreath around each nameplate and another on the smokebox door. Always working from Gorton shed for this auspicious occasion, the engine took part in the then customary two minute silence at 11 o'clock in the morning having worked an up express from Manchester. The first two of these annual events are reported as having taken place at Leicester, the ceremony was then transferred to Sheffield, where the memorial to the Great Central's 1,304 war dead was erected.

*Collection of Brian Hilton*

Of the sextet that formed the 9P Class only two engines – *LORD FARINGDON* and *VALOUR* escaped rebuilding of one form or another. Great Central No.1166 *EARL HAIG* was born-again in 1943, shorn of her name and the sole member of class B3/3. The engine had appeared in August 1920, one month after 1165. For reasons which are not apparent, Robinson rather curiously reversed the progression to a side-window cab with extended roof which had appeared on No.1165. In full Great Central livery the engine appears in 'as built' condition, unsullied as yet by oil-feed pipes and snifting valve. Her tender is the original pattern, showing the narrower body with Iracier axleboxes. Because of their appearance at the end of the Great Central's existence, comparatively few pictures exist of the 9P 4–6–0s in their pre-1923 form. We should, therefore, be more than grateful for views such as this one – an outstanding portrait of No.1166 at Guide Bridge awaiting departure with an up express. One feels, when confronted with a picture like this, to be almost lost for words, such is the sheer magnificence of the machine. Notice the later pattern of Great Central corridor stock, equipped with Robinson's anti-collision steel fenders.

In July 1923 *EARL HAIG* had been the first known Great Central engine to work a Great Northern line express train as such. Much of the atmosphere of those heady days when old rivalries were no doubt still emotionally charged are captured in this fine view taken near Hadley Wood. Maximum power is being extracted from No.1166 as she charges along at the head of the 4.00 pm out of Kings Cross, a down Leeds express; this was a Doncaster shed duty and 1166 was allocated to that shed from the 20th to 26th July 1923. The train is made up to at least twelve coaches, the fourth and sixth are examples of the Great Northern company's magnificent 12-wheel clerestories.

tions for early 1921 show Nos. 1164 and 1168 at Immingham with the other four engines based at Gorton. It is interesting to note that the 4–4–0 Directors maintained their supremacy on the fastest of the Manchester – Marylebone trains, the new 4–6–0s being allocated to slower workings such as the 3.50 pm from Manchester London Road and 8.45 morning train down from Marylebone. The up afternoon train from Manchester is shown in the 1922 timetable as making no less than 12 stops and taking 5 hours 5 minutes for the 206 mile journey. Doubtless the extra performance from a four cylinder engine, allied to a six coupled wheelbase would have been an asset on such workings.

Certainly the most interesting work given to these engines, the last of the Robinson express passenger 4–6–0s, was between 1923 and 1927 on the Great Northern main line out of Kings Cross. Upon the Grouping the Great Central's Running Superintendent W.G.P.Maclure had been given the same position in the newly formed LNER Southern Area based at Liverpool Street.

Three B3 class locomotives were involved at first on the Kings Cross workings – 1165 'Valour', 1166 'Earl Haig' and 1167 'Lloyd George.' The first engine recorded at work on the Great Northern line was 'Earl Haig' on July 19th. Driver Willoughby Lea, a Gorton man, was in charge arriving at Kings Cross at 4.00 pm with an express from the West Riding. Little respite was given, the big 4–6–0 heading northwards at 5.30 with the Newcastle Dining Car train. 'Earl Haig' followed this on the two successive days, July 20th and 21st with an entry into Kings Cross at 1.55 in the afternoon. At 4.00 the engine was at work again, at the head of the heavy Down Leeds express. To set the transfer of these engines into perspective it is necessary to state the position regarding motive power on the G.N. main line at this time. By midsummer of 1923 construction of Pacifics had totalled only eight, although four more would appear that year. The celebrated large boilered Ivatt Atlantics were still handling the heaviest trains with loads of up to around 500 tons, certainly not the traffic for which the B3s had been designed!

Considering the marked contrast in design between the B3s and the Atlantics and Pacifics with their wide fireboxes, the Great Central engines would appear to have coped with their new work and environment with not unreasonable success. 'Earl Haig' was recorded as passing Finsbury Park, 2.6 miles out from Kings Cross, in around six minutes with the 4 pm Doncaster train, loaded to at least 500 tons. 'Valour' is on record as having run the 29 miles from Grantham to Peterborough in a shade under 27 minutes (pass to pass time) with a 330 ton load, achieving 85 m.p.h. in the process. Comparison with contemporary Great Northern motive power is interesting: the B3 with its Belpaire firebox had a comparatively small grate area (26 sq.ft.), the Ivatt Atlantic possessed 31 square feet of grate and the Gresley A1 Pacific a massive 41.25 sq.ft. The tractive effort of the Robinson 4–6–0 was roughly 20% higher, however, than the superheated G.N. 4–4–2. A general impression appears to be that the Robinson 4–6–0s gave good results provided they were fired and driven carefully.

The G.N. line workings from midsummer 1923 were the start of a four year foray into what had hitherto been foreign territory, but now a route belonging to the same company. At this time other B3s were finding their way into Kings Cross on the celebrated and highly popular Eason's Specials from Grimsby to London. J.W.Eason, a Grimsby travel agent, had begun his excursions as far back as 1905. Something of a cut above other excursions

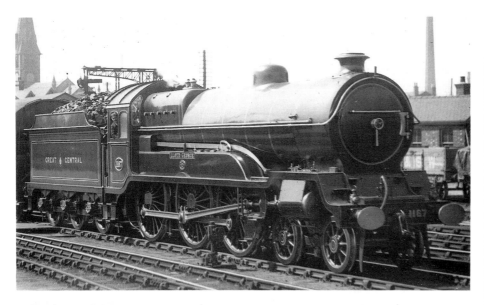

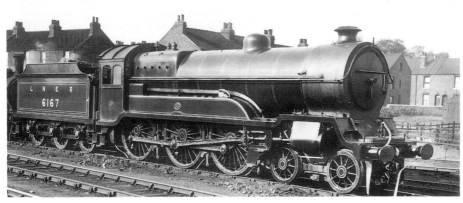

(top) A politician at work on the Great Central: No.1167 *LLOYD GEORGE* at the head of an up express at Guide Bridge. The locomotive had, briefly, been fitted for oil-burning in the 1921 coal strikes. (2nd from top) The sight of former 9P No.6167 nameless at Doncaster recalls a story that has passed into railway folklore, although, no doubt, there are still many who may not have heard the whole tale. The Great Central under Robinson had taken the practice of naming fairly gently. Among the early classes only a few of the 4–4–0s and the four Compound Atlantics bore titles and it was not until the appearance of *SIR SAM FAY* in late 1912 that the company's express locomotives carried titles almost as soon as they left the works. Something of a mystery and one or two apochryphal stories surround 9P No.1167 *LLOYD GEORGE*. In the first instance it seems uncertain as to whether the locomotive should have carried that title at all. One reliable source suggests that the engine was turned out in 1920 carrying the name: 'Rt.Hon.David Lloyd George'. Though no photograph appears to exist to support this supposition, it is known, of course, that No.1167 emerged in the end as plain 'Lloyd George'. He was included as the civilian war leader, on the same basis as Beatty for the Navy and Haig for the Army. Perhaps the railway companies' innate conservatism inhibited their use of names of personages that were, at best, often only of a transient nature and lacked the solid, historical lineage of monarchs and noble buildings. Sir Frederick Banbury, Chairman of the Great Northern, is said to have taken umbrage at the appearance of 'Lloyd George' in the summer of 1923 and ordered the nameplates to be removed. Another version of the story suggests that the engine was due to haul a special train carrying Queen Mary and was rendered anonymous for the occasion. Whatever the real reason was, whoever got hold of them made sure they were not going to be found easily. The plates were eventually discovered inside a partition wall at Kings Cross Top Shed when demolition work was in progress in 1963! They had in fact been taken off at Gorton who must have expected they were to be re-fitted, otherwise they would not have returned them to Top Shed. Lloyd George had resigned in 1922 and was never to hold public office again. Here, the engine named after him stands seemingly silent and out of traffic, its name removed and only the Gorton works plate adorning the elegant splasher panel. Renumbered, the engine retains Great Central boiler mountings and short ash ejector. Notice the lack of oil feed pipes alongside the boiler casing; the tender is the later wide-bodied pattern with self-trimming coal space and plain axle boxes. (2nd from bottom) The following two views of this somewhat enigmatic locomotive show it in its LNER existence and prior to conversion to Caprotti valve gear in 1938. Displaying the later LNER green livery with engine number on the cabside, No.6167 has in this view, a lower dome cover, 'flowerpot' chimney and snifting valve. Oil feed pipes from the Detroit lubricator appear along the boiler casing and the long pattern of ash ejector has been fitted. The opposite-hand view (bottom shows other changes; this time the smokebox has been renewed, notice the rather prominent snaphead rivets around the circumference. The cab windows carry a sight screen between them, a feature applied to other ex-GC engines also. Taken at Neasden, the picture can be part dated by the appearance of the self-trimming tender, the original with Iracier bearings being re-fitted in 1927.

(top) 9P No.1168 was named *LORD STUART OF WORTLEY* upon completion in October 1920. Charles Beilby Stuart-Wortley was a director of the Great Central, a successful MP and a notable patron of the Arts (Q.V. Director Class). The name: *CHARLES STUART-WORTLEY* had been carried by 11E 4–4–0 No.437, one of the first batch of the celebrated 'Directors' built in 1913. This gentleman had been created a Baron in 1917 which privilege accorded him a different title. Here, in 1924, the engine bearing his later title enters Kings Cross with the *Harrogate Pullman*. Notice the oval numberplate on the cab side with the locomotive re-numbered by the 5000 addition in the first LNER style. GC boiler mountings are still apparent with short ash ejector and the high coal plate of the swapped wide-bodied pattern tender is just visible behind the 'ship's wheel'. *H. Gordon Tidey*. (middle) In the same period as the preceding picture, No.6168 has reversed onto the new turntable at Kings Cross station loco yard. Though no longer stating its Great Central ownership No.6168 is still a magnificent-looking machine, its strong Robinson character manifestly apparent. Now in LNER lined apple green this study makes an interesting comparison to 'Valour' in the same location. The oval numberplate bearing the LNER number is now in the North-Eastern Railway style and shows place and year built. This type of numberplate became attached to other former GC engines in this era, although this engine and No. 6166 appear to the only members of the 9P class so honoured. (bottom) 6168 at speed on the G.N. main line near Greenwood with a 12-coach train of Gresley corridor stock. *P. Ransome–Wallis*.

which often relied upon superannuated rolling stock, Eason's trains were made up with corridor stock, guaranteed seating and meals served in both directions. Eason's were not the only concern to venture into this field, Dean and Dawson, who had long–established links with both the MS&L and the Great Central and, of course, the LNER themselves also ran such trains.

Prior to Grouping, the Eason excursions had been the prerogative of the Great Northern, but in September of 1923 B3 No. 1169 'Lord Faringdon' arrived in Kings Cross at the head of a Grimsby excursion, such duties now being worked by former Great Central engines and crews throughout.

The following year, 1924, saw the transfer of further B3s to the Great Northern line and all six engines were then deployed on workings in and out of Kings Cross. Notable was their use on the newly introduced Pullman trains to Leeds and Harrogate. These trains ran non–stop to Leeds

and averaged 54 m.p.h. Allocations in this period were split between Kings Cross shed and Copley Hill, Leeds. Aside from the Pullman workings the B3s also saw service on Kings Cross to Hull expresses as far as Grantham returning with a less prestigious duty in the form of a milk train. Engines based at Leeds also ventured as far as Doncaster. 'Lord Faringdon' took part in the 1925 centenary celebrations for the Stockton & Darlington Railway.

All six of the B3s were repatriated to Gorton in 1927 although Nos. 6166 and 6169 were sent to Neasden later that year, the first time one of the class had been based there. In the 1927/28 period No. 6164 was rostered to work the 3.20 pm express from Marylebone with a 4 hours 32 minutes timing to Manchester and was noted as having put up some fine performances. This appeared to be the last time the engines had worked regularly between Marylebone and Manchester. Though this London shed retained B3s on its books

until the end of the Second War (apart form a brief intermission in the 1930s) workings appear to have been confined to trips between Marylebone and Leicester or Nottingham – fast running with loads of around 300 tons being recorded with night mail and newspaper trains.

Some time after their transfer away from the Great Northern line Immingham received an allocation of B3s which remained on set duties up to around the start of the Second World War. Notable amongst these workings were the mid–day Cleethorpes to Leicester train and a summer turn, boat trains from Immingham Dock up to Marylebone. The Eason's specials, mentioned previously, continued to be worked over the erstwhile Great Northern line by members of the class by a select link of men familiar with the G.N. road via Boston and Peterborough.

By the outbreak of war the B3s were split 50/50 between Neasden and Woodford, the latter's allocation having been

**No.6168 *LORD STUART OF WORTLEY* was the first of the former 9P 4–6–0s to be rebuilt, in September 1929. This study gives a good impression of the massive outline of this last Robinson express 4–6–0. Although the Caprotti gear spoilt the original lines of the 1917 design, there is, nevertheless, an overwhelming impression of brute power and solidity apparent. The altered handrail profile around the smokebox is immediately obvious; this was subject to some later modifications (*q.v.*). Not to be confused with the handrail, the longer-pattern ash ejector lies on the right-hand side of the smokebox between the vacuum ejector pipe and the raised section of the front handrail. The rebuilding also provided an altered arrangement of footsteps at the bottom of the smokebox, a single step appearing in line with those on the cam box covers. Withdrawn in September 1946, 6168 was allocated No.1499 but never carried it.**

The cam boxes for the Caprotti valve gear applied to the B3s did little to enhance their rather splendid proportions. With the appendages in place one could argue, perhaps, that the frontal appearance of the locomotive took on an atmosphere of brute force and power. Side-by-side at Nottingham Victoria are the first two Caprotti B3 conversions, 6166 *EARL HAIG* and 6168 *LORD STUART OF WORTLEY*.

*N.E.Stead collection*

cquired by transfers from Immingham. Woodford engines were kept busy with West of England trains between Banbury nd Sheffield while their counterparts at he London shed were hauling loads etween Marylebone and Sheffield, duties hat had been handled by Pacifics.

1942 found B3s, Nos. 6164 & 6165, sta-oned again at the Leeds shed of Copley Hill. 6164 was in reputedly poor shape at his time and was swapped after a short while for 'Lord Faringdon' – No. 6169. 165 distinguished itself when, after depu-sing for a failed V2, it hauled a load of ome 540 tons from Leeds to Kings Cross s far as Grantham. Later on in 1942 the wo Leeds engines moved west to Man-

chester filling in at Gorton for Pacifics that had been sent back to the G.N.line. In 1943 the rebuilt 6166 was also sent to Gor-ton, its slot at Neasden being taken up by No. 6164. By the end of 1945, however, the rebuild was back at its former London shed. These wartime peregrinations were further complicated when, at the end of 1944, two of the Gorton B3s were sent south to Neasden giving this depot, albeit only briefly, all but one of the six members of the class.

The B3s had now entered their twilight years. In 1946 No. 6168 'Lord Stuart of Wortley', the first of the Caprotti rebuilds, was withdrawn from Neasden shed. In June 1947 'Lord Faringdon' and 'Valour'

(now renumbered 1494 & 1496) were transferred to Lincoln, and Immingham shed received the remaining three engines from Neasden. Express working seems to have been retained by the class right up to the end and they appear to have been spared the indignity of many top link engines which departed this life having spent their last breaths of steam on mun-dane freight turns. Inevitably, the last engine to go was the solitary B3/3 rebuild – the Thompson B1 lookalike of 1943. So departed the former Great Central No. 1166 'Earl Haig' in the April of 1949.

The second Caprotti rebuild No.6166 *EARL HAIG* at Neasden shed. Apart from the oil feed pipes, which had appeared before rebuilding, the external lines remained relatively clean looking. The chimney, it hardly needs saying, is the 'flowerpot' allied to the lower pattern of dome cover.

*Collection of Brian Hilton*

The original Caprotti rebuilding provided for the new valve chests and cam boxes to be completely enclosed. Although this resulted in a fairly neat, uniform appearance it caused overheating of the boxes. To alleviate this a partial removal of the covers was initiated. At first, the side covers were removed and holes were cut in the front of the casings. This, however, was only partially successful and eventually the sheet metal casings were removed altogether. No.6166 *EARL HAIG* rests amongst sister GC engines and is displaying the Caprotti arrangement in the first modification, with side covers removed and holes drilled in the casing front.

*Collection of W.A.Brown*

A view of the untidy conglomeration that resulted with the removal of the covers over the Caprotti gear. 6168 displays a distinctly utilitarian front end as it passes through Harrow with an up slow train from Leicester. Both this and the subsequent view of No. 6168 show the later pattern of chimney which echoed somewhat the Great Central version.

*C.R.L.Coles*

Although sparkling clean in the later LNER apple green livery *LORD STUART OF WORTLEY* looks distinctly untidy round the front-end. Several details are worth perusal in this Gorton picture taken in June 1936: Both this engine and No.6166 had one-piece reversing rods and displayed a different profile of cover to the outside steam pipes. The picture also shows the lower pattern of dome cover coupled with the retention of the G.C. pattern of chimney with snifting valve behind. This later picture reveals the smokebox door handrail put back in its original position, and notice the top lamp iron too has now re-gained its Great Central position. The tender is the wide-bodied pattern with standard axle boxes.

Nos.6167 and 6164 *EARL BEATTY* were rebuilt to the Caprotti arrangement in June 1938 and 1939 respectively. Comparison with the previous pictures will reveal some mechanical subtleties. The former Liberal Prime Minister poses for the late Mr.William Lees alongside the down platform at Wilbraham Road Station en route from Gorton shed to Manchester Central via the Fairfield Loop line. No.6167 is in spanking condition and the picture was probably taken when the engine was 'ex works' after rebuilding in 1938. Manifest is the two-piece reversing rod with universal joint in front of the Belpaire shoulder and the later version of the steam pipe casing, almost an inversion of the original pattern.

*W.Lees*

Seen at Neasden on a grey March 18th 1939, the hump alongside the top feed of 6167 can be discerned. This covered the live steam feed to the cam boxes required to return the valves to their seats after each opening. This contrasted with the 1929 arrangement which used springs for the same operation. Sight screens, as displayed here, were fitted between the cab windows on the B3 class in the 1930s.

*Collection of Brian Hilton*

March 11th 1948: Sad and forlorn-looking, the former 'Lloyd George' now numbered 1498 waits alongside the former GC carriage works at Dukinfield to be cut up some three months after withdrawal from traffic. Inevitable comparisons with the beautifully polished machine at Guide Bridge seen in our frontispiece will be made and sentimentality is easily drawn. Realistically though, the steam engine was a mere device to move passengers and goods from one point to another.

*H.C.Casserley*

Every inch a B1, or almost so. Only the tender gives the lie to the fact that this could have once been a Great Central locomotive. Tender apart, the only tell-tale difference between the rebuilt *EARL HAIG* and the Standard Thompson 4–6–0 are the slightly wider-spaced bogie axles (+ 3″) and the longer wheelbase between the bogie and leading coupled axle (+ 5″). Taken at Gorton after rebuilding in October 1943, the photograph shows the utilitarian wartime black livery with plain 'NE' initials on the tender. LNER Group Standard buffers replaced the oval Great Central ones, but the GC swivelling drawhook was retained.

*Collection of Brian Hilton*

No.6166 became 1497 in September 1946. Carrying this intermediate number the locomotive is seen outside the shed at Neasden on April 10th 1947 having its tender tank filled. The truncated company initials have been all but obliterated under a carpet of grime.

*H.C.Casserely*

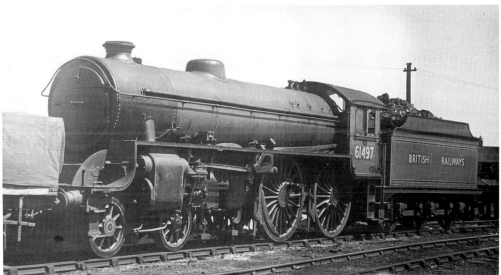

The solitary B3 rebuild became BR No.61497 in April 1948 during a works visit. Seen here at Immingham on May 17th 1948, the engine is in lined green LNER livery but lettered BRITISH RAILWAYS with LNER ownership discernible beneath. Cabside lettering is the modified Gill Sans style with 12″ numerals, but the BR smokebox numberplate is yet to be fitted. A dropped leading coupled axle and withdrawn motion may have been to attend to a cracked frame plate, to which the locomotive was apparently prone. 61497 remained the sole B3/3, and did not serve her new owners for long, being withdrawn in April 1949.

*A.B.Crompton*

## SUMMARY OF CLASS 9P 4–6–0 (LNER B3)

| NUMBER | BUILDER | DATE BUILT | NAME | WITHDRAWN |
|---|---|---|---|---|
| 1164 | Gorton | June 1920 | EARL BEATTY | September 1947 |
| 1165 | –'– | July 1920 | VALOUR | December 1947 |
| 1166 | –'– | August 1920 | EARL HAIG* | April 1949 |
| 1167 | –'– | September 1920 | LLOYD GEORGE† | December 1947 |
| 1168 | –'– | October 1920 | LORD STUART OF WORTLEY | September 1946 |
| 1169 | –'– | November 1917 | LORD FARINGDON | December 1947 |

*NOTES:–*

a) Nos. 1164/1166/1167/1168 all rebuilt with Caprotti valve gear (see above).

b) 1166 rebuilt again into class B3/3 in 1943–see separate feature.

c) 9P Class (B3) were allocated numbers 1480 – 1485 under initial LNER re-numbering scheme of 1943 but numbers never carried. 1946 scheme provided numbers 1494 – 1499 and carried by all engines except No.6168.

d) Only one engine, the 1943 B3/3 rebuild, carried its British Railways number of 61497.

* Name removed when rebuilt to Class B3/3 in 1943.

† Name removed in August 1923.

Showing at once the massiveness of the design, the pioneer 8M No.412 stands on the sidings known as 'The Park' at the west end of Guide Bridge station. Subtleties marking out the upper quarters of the class from the 8K are readily identifiable: top feed on the boiler, Ross 'pop' safety valves and rear sandbox below the cab. Notice too, the extra footstep between the first and second pair of coupled wheels and the single spectacle in the front of the cab. No.412 and the next engine in the 8M series, No.413, were both rebuilt in July 1922 with the smaller No.6 standard boiler fitted to the 8K. Becoming Class O4/1 in LNER days, 412 was withdrawn as British Railways No.63902 in April 1965.

# Class 8M 2–8–0 Heavy Goods

The brilliant and successful 8K 2–8–0 heavy goods engine had been introduced by Robinson in 1911, itself a development of the previous Great Central heavy goods design – the 8A 0–8–0 tender engine of 1902.

During the First World War the 8K 2–8–0 had undergone something of an apotheosis in the guise of the R.O.D. version – essentially the Robinson 1911 engine but with detail modifications (q.v.). Doubtless fired by the pressures of wartime traffic and the success of his 8K, Robinson worked out a design for a larger–boilered version of what was undoubtedly one of his best efforts to date.

Engine building at Gorton had slowed to a mere trickle during the First War, a meagre twelve locomotives emerging in 1917 – the last full year of hostilities. The 8M design appears to have been mooted by Robinson in early 1916: batches of ten engines apiece were ordered in the March of that year and August 1917. The first engine, No. 412, appeared in January 1918 as part of a projected batch of ten*. Delivery of the second batch commenced with No. 422 in June 1919 but, no doubt due to the privations of the post–War period, the last of the class, No. 22, did not appear until February 1921.

* In the interim, in July 1918, one of the projected 8Ms had emerged as a 4–6–0 and thus became the pioneer of yet another Robinson class using this wheel arrangement, the 8N; although only two further examples of this class followed on.

Let us use the familiar family tree to show the evolution of the 8M 2–8–0, bringing into play some principal dimensions for comparative purposes.

January 1918 saw the arrival of the first 8M. The 'Locomotive Magazine' for August 15th of that year described it as 'a new Consolidation locomotive for goods and mineral traffic.' A large boilered version of the 8K, mechanically identical to its parent and incorporating several Robinson refinements which had been built–in to both the 8K and the R.O.D. engines. Above the motion, these comprised the superheater header discharge valve and the second version of the combined blower and steam circulating valve. Top feed for the boiler, which had made its appearance on some of the later 8K series, was standard as was Robinson's well–tried and established hydrostatic lubrication system, the 'Intensifore'. A modification to the boiler carried over from the R.O.D. locomotives was the use of Ross 'pop' safety valves in lieu of the Ramsbottom pattern used on the 8K.

In September 1915 Robinson had patented a small tube superheater with 36 elements. This had been followed just over a year later with another version, again with 36 elements. Ever imaginative, Robinson had filed a whole succession of patents between 1911 and 1916 for one version of superheater after another and was in the front rank of British locomotive engineers in the field of superheating. Yet another version of the small tube superheater was applied to the 8M – Nos. 10 – 13 and No. 421 turned out in 1919. Possessing 42 × ¾" elements, this superheater occupied no less than 98 3" boiler flues. Though small tube superheaters had been applied to other Robinson engines (q.v. Vol I), the 8M design provided the only example of its use on new engines. The remainder of the class (14 engines) were fitted with the more conventional 28 element design and the small tube engines were eventually reboilered. Whether any

trials were conducted to obtain results as to the efficacy of the small tube superheater is not known. Little imagination is needed to realise that boiler maintenance must have been hindered by the presence of so much tubing occupying an inordinate amount of space and cleaning and maintenance suffering as a result.

Whereas the 8K appeared as a slim, well proportioned design, its successor looked almost paunchy by comparison. The larger boiler and wider cab lent a feeling of size somewhat reminiscent of the lines of the Sir Sam Fay 4–6–0 of 1912. To accommodate spectacles of a reasonable width the 8M cab was widened by 7" to 8' 3". In contrast to the 8Ks, only one spectacle was provided, the small, square lower spectacle of the latter being done away with. This detail difference was retained upon later re–boilering, providing evidence of the engines' former parentage. Although wider and taller, the cab had to be shortened by 5" to clear the firebox washout plugs. A consequence of this was the provision of a steel casing on the right hand side of the cab front to cover the screw reversing gear. Under the cab appeared the sandboxes for reverse running, another visual difference from the 8K which had housed the boxes in the longer cab. 7¼" was lopped off the chimney which appeared somewhat squat at 1' 3".

In the manner of the later 9P engines, the last five of the 8Ms – Nos. 14, 15, 17, 19 and 22 of 1921/22 – had what might be termed an improved cab with two side windows and extended roof. Again, this was a feature retained upon re–boilering in later years, though with some alteration to the front spectacles. A mechanical modification applied to five of the last 8Ms concerned the balancing of the coupled wheels. On these engines (Nos. 13, 14, 15, 19 and 22) the earlier weight, of crescent shape, was dispensed with and a much wider version, integral with the wheel boss and bearing a characteristic hole, was used. Colloquially known as the 'battleaxe' type of balance weight, the application of this unusual shape may well have been an attempt to bring about higher speeds from the 2–8–0 type.

As far back as 1912 Robinson had seen the need to speed up the Great Central's freight traffic as congestion was occurring on busy parts of the system. His address to the Locomotive, Carriage and Wagon Committee of October 4th. 1912 might be taken as something of a hint:

......*I have no desire to say one word against the present eight–wheels coupled engines as I consider they are ideal for the work for which they are designed and they are doing excellent work, but as the size of the wheels*

**ROBINSON TENDER LOCOMOTIVES FOR HEAVY GOODS TRAFFIC**

**8A 0–8–0** (1902)

4' 9" boiler *(minority only superheated and not until 1914)* 15' 0" barrel
19" cylinders

**8K 2–8–0** (1911)

5' 0" boiler with 15' 0" barrel, all superheated – designated No.6 Standard, shared with Atlantics *(some detail differences)*
21" cylinders.

**8M 2–8–0** (1918)

5' 6" boiler with 15' 0" barrel, all superheated (though not with same pattern) same outside diameter as 'Sir Sam Fay' boiler but using shortened barrel and deeper firebox. Boiler designated No.8 Standard
21" cylinders.

One 8K engine (No.966, the pioneer of the class from September 1911) was rebuilt with 6' 0" round topped boiler in 1921, in conjunction with pulverised fuel experiments.

Cab views of Robinson engines would appear to be somewhat thin on the ground and, with so little of the Great Central surviving into preservation, enthusiasts and modellers in particular have little to draw upon. The views show, again, the pioneer large-boilered engine No.412 in original condition. Prominent on the right-hand are the regulator handle, reversing gear and vacuum brake handle. Either side of the fairly high firehole door are the pipes for the two injectors, the overflow pipes for these run either side of the space below the cab floor terminating under the footsteps. Just visible on the fireman's side behind the side opening and the spectacle are the sight feeds for the 'Intensifore' lubrication system. Adjacent to the cab side sheets are two rectangular steel plates; these were equipped with small doors which gave access to lockers on either side for tools etc. Almost equally full of interest is the view of the front of No.412. Missing is the twin crossbar arrangement into which the 'dart' of the smokebox handle engaged to be tightened in order to facilitate an airtight seal, a 1″ rope of asbestos providing the necessary packing around the contact face. Behind the bell mouth of the petticoat pipe can be seen the superheater

header, the 28 elements dropping down in seven sets of four pipes each. Only the bottom row of pipes is visible, the remaining three sets of pipework are stacked up, out of sight, behind. The superheater header is of the 'front cover' pattern which Robinson filed a patent for in 1916. Saturated and superheated steam chambers alternated along the width of the header, the ends of the pipes being expanded to a steam-tight joint directly into the base of the header. From the left-hand side of the smokebox the pipe supplying steam to the blower can be seen, the latter standing directly on top of the blast pipe. In the centre of the buffer beam or 'plank' is the drawhook complete with screw coupling. A longitudinal slot allowed the drawhook to swivel sideways, a Robinson standard feature. Standing just to the right of this is the connection for the steam heating pipe; the operating cock is visible but the pipe has been removed. Clearly seen below the platform is the axle of the pony truck with its cross-stay, guard irons and side coil springs. Oval head buffers complete the picture.

GREAT CENTRAL LOCOMOTIVES

*will not allow them to haul these heavy trains at greater speed than from 15–20 m.p.h., I recommend that we build some engines to meet the conditions already stated.....*

The five engines mentioned appear to have had the altered balance weight arrangement from new. No. 420 acquired the revised arrangement later on its career. As LNER 5420 it had received the 'battle-axe' pattern by 16th June 1935. Conversely, No. 13 (as 5013) had lost these weights by 7th April 1928 (an ex-works date). No. 22 ran with this pattern up to at least May 1952. Observation of works dates for No. 5420 (it received a general repair from 18th May 1929 to 8th June 1929) indicate that it could have received the 'battleaxe' wheel-set from No. 5013 which underwent a change of boiler at around that time. No. 5015 lost its 'battleaxe' wheels by 1952 (as No. 63917) and a photograph exists of O4/3 No. 3870 (ROD No. 2084) with a 'battleaxe' set too. No. 5014 still retained the revised arrangement when later rebuilt to O4/6.

A further sidelight on the business of balancing concerned the report from the Bridge Stress Committee of 1928 which found the 8K 2–8–0 had considerable hammer blow at elevated speeds. The Committee had started work some 6–7 years earlier and had also cited the Simple Atlantics and the L1 tanks as culprits for excessive hammer blow.

Braking apparatus, as with almost all Great Central engines, was the standard arrangement of steam brake for the locomotive and vacuum ejector for the train. Screw couplings were provided on most of the later (1920/21 batch) and are thought to have been added for the purpose of working passenger trains on running–in duties in the Manchester area. In like manner, steam heating connections were also added to the locomotives. Both these fittings were removed in later LNER days.

The work and duties of the 8K 2–8–0 was described in Volume I and it is logical to state that the nineteen 8M variants of the class covered much the same ground as their somewhat smaller antecedents. This statement is, however, pre–empted by the fact that Robinson had two of the 8Ms (Nos. 412 & 413) rebuilt with the smaller No. 6 Standard boiler as early as summer 1922. All the 8Ms were eventually rebuilt with the smaller boiler. This was a rather protracted process and was not completed until January 1943. From 1939 the generous Great Central cabs were cut down to enable through running over other lines in the event of war. Upon alteration to LNER standard gauge the cab spectacles were made wider (q.v.). Previously classified O5 by the LNER, the small boiler rebuilds were classed as O4/1 at first and O4/6 after the end of 1938.

Two other members of the class, Nos. 420 & 422, were selected by Robinson to be part of a quartet of 2–8–0 freight engines, used as Guinea Pigs for what nowadays might be termed 'alternative fuels'.

## ALTERNATIVE FUEL EXPERIMENTS – CLASSES 8K AND 8M

Robinson's flair for innovative engineering was manifest right throughout his period of tenure on the Great Central. Not confining himself solely to locomotive work, he was also an engineer in the broadest sense; his work with superheaters, for example, extended into the marine field. In this broad vein he had become profoundly interested in the quest for fuel other than coal to power locomotives. The First World War had seen a period of inflation unprecedented in contemporary British history and the price (and quality) of coal was always uppermost in the minds of railway managers and engineers.

So Robinson's two prime objectives in his search for an alternative were: coal of lower grade that was obviously cheaper, and to ensure as near complete combustion as possible, with an obvious saving in maintenance and turnround. These innovations, though short–lived, represent a landmark in Great Central locomotive development and are worthy of a reasonably detailed study.

The first engine selected for experimentation was a standard 8K, No. 353. Pulverised coal was selected for this preliminary attempt, the finely divided fuel being obtained from collieries as the residue from the coal screening apparatus. No special drying facilities were available in this wartime period and the fuel was dried by exposure for a few days to the heat from a battery of Lancashire boilers. Now in a powdered state, 80–90% of the weight of the fuel would pass through a screen of 200 meshes per linear inch; in more practical terms, it was stated that no particle was more than $\frac{1}{400}$ of an inch in size, with the bulk of it a great deal smaller.

This medium was to feature in all Robinson's alternative fuel experiments in one form or another. As will be seen, the third attempt was to mix the powdered coal with oil to form what was termed 'Colloidal' fuel.

Robinson's prestige and fame as a locomotive engineer was riding high indeed in the period following the First World War. The technical press of the day were lavish in their coverage of his work and both 'The Locomotive' and 'The Engineer' carried full–length articles on the converted 353.

On this engine, pulverised fuel was housed in the normal coal space in the tender, which was specially adapted for the purpose and readily identifiable by the inwardly sloping watertight doors visible

above the coal plates. An air intake, a bit like a periscope, faced inwards in front of the fuel bunker to supply the necessary air for combustion. In the bottom of the tender coal space (or hopper as it was described) were placed two horizontal conveyor screws which were rotated through worm and spur gearing driven by a small horizontal two–crank steam engine (a small 4–cylinder petrol engine had been used initially). Care was taken to ensure a fairly high piston speed to avoid condensation losses when the lowest rate of feed was used. So far, the principle was simple and more or less akin to the action of a household mincer or the Archimedean screw, a device used from time immemorial for the raising of water. On leaving the feed screws the fuel was met by a blast of air supplied from a blower or fan driven at around 2,500 r.p.m. by means of a De Laval steam turbine. Dog clutches were provided to the fan drive, enabling it to be disconnected in case of any malfunction. In the event of this, the fan would become chain–driven from the steam engine that drove the feed screws. On leaving the tender, the fuel/air mixture passed through flexible pipes some 5″ in diameter. To accommodate the new fuel the firebox was modified; the grate and ashpan were removed and two openings of 7½″ in diameter were made through the water space and sited between the foundation ring and below the cast–iron footplate. Wrought iron rings were used for the openings, rivetted to the inner and outer firebox backplates. The lower part of the firebox was lined with firebrick and a series of holes or 'ports' therein drew air for combustion of the fuel. Ducts along the firebox sides admitted air to the ports, the flow of air itself being controlled by dampers, in conventional fashion, from underneath the firebox. In order to obtain the best pattern of combustion, the ports at the back of the firebox were made larger, the idea being that secondary air would be admitted in greater quantity to meet the issuing jet of fuel from the tender as soon as it entered the box. This would shorten the flame and help to ensure almost complete combustion. Inside the firebox the normal brick arch was retained. It was supplemented by a second arch which projected from under the firedoor for just under half the length of the firebox. Unburnt products from the fuel dropped into what was termed a 'slag box', in effect an ashpan, situated below the front of the firebox and occupying about one third of its length. In place of the normal firebox door a brick–lined door, normally kept fastened whilst the engine was in operation, took its place. A sight hole to monitor the proceedings was built in to this door.

Trials were conducted with No. 353 and a conventional coal–burning 8K on the line

The last five of the 8Ms, Nos.14/15/17/19/22, were completed between November 1920 and February 1921. They differed visually from their predecessors in having side-window cabs and extended roofs. This much improved cab had made its appearance with the second batch of 'Directors' (11F) in 1919. The crew of No.14, the first of the side-window cab engines, pose for the camera in between movements on the 'Park' sidings at Guide Bridge. Below footplate level the application of the later pattern of balance weights known as 'battleaxes' can be observed. The looped pipe to the pyrometer projects from the rear of the smokebox. A subtle change in livery for these later engines was the panel, lined red and white in the standard Great Central black goods style, below the cab windows. A further small change brought the handrail down below to extend the width of the cab. No.14 ran until January 1933 with the large boiler and was then, like all the remainder, rebuilt with the smaller boiler. She had only a brief career after rebuilding; ninety-two of the Robinson O4's were requisitioned by the Government in 1941 as engines for the war effort overseas. Robinson's freight engines had an excellent track record for this type of work, the R.O.D. series are but one example. Leaving LNER stock in the October of 1941 the then No.5014 became W.D.787 and was despatched for work in the Middle East where she saw service on the Egyptian State Railways. Her final date of withdrawal is not known.

Looking grimy by comparison with the previous view, No.14 is engaged in freight movement at the east end of Guide Bridge station. The 'stopping passenger train' headcode would seem somewhat inappropriate!

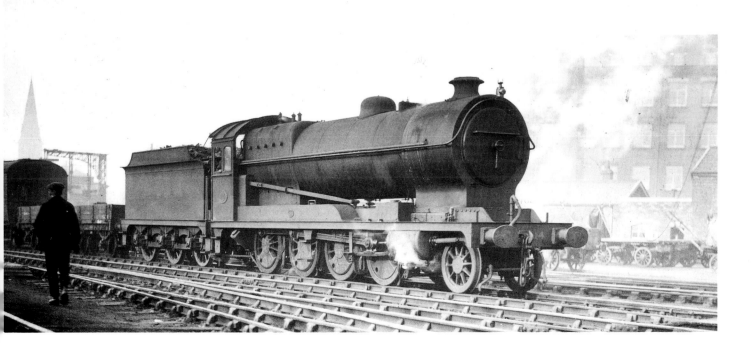

Three 8Ms for the price of one. Nos.415, 418 and one other (unidentified) member of the class are lined up for display. Neither of the first two engines appear to be coaled and No.415 has lost its steam supply pipe to the combined blower and steam circulating valve. A further small point concerns the lack of company crest between the lettering on No.415's tender.

An unusual photograph taken at the Manchester end of Sheffield Victoria station on October 7th 1922. Perhaps before passing to the two locomotives we could comment on the splendid G.C.R. bracket signal and the ex-M.S & L. fluted water column complete with brazier for cold weather use. Two of the later series of 8Ms, Nos.19 and 15 are passing across the station throat in tandem. Both engines are in steam with No.19 leading whilst the driver of No.15, behind, observes the duo's progress. No.19 was re-boilered in September 1933 and was sold out of service to the Egyptian State Railways in 1944. No.15 was rebuilt in June 1935, and was re-numbered LNER 3917 in August 1946. As British Railways No.63917 she was withdrawn in June 1962.

The LNER inherited seventeen of the large-boilered 8Ms from the Great Central, two of the original nineteen having been rebuilt as described. Becoming Class O5, the erstwhile 8Ms had 5000 added to their numbers in common with all other G.C. locomotives. Thus, one of our pair from Sheffield had become No.5019, photographed at Retford on July 3rd 1932. The engine wears the plain all-over black livery and looks far from well kept into the bargain. Lacking tail rod covers to the pistons and top-feed, No.5019 has acquired the Doncaster pattern of chimney which, though the same height as the original Robinson fitting, did little for the appearance of former Great Central locomotives. Gone too are the combined blower and steam circulating valve and superheater header discharge valve from the left-hand side of the smokebox.

Whilst the previous photograph showed an 8M with detail alterations this view shows a completely different locomotive, an 8M rebuilt with the 8K (GCR No.6 Standard) boiler. No.15 had also appeared in our Sheffield photograph but now looks a very different animal indeed. At Neepsend on September 9th 1935 what we have now is, effectively, a former 8K engine with a large side-window cab but lacking the lower front spectacle. Wakefield mechanical lubrication has supplanted the Intensifore system, a change completed for the former 8Ms by mid-1937. A Robinson-pattern smokebox door is fitted complete with wheel and single handle, but the smokebox wrapper now carries snap-head rivet fixtures seemingly anathema to Robinson. With the coupling rods almost on back dead centres the later, much fuller balance weights can be discerned. The chimney is the Gorton 1′ 5½″ variety, a pattern not totally dissimiliar from the original Great Central design. This view should be compared with the engines from Class O4/6.

between Gorton and Woodhead. A clear road was obtained for the eighteen miles from Ashburys onward (one assumes this was a Sunday); the train load comprised 545 tons made up from eighty empty 10 ton mineral wagons and a brake van. This test loading was the maximum permitted over the Woodhead line at that time which, of course, was noted for its almost unremitting gradient in the up direction.

An average horsepower of about 1000 was extracted from 353 on test. In terms of the efficacy of the pulverised fuel, the tests revealed that for every pound of fuel consumed the boiler evaporated just 0·25lb. more of water, less than a quarter of a pint (!), than its partner burning lump coal. Tests in the reverse direction were made between Sheffield and Dunford Bridge with a load of 686 tons made up from forty one loaded wagons and a 15-ton brake van.

On February 1st.1919 Robinson reported to the Locomotive, Carriage and Wagon Committee '...of successful experiment in adapting engine No. 353 to burn pulverised coal. Resolved, to obtain tender for coal pulverising machine.'

Although the trials were heralded as a success in the engineering press of the day, the savings made on fuel could hardly have warranted the trouble, not to mention cost, of grinding, storing and handling the new fuel. Aside from this, the cost of converting the locomotives and training of footplate crew would have had to be considered. Advantages of course, could be seen as plentiful: 'The Locomotive' for July 1919 waxed lyrical:

*With pulverized fuel far higher rates of combustion can be obtained when the engine is at rest than when solid fuel is used, and in consequence the process of steam raising can be very much accelerated. The fireman's duties are greatly relieved, as the physical labour of firing is entirely eliminated, and this very real limit to the sustained power of a large engine is removed.*

*It is neither necessary nor indeed desirable to use high-class round coal such as is necessary for hand firing, and fuel of such a nature as to be practically unworkable when fired in a grate by reason of its clinker-forming properties and high ash content can be satisfactorily employed in the pulverized form.*

*But little ash or slag remains in the furnace or smokebox, as the ash and clinker are in such minute particles that the draught readily discharges them through the chimney. Sparks are entirely absent, and the air and fuel supplies can be readily regulated so as to give practically smokeless combustion with any class of fuel.*

Pulverised coal had been used as a fuel for cement kilns, industrial furnaces, stationary water tube boilers and other purposes both in Europe and America for some time with considerable success and Robinson was convinced that there was still mileage to be obtained in its use as a locomotive fuel. As with compounding, water tube boilers and turbines though, the transfer of one principle to another, altogether different medium with its own very special peculiarities, is never accomplished easily. Robinson, in his typically empirical style, pushed ahead.

In converted state No. 353 notched up a meagre 2,747 miles and remained in this form until January 1920 when she was rebuilt back to conventional firing. The next locomotive to be used for alternative fuel experiments was 8M No. 422, again with pulverised coal as fuel. This time, however, with the war over, reliance on outside sources for the coal dust was avoided. On March 7th 1919 the Locomotive, Carriage and Wagon Committee confirmed 'the order placed with the Powdered Fuel Plant Company Ltd. for a Bonnet pulveriser mill to enable the company to experiment with low-grade fuels. Nett cost £680, delivered to Gorton Works.'

Having the advantage of larger firebox volume, and with the previous experience with 353, the experiments should have had a better chance of success. In particular, improvements were made to the supply of secondary air inside the firebox. This time the fuel emerged inside the firebox via holes underneath the foundation ring and the fuel was exposed to further air by means of a pipe located beneath the cab. Ports and dampers, as with No. 353, admitted further air – the base of the firebox being lined with firebrick as before. No. 422 was provided with a larger tender during its experimental period. Carrying 4,150 gallons of water and 7 tons of the pulverised fuel in an enclosed hopper, it was a curious thing; carried high on two four wheeled bogies it had a distinctly American air about it. Mounted behind the tender bulkhead were two vertically mounted twin-cylinder steam engines, one to drive the feed screws to push the pulverised fuel forward and the other on the opposite (left hand) side to drive the fan supplying air under pressure to blast the fuel forward towards the firebox. As before, an arrangement of dog clutches provided for the one steam engine to power both sets of mechanism should the other fail. Provision was also made to ensure that the fan was always set in motion before the feed screws began turning. A simple steam regulating valve was provided to control the speed of both engines. Additionally, a two speed gearbox was installed to give full control over the speed of the two feed screw worms.

A much higher mileage was obtained from No. 422 – 22,638 miles in the period 1919–1923. And, although full technical details of the engine were published in 'The Locomotive' early in 1920, no details of test runs, comparative power outputs or fuel savings appear to have been made available. No. 422 was converted back to

We can complete the picture of the rebuilt former 8Ms by looking at the opposite side of one of the engines, this time the second of our Sheffield pair former No.19, now 5019. This Gorton picture shows, again, a side-windowed cab engine with a small boiler (fitted August 1933) but displaying the 'flowerpot' chimney, the 1' 9" pattern with Gresley snifting valve behind. As with the previous view, tail rods and associated covers have been removed from the two outside cylinders and snaphead rivets adorn the smokebox wrapper plate.

The noisy clamour of Gorton shed yard is the venue for our penultimate look at the original engines in LNER days. Here No.5422 (422 of June 1919) stands, in steam, fully coaled but in a rather grimy state. Only the missing tail rod covers mark the locomotive from her Great Central days. 5422 was one of the later rebuilds, not receiving her small boiler until January 1943 (then becoming a member of class O4/6.) As British Railways No.63911 she was withdrawn in December 1962. In the background J10 class 0-6-0 No.5097 (one of the Robinson series from 1901) can be seen.

On June 16th 1935 No.5420 stands on shed at March. The slightly rearward perspective gives a good view of the cab fittings and the back of the tender. Well over twelve years after the demise of the Great Central the company's name still appears, ghost-like, on the tender side with the double lining managing to show as well. This engine, along with No.5421, had arrived at March from Mexborough in the Spring of 1932 for duties on the Whitemoor 'hump' yard. Both remained there until withdrawal in 1941 for overseas work. Notice the rolled tarpaulin on the cab roof with the attendant rail above the tender bulkhead. The later pattern of balance weights on the coupled wheels show quite clearly, the 'battleaxes' thought to have been acquired from No.5013 in 1929. 5420 was rebuilt to O4/6 in September 1941. She was one of the O4s requisitioned by the Government in 1941 for service overseas and written out of LNER stock at the end of 1943.

*L.Hanson*

No.420 was the third Robinson engine, and the second 8M, to be converted to burn what we have described as 'alternative fuels'. Because of the use of compressed air to mix together the solid and liquid parts of the colloidal fuel it was possible to use a standard Robinson 4,000 gallon tender – no feed screws or stationary steam engines being required. Visually, the only noticeable difference was the presence of the oil tank on top of the tender. Though the photograph, taken outside Manchester London Road station, clearly shows the tank to be present, it can only be speculated upon as to whether this engine was burning colloidal fuel at the time, as it is believed that No.420 ran for a period as a straight oil burner as well. The engine carries a pyrometer, a device that seems to have fascinated Robinson with his particular penchant for superheating and which was applied to all four of these 'alternative fuel' locomotives.

burn conventional fuel in March 1923; she was rebuilt to class 04/6 in January 1943 and withdrawn from service as B.R. No. 63911 in December 1962.

A further 8M, No. 420, became the next candidate for Robinson's experiments. This time the engine, built in April 1919, was equipped to burn an altogether different fuel. This was the Colloidal mixture – a combination of liquid fuel oil and pulverised coal held together as an emulsion, the very fine coal dust being suspended in the liquid. As well as burning the combination fuel, the locomotive could also run as a straight oil–burner which is believed to have been the case for a short period. In addition to the use of oil in combination with coal dust, pitch and creosote were also tried, low–grade fuels indeed!

In contrast to the previous two conversions, little modification to No.420's firebox was necessary. The grate was lined with firebrick, the front portion being covered with broken firebrick through which air was admitted in the normal manner. Two dampers, front and back, controlled the airflow to the burner. This was of the Triplex type consisting of three identical fuel injectors and atomisers housed in one body. Superheated steam was drawn from a separate header in the smokebox and was available to be piped to the burners to obtain the necessary atomising and injection action. Steam was also fed to a heating coil in the tender oil tank to lower the viscosity of the fuel in cold weather. A heater under the footplate warmed the fuel as it was fed through to the burners. The Triplex arrangement provided for all three burners to be working together, the central one working alone, or the two outer ones as a pair. A combination steam valve on the left hand side of the firebox backplate enabled either superheated or saturated

steam to be piped to the requisite positions, although superheated steam was the preferred medium for the burners. To operate the burners for steam–raising purposes a connection was made for the provision of an external steam supply.

No. 420 was paired with a more or less normal–bodied tender, in contrast to the previous two conversions; the only visible sign of any modification was the large fuel oil tank extending almost to the limits of the loading gauge and occupying the whole of the top of the coal space in a manner similar to the 1922 G.C. oil burners. Compressed air was used to agitate the fuels and unite them in an even mixture before they were blown along pipes to the burners. Though a full account of this conversion was carried by 'The Locomotive' in July 1922 complete with drawings, no explanation was offered as where the compressed air was derived from. As well as coping with somewhat unusual liquid fuels trials were also conducted with 50–50 mixtures of coke breeze and fuel oil and 65–35 mixtures of smokebox ash and fuel oil. 50–50 and 60–40 mixtures of fuel oil and coal dust were also tried.

Using a mixture of 60% Elsecar coal dust and 40% fuel oil, trials were conducted with No. 420 between Dewsnap Sidings (adjacent to Dukinfield carriage works) and Dunford Bridge – a distance of 16 miles, 35 chains. Eighty empty coal wagons and a brake van were taken up, the load being equal to 510 tons. The average gradient on the line was 1 in 166 with a maximum of 1 in 100. To ensure a reasonable comparison 8K No. 419 was used (burning ordinary coal) along with No. 422 on the pulverised variety. Though a higher superheat temperature was drawn from the colloidal engine, no significant savings in fuel or water were apparent. Altogether 38,725 miles were run with No. 420 during

her conversion. She was rebuilt back to conventional form in October 1923.

A fourth, and final, conversion came in 1921 when an 8K, No. 966 (the pioneer of the class from September 1911), was rebuilt with a 6′ 0″ diameter boiler. Robinson must have been convinced he was on to a good thing with his pulverised and colloidal fuel theories and with this last attempt he no doubt hoped to vindicate himself. The boiler with which No. 966 was equipped was of special design and equipped to burn pulverised fuel only; the round topped firebox had water spaces that extended below the level of the fire. At this point the firebox had an appearance in cross section similar to that of an electric light bulb, the waisted area narrowing in the region of the tubeplate. Constricted corners in the region of the foundation ring were avoided and the build up of mud and solid deposits from the water was thus minimised. Feed water was delivered to the boiler in this space, in contrast to the top feed that Robinson was employing at that time. Scale–forming solids were precipitated there and mud doors and access holes were provided in this region, which took a rounded form. No fire grate was provided, the fuel entering at a low level in the form of a flat sheet or ribbon along with 25–30% of the air necessary for combustion. Two brick arches were provided; the first, or primary arch, covered approximately one third of the rear of the firebox, the second was situated below the front of the firebox extension. The mixed fuel and air ignited spontaneously. On reaching the forward part of the firebox the gases, then partially consumed, met with air drawn in from the smokebox blast and passed through a ring of refractory material into what was in effect a combustion chamber – narrow neck or extension of the firebox. It is worth mentioning that this in itself was a novelty

**Little, if any, visual differences marked out No.422 as a locomotive from its coal burning compatriots. Little different that is, until one looked at the tender! Carrying seven tons of fuel and 4,150 gallons of water, on-board steam engines and fuel feed apparatus, the double bogie affair was quite a monster. Bogie tenders were not new to the Great Central, having made their debut behind the Baldwin engines from the United States that had first appeared in 1899. Their massive appearance was increased by the profile of the large bunker doors which reached almost to the height of the cab roof. Taken at Guide Bridge, only the limited period of operation of No.422, 1919 – 1923, provides a clue as to the date of the photograph. The keen eyed should have observed the panel in front of the main tender tank, lined around with a single white line.**

*W.H.Whitworth, collection of W.A.Brown*

Travelling some five miles up the line to Guide Bridge, a halt is made at the west end of the station to view No.420 displaying a rearward view as she prepares to depart for Manchester with a down stopping train. Using a fairly long exposure the photographer has caught the two figures on the footplate as 'ghosts' and at the same time given us a rare opportunity to view the controls inside the cab. Modellers should make the most of a picture like this, showing as it does such neglected areas as the back of the tender and the detail around the tank filler.

The first of two of the very few pictures of No.966 in action. How far afield the engine travelled during its 9,648 miles of duty in its converted state between September 1921 and January 1924 is not recorded. The presence of a G.N. wagon at the head of the train suggests a revenue earning duty, possibly an up freight on the Chorlton Junction – Fairfield line, and not one of the test workings over the Woodhead route mentioned in the text. Notice the plume of steam being emitted from the tender indicating the fan and/or the feed screws for the pulverised fuel in operation.

This photograph shows the opposite side of No.966 as it leaves the north side of Guide Bridge station with an up freight train. The massive boiler, the largest ever carried by a Great Central locomotive, looks strange on a Robinson engine and is (prophetically) reminiscent of the later LNER rebuilds carrying the Doncaster round-topped boiler. The low elevation of the photograph heightens the 'water cart' appearance of the bogie tender. Enthusiasts may wish to know that the 10 ton GC cattle wagon at the head of the train is numbered 24073.

at the time, such devices finding favour with Gresley and Bulleid only in later years. A sight hole was provided in a brick lined door, in turn fitted in the position of the normal firehole door.

No. 966 is thought to have acquired her bogie tender from No. 422 in the May of 1922 and could well have run throughout the previous months coupled to the oil–carrying tender from No. 420. Just to complicate matters, 420's tender ended up being coupled to No. 422 and No. 966's ordinary tender (the original six–wheeler) was attached to No. 420! A complicated business indeed, further confused by a lack of dates.

Trials were conducted (in addition to those mentioned in connection with No. 420) between Ashburys East Junction and Crowden, again over a steeply graded route. Eighty empty coal wagons and a brake van, equivalent to 510 tons, was once more provided as a test load. The published results show a disappointing contrast to those obtained under similar condi-

tions from No. 420 burning colloidal fuel in a more or less conventional boiler. The detailed statistics are somewhat tedious, but put simply the colloidal engine evaporated just over 9lb. of water per lb. of fuel compared to just under 7lb. for No. 966 with its special boiler. Overall efficiency was quoted as 72% for the colloidal engine and 66% for No. 966.

Engine No.966 changed tenders from T966 to T422 on the 12th May 1922 whilst engine No.420 changed from T420 to T966 on the 9th May 1922.

No. 966 was rebuilt back to its original form in June 1924 having managed a meagre 9,648 miles in its converted state. The tank of the American-looking tender was used for oil storage and the bogies found duty at Dukinfield Carriage Works in the construction of a well trolley wagon in 1926. The boiler, one of the boldest designs to date, could not be used for other locomotive purposes and was scrapped in August 1927.

The outline of the pulverising mill could

be seen at Gorton for many years and appears on some of the photographs used in these volumes. It is fairly easy to dismiss the experiments at this date as an expensive mistake. However, problems with fuel supplies were the bane of the locomotive engineer's life and no other real economic alternative to coal as a fuel was then available. Railway companies had to stand on their own two feet, though even then there were some rumblings about Nationalisation. The cost of processing the pulverised fuel was a considerable factor in ensuring the demise of the process and none of the savings shown could be said to have been significant.

Many further experiments would be made in the field of steam locomotive engineering in the ensuing years. Most of these, too, would prove to be fruitless; but all this is said with the blessing of hindsight. And in the great field of human endeavour, the man who never made a mistake never made anything at all.

## SUMMARY OF CLASS 8M 2–8–0 LOCOMOTIVES

| NUMBER | BUILDER | DATE BUILT | REBUILT | WITHDRAWN |
|---|---|---|---|---|
| 412 | Gorton | January 1918 | July 1922 | April 1965 |
| 413 | –'– | March 1918 | July 1922 | November 1941* |
| 414 | –'– | April 1918 | November 1936 | November 1961 |
| 415 | –'– | May 1918 | October 1936 | April 1959 |
| 417 | –'– | June 1918 | February 1937 | January 1965 |
| 418 | –'– | August 1918 | February 1936 | May 1964 |
| 419 | –'– | September 1918 | April 1935 | October 1963 |
| 420 | –'– | April 1919 | September 1941 | September 1941* |
| 422 | –'– | June 1919 | January 1943 | December 1962 |
| 421 | –'– | July 1919 | October 1941 | October 1941* |
| 10 | –'– | August 1919 | July 1941 | December 1962 |
| 11 | –'– | August 1919 | May 1936 | June 1965 |
| 12 | –'– | September 1919 | August 1926 | May 1964 |
| 13 | –'– | October 1919 | June 1940 | June 1961 |
| 14 | –'– | November 1920 | January 1933 | October 1941* |
| 15 | –'– | December 1920 | June 1935 | June 1962 |
| 17 | –'– | December 1920 | October 1932 | October 1941* |
| 19 | –'– | January 1921 | August 1933 | September 1941* |
| 22 | –'– | February 1921 | October 1935 | August 1962 |

NOTES:

1) The broad classification for Nos.414 onwards to No.22 in LNER days was 05. As the engines were rebuilt this changed to the various 04 sub-classes indicating different heights of chimney, type of cab, type of tender and number of boiler tubes.

* These locomotives were sold to the War Department and written off from LNER loco stock. They had, however, all been on loan to the government from 1941-1942.

(opposite) **Clearly, one company at least still maintained faith in the concept of pulverised fuels. This advertisement appeared in the** Beyer, Peacock Quarterly Review **for July 1929. Shown is 8M 2–8–0 No.420, its fuel tank clearly visible on the tender. The engine had been converted back to burn lump coal almost six years earlier!**

No.53 was put into traffic in April 1921 and was photographed by P.F.Cooke in Fallowfield station goods yard whilst the engine was undergoing running trials shortly after completion. This first view shows No.53 at the back of the yard, facing west. Every major detail of the locomotive is visible and the condition is truly immaculate; a state of the art example of a Robinson engine wearing the lined black goods livery. The later variety of cab, with side windows and rear extension provides an interesting contrast with the earlier pattern fitted to No.416. In the 'daylight' under the boiler can be seen the two feed-water pipes to the top feed. With typical precision, Robinson had arranged for these pipes to be covered by the boiler lagging plates. Tenders for the trio were the standard 4,000 gallon pattern with a nominal 6 tons coal capacity and water pick-up apparatus (save for No.416 with the Iracier axleboxes). Clearly visible here is the curved bulkhead plate distinguishing this tender from the improved version with self-trimming bunker.

*P.F.Cooke/Author's collection*

# Class 8N 4–6–0

Mention was made in the description of the large boilered 8M 2–8–0s of the emergence of one of the locomotives, in July 1918, as a 4–6–0. Such practice was not new to Robinson; the 4–4–2/4–6–0 engines of classes 8B/8C of 1903/04 established a precedent and such swapping of wheel arrangements was to appear in later LNER locomotive design as well.

Emerging in July 1918, the one 8N was the only mixed traffic engine to appear on the Great Central since the completion of No. 280, the last of the Glenalmonds (Class 1A), in January 1915. The latter had appeared to suffer from overheated driving axleboxes caused by a restriction on axlebox size, a consequence of the large inside cylinders.

Using coupled wheels 4″ larger than the 1A, Robinson placed the cylinders outside the frames – removing at a stroke the restriction on axlebox size. The coupled wheelbase, at 6′ 9″ + 8′ 6″ was a hybrid for a Robinson 4–6–0, not conforming to any particular configuration that had existed before and differing by several inches from the succeeding 9Q (B7). The total coupled wheelbase was, however, 3″ shorter than that of the 9P which stretched to 15′ 6″.

Thus, a mixed–traffic design was laid down, dispensing with the 1A boiler and substituting in its place the enlarged 8K design. This boiler (No. 8 Standard) was 2′ 3″ shorter than the 1A giving a reduction in total heating surface, but a small increase in firebox heating surface. A free steaming boiler resulted and the locomotives appear to have been a success. Following the emergence of No. 416, almost three years elapsed before succeeding engines appeared and these numbered only two – Nos. 52 and 53 built in the spring of 1921. That the class were never multiplied beyond these three examples is no doubt due to Robinson's conviction that a more powerful engine was required than the two cylinder 8N; this conviction manifested itself in the emergence in the interim of the 9Q (B7) 4–6–0 which was quickly multiplied. A salient point in respect of the three 4–6–0s concerns their retention of the 8M boiler throughout their lives. Whereas the 2–8–0 engines had all been reboilered by 1943 (and two dealt with before Grouping), the 8Ns retained the original boiler until withdrawal took place in 1947. Some spare boilers were thrown up as a result of the reboilering of the 2–8–0s, and inter-change of boilers between the two classes whilst they were under repair (which was logical) is known to have taken place. As late as 1941 two new boilers were built for the class.

In like manner to the 2–8–0s and all the Robinson post–First War engines the 4–6–0 variants were fitted with top feed and the patented Intensifore lubrication system. Standard fittings to look after the superheater were the application of the header discharge valve and the combined blower and steam circulating valve, apparatus that by now should be familiar to observers of Robinson locomotives of this period. For reasons not apparent, ash ejectors were never fitted to these locomotives. Like the remainder of Robinson's engines in the LNER period the header discharge and steam circulating valves were taken off, replaced, in due course, by Gresley's snifting valve sited behind the chimney. Another casualty was the Intensifore lubrication system – removed in the 1934/35 period and substituted by Wakefield mechanical lubricators and not, as with many other Robinson engines, by hydrostatic arrangements such as the Detroit or Eureka systems, characterized by their awk-

No.416 viewed from rail level at Neasden shed in all the pristine glory of its Great Central livery. The massive presence of the later Robinson engines comes over strongly from such a viewpoint, the machines seemingly exuding power and strength. Superheater header discharge valve, blower and steam circulating valve show clearly, along with minor points such as the tallow cup lubricators above the cylinders. A curiosity on these engines was the omission of the company crest between the words 'Great Central' on the tender side, a vagary shared by the 8M 2–8–0s.

*Collection of W.A.Brown*

No.416 is busily engaged on freight duty at the east end of Guide Bridge station in 1923. Appearing with the early LNER style of company insignia, with full stops and ampersand between the lettering, the Great Central numberplate adorns the cab whilst the number 416 graces on the tender side. GC livery style of red and white is still carried with such nicely produced appendages as polished cylinder covers, smokebox fittings, motion and handrail.

Saturday, February 24th 1923 saw the well-known railway photographer W.H.Whitworth in action at Gorton to catch 416 alongside the coaling stage. Appearing in exactly the same livery style as the previous picture, the neat and workmanlike outlines of the prototype show well. Clearly visible is the hybrid wheel spacing of the locomotive's coupled wheelbase, the extra 3″ between the middle and rear axles making for something of an unbalanced look. The tender coupled to No.416 was fitted with Iracier axleboxes, notice the shield shaped covers, the same pattern as those carried by the original 9P tenders. No.416 was paired with this tender until 1932 when it got tender no.5509 which it kept until withdrawal. Reminders of earlier Robinson classes are recalled by the cab with its side cut-out a feature distinguishing this from the two later engines.

*W.H.Whitworth/Author's collection*

GC 416, now 5416, in later LNER days when it had received a Doncaster pattern chimney and lost its superheater header discharge valve with attendant blower and steam circulating valve. No snifting valve yet appears behind the chimney and the engine retains its original lubrication system, this was changed for Wakefield mechanical lubricators in the mid '30s. Piston tail rods have gone, as has the tender with Iracier axleboxes; a standard Robinson 4,000 gallon pattern is now fitted, the curved front plate indicating a normal pattern of coal bunker (non self-trimming).

5416 became No.1346 in September 1946, an intermediate number of 1328 being allotted but never carried. Though the pioneer locomotive was taken out of service in November 1947, the picture can serve to illustrate the time lag between withdrawal and scrapping dates, the photograph having been taken on March 11th 1948. The scene is Dukinfield Carriage Works, a venue for the scrapping of several Robinson engines after the war, there being insufficient room at Gorton. A truly woebegone picture is presented here: the front left-hand of the engine looks severely damaged, with the running plate bent down and buffer drooping as the result of a collision, boiler handrail crooked and dome cover loose. The chimney is of the third variety carried by the class, showing something of the outlines of Robinson's design. 'RA 5' denoting route availability 5 can just be discerned below the still new-looking number. This engine was the only one of the trio to retain its centre footsteps to the end. To complete the melancholy, two further Robinson engines, one an Atlantic, appear in the background, now mere mechanical cadavers enveloped by the passage of time.

*H.C.Casserley*

No.416 ran as a lone example for well over two years before being joined by Nos.52 and 53, outshopped from Gorton in March and April 1921. Mechanically identical to their predecessor, these two later locomotives differed in appearance by the fitting of a side-window cab with extended roof. On February 10th 1922 No.52 stands at the head of an up express, framed by one of A.F.Bound's distinctive lattice-post signal gantries at the east end of Guide Bridge station.
*W.H.Whitworth/Author's collection*

ward–looking oil feed pipes along the boiler casing. Piston tail rods, standard features on all the Robinson outside cylinder locomotives, were fitted to the 8Ns and lasted into the LNER era, unlike the other classes so fitted, where removal occurred before Grouping.

Other boiler mountings were replaced also. It is hardly necessary to reiterate the Robinson chimney story again, only to record the substitution of the original fittings by the Doncaster 'Flowerpot' and then the fitting of replacement chimneys in the 1930s, of a type akin to the originals. Top feeds, another standard Robinson fitting by this time, were discarded too by the new company. Reports exist of engine crews using coal hammers on them in order to dislodge sticking clack valves. Dome covers on these three engines seem to have had more than their fair share of interchanging: No. 416 was built with a cover of a type approximating to that of the 9P class. The two 1921 locomotives carried a cover of a lower shape and this was manifest in the parent 8M 2–8–0s as well as the 9Qs (B7) being built at that time. Dome covers of a more squat pattern were fitted to the later boilers (built in 1941).

As built the first 8N had a cab side with a single large cutout, an outline that resembled the bulk of Robinson's engines up to that date, Sir Sams, Glenalmonds and first 8Ms. Then, in the manner of the later post–war Robinson engines, the 11E, subsequent members of the 9P, 9Q and 8M classes a more commodious cab was fitted with extended roof and two glazed side windows. The improved cab was carried by both of the 1921 engines, Nos. 52 and 53. No. 416 retained its original cab side throughout its life and none of the trio's cabs were ever reduced in height to conform to the more restricted LNER loading gauge. Another subtlety manifest on the 1921 duo was the provision of larger axlebox journals for the driving and leading coupled wheels than on the original – No.416.

Something of a nomadic existence was shared by the trio. The pioneer loco, No. 416 began its working life at Gorton before moving south to Neasden. When new, the two successors, No. 52 and 53, were sent to Woodford where they were joined by the parent engine. From Woodford the 8Ns worked West of England expresses between Banbury and Sheffield before they were supplanted by 9Qs (B7s) then appearing as new engines. At Grouping the trio were all based at home, so to speak, spending the next two and a half years or so at Gorton. Goods workings eastwards over to Hull appear to have been the order of the day in this period. The next two years saw migration east to Sheffield, a process complete by early 1927. A tour around the West Riding of Yorkshire was the next agenda item with Ardsley, Copley Hill and Bradford playing host until, by 1930, all three were officially allocated to Bradford itself. Out of Bradford passenger workings to east and west coast destinations were undertaken as well as duties south west to Banbury. It was in this period that Ted Hailstone, a former Great Central driver from Bradford, was associated with the trio. Ted Hailstone, of course, achieved lasting fame in B.R. days with his work with Gresley A4s, 'Silver Link' in particular.

In 1934 the three 8Ns, by then classed B6, were moved yet again, this time to Sheffield. This was their last pre–War depot and, as before, a variety of duties, as befitted their status, was allotted them. The Second War over, the trio were moved for what was the last time. At Ardsley shed the three spun out the last eighteen months of their working lives on goods trains before being withdrawn in the last two months of 1947.

## SUMMARY OF CLASS 8N 4–6–0

| NUMBER | BUILDER | DATE BUILT | WITHDRAWN |
|--------|---------|------------|-----------|
| 416 | Gorton | July 1918 | November 1947 |
| 52 | – ' – | March 1921 | December 1947 |
| 53 | – ' – | April 1921 | December 1947 |

The second engine, now numbered 5052, appears over the ashpits at Neasden shed in pre-1928 LNER livery: 7½″ letters and 12″ numerals, plain black with apparently no lining; pre-1928 livery had in fact a single red lining which negatives then could not distinguish. The original chimney is carried, with top feed behind, while piston tail-rods have been removed along with the centre footsteps.
*Collection of Brian Hilton*

Taking the history of the class forward to the mid-1930s we see 5052 at Gorton in September 1935. The elegant Robinson chimney has been replaced by the Doncaster inspired 'flowerpot' with a Gresley-pattern snifting valve behind it and the boiler top-feed has gone. At this point in their history all three engines had been fitted with a new design of piston valve with narrow rings.

Out of traffic and out of steam, No.1347, formerly No.52 waits forlornly outside Dukinfield carriage works for the cutter's torch. Again, the date is March 11th 1948, some three months after withdrawal. Though not wishing to replicate the agony of No.1346, the view shows three features peculiar to this member of the trio, taking us right through to Omega as far as the class history is concerned. The squat dome cover was introduced on the two new boilers built in 1941 for the class and was carried by 1347 to the end. Alone of the trio, 1347 lost its Robinson handwheel on the smokebox door and had the twin handles substituted. A third subtlety was the lowering of the top lamp iron to the position seen here, sited just above the horizontal handrail.

*H.C.Casserley*

Having moved around for this picture, No.53 is now standing behind the down platform with Fallowfield's signalbox sprouting behind the tender. Viewing the engine from its right hand side provides the opportunity to comment upon the lack of ash ejector, one Robinson device never carried by this class. Though not apparent on a photograph, the two later engines were fitted with bigger axlebox journals to the leading and driving axles. Notice the provision of sand boxes for all the coupled wheels, along with the precise curvature of the sand pipes, no steam assistance being fitted. Such an excellent picture offers any potential modellers assistance in respect of normally forgotten rivet detail around, for instance, the box over the reversing rod, the cab roof, spectacle beading and rear Belpaire casing. After posing for Mr. Cooke the crew would have returned home up the Fallowfield line to Gorton via Hyde Road and Gorton junctions.

*P.F.Cooke/Author's collection*

Still in the Great Central era which, for this particular locomotive, was less than twenty-one months, we travel over to Guide Bridge to look at a slightly work stained No.53. The shifted perspective allows for a view of the whole front of the engine, the characteristic steps on the front left-hand side and the white lining-out details of the front buffer beam and buffer headstocks are points in evidence. A point of interest concerning Robinson's engines was the number of washout plugs alongside the firebox: five on the right-hand side, as seen here with two 'blisters' above on the Belpaire shoulder. This contrasted with four plugs on the left-hand side of the engine and three 'blisters' above.

No.53 became 5053 in October 1926. The engine was photographed at the head of a nine coach Grand National special in March 1939 at Glazebrook (CLC). This immediate pre-War view shows well the condition of the class at that time: later pattern chimney approximating to the original with snifting valve behind, new smokebox with snap-head rivets and mechanical lubrication and plain all-over black livery. 53 herself carries the taller dome cover of the type originally fitted to No.416. As LNER 1348, the engine was withdrawn in the December of 1947.

W. Potter

No.506 *BUTLER – HENDERSON* when new at Neasden. Frame profile, cab and Ross 'pop' safety valves all mark the it out from its predecessors, the 11E's. Notice that no ash ejector is fitted at this early point in the locomotive's life. Tenders for the first batch of 11Fs were the conventional Robinson 4,000 gallon/6 tons of coal pattern as seen here: this type was characterised by the curved top to the bulkhead in front of the 'ship's wheel' for water pickup.

# Class 11F Improved Directors

The 11E engine, developed out of the final front end of the 11D 4–4–0 and built in the shadow of the enigmatic Sir Sam Fay 4–6–0, had proved itself to be a winner right from the start. Though Robinson still had a foot in the big 4–6–0 camp, he obviously saw the 4–4–0 type as still having potential. The succeeding engine, classed 11F and introduced from the end of 1919, proved itself even more popular than the 11E. History has rated this locomotive, along with the 8K 2–8–0 as Robinson's best and most successful designs. The 11F Director was perpetuated in 1924 when two batches of twelve each were authorised by Gresley for service in Scotland on former North British routes. It is intended to cover these later machines as a separate sub–section.

A further order for more Directors had originally been placed in March 1916. Study of the Great Central Locomotive, Carriage and Wagon Committee reports for that time, however, show Gorton Works to be in something of low water, with labour problems, a pre–occupation with munitions work and, above all, difficulty in obtaining materials (see Introduction). Given this situation, then, it is hardly surprising that the proposed engines had to be deferred until the situation eased.

Robinson would have had cause to be satisfied with the original Director. Put to work straight away on the company's best services, the London – Manchester trains over the London Extension, the 11E had proved itself master of the task in hand; but still there was room for improvement. The 11E had inherited a cylinder block and valve gear layout from the final version of his first 4–4–0 (11D class). Imported into the Director, this cylinder block required outside admission of steam, as in the 11D, if the same valve gear was to be used.

With this transposition behind him, Robinson reverted to more conventional mechanics with his 11F. Cylinders with inside admission were used, with the drive to the valves via rocking levers, a practice used on most of his other inside cylinder locomotives – 11C, 1, 1A, 1B, and 9N. In consequence it was necessary to raise the pitch of the boiler by 1½″ to 8′ 10½″. The 11E had used direct drive to the valve motion, hence the boiler could be set at a lower pitch, no clearance for rocking levers being required. Piston valves, 10″ in diameter were retained for the 11F.

Like their predecessors, the 11Es, the engines were named. The first five carried on the tradition that had given the class their title of Director, after members of the Great Central Board, two of whom had joined after the introduction of the first

class in 1913. The First War had left indelible stains on the country's memory and it was considered appropriate to name the six 1922 engines after places synonymous with events from that great conflict. Where the popular sobriquet 'Improved Director' came from is not known. Although the logic of the title is irrefutable, there seems to be no official use of the name, only the application of class initials.

The 11E boiler had been developed from that used on 'Sir Sam Fay.' Between the emergence of the two classes of Director Robinson had introduced his 1B 2–6–4 tank engine (in December 1914). The boiler for this ungainly machine was a development of that used for the 11E; the small tubes reduced from 175 to 157 and the superheater modified by the introduction of elements with shorter loops. This modified boiler was used for the new locomotive and became standard issue for both classes. The 1922 engine diagram shows the same tube and superheater layout for 11E and 11F alike.

That the Class 11F was instantly popular with engine crews may be due in no small measure to the provision of the side window cab with its rearward extension to the roof. Introduced on this class and something of a Robinson hallmark on his post–World War I locomotives, this commodious feature made the succeeding Director instantly recognisable from its predecessor. Another feature abandoned in the development were the Ramsbottom cased safety valves, substituted, as on the R.O.D. and 8M 2–8–0s, by Ross 'pops' from the outset. Some differences ensued in the size of these valves between the

earlier and later batches. The 11Es had begun life with superheater element protection in the hands of Robinson's steam jet draught retarder, changed later on for the arrangement of the header discharge valve and the combined blower and steam circulating valve. These later devices were built in to the 11F from new, although, as with the 11Es, they were changed in the LNER years for Gresley snifting valves.

Robinson had equipped the first Directors with Wakefield mechanical lubricators and then substituted these by his own Intensifore hydrostatic system. This was followed through by equipping the 11Fs with the Intensifore from the start; like the earlier engines, Detroit or Eureka systems ousted Robinson's system in LNER days, identified by the oil feed piping running along the boiler casing.

Like their predecessors, the Improved Directors had the space below the raised footplate filled in from new. Again, a major visual change in early LNER days was the cutting away of this platework, an obvious advantage being the improved access to the coupling rods for oiling up and maintenance work.

A beautiful livery scheme was an asset shared by all Great Central passenger locomotives. The 11Fs were finished in the rich Brunswick green of the company, lined out in black and white. As with the Atlantics the rich maroon complementary colour was used, although with the Directors it was used on the coupling rod valances, front mainframes and tender frames and not, as far as can be ascertained, on the driving wheel splasher itself. A major difference with the second series of locomo-

*BUTLER – HENDERSON* **has its coupling rod bearings 'oiled-up' at Neasden towards the end of the Great Central era, with 9Q 4–6–0 No.464 for company in the background. Notice the presence of the short ash ejector at the back of the smokebox. The splendid GC livery shows up well, and the picture makes an interesting comparison with our later views of the preserved locomotive.**

tives was the side window cab which called for a different layout of the black and white lining scheme. Once more, brass beading adorned the splasher panel and the wheels, appearing again in green, were lined white. An altogether magnificent ensemble.

The engines suffered in the post–1928 economies through an enforced black livery. Even after this period all was not lost, as some rather striking appearances were managed, dare I say it, in B.R. days in the black LNWR–style livery!

Beginning in 1937 the 11Fs were given new piston valves of longer travel. Parallel with this innovation was the fitting of a cylinder block similar to that designed for the Gresley J39 0–6–0 goods engine. The J39 cylinder block used piston valves of 8″ diameter and the smaller valve became standard thereafter; a slightly retrograde step which does not appear to have inhibited the performance of the class. Nine of the original eleven locomotives were thus equipped, the exception being the prototype 'Butler-Henderson' which has, of course, survived into preservation. Only one engine was modified initially, Great Central No. 505 'Ypres' in 1937. Savings in fuel of around some 5% were recorded in trials held on runs between Marylebone, Leicester and back. The conversion process was not completed until as late as 1952.

*Dates of rebuilding are:–*

*5501 — February 1952*
*5502 — August 1947*
*5503 — October 1945*
*5504 — November 1946*
*5505 — January 1937*
*5507 — June 1944*
*5508 — May 1949*
*5509 — December 1945*
*5510 — September 1945*
*5511 — May 1945*

Engines in the unmodified state can be identified by the ends of their reversing (or 'reach') rods; as built these had straight ends, modified engines had the ends curved down towards the valve motion inside the frames. Differences also ensued in the arrangement of cylinder mounting bolts on the mainframes under the smokebox. Another alteration carried out in respect of valves was the fitting of four narrow piston rings on each head in place of Robinson's single, broad ring *(see also 11E section)*.

Boilers with lower dome covers were fitted in LNER days (1930s) to ensure compliance with the composite loading gauge and the celebrated Robinson chimney with its elegant, curved outlines was removed under post–1923 ownership in favour of the (almost as celebrated!) Flowerpot pattern inspired by Doncaster. The chimneys were replaced, as on other larger ex–G.C. classes, by a more aesthetically pleasing design that had some overtones of Robinson thinking in it. Another visual change, unnoticed by nearly all observers, was the fitting of replacement smokeboxes with snaphead (raised, rounded) rivetting around the wrapper plate. To one Robinson admirer at least, it is the presence of this anomaly that slightly mars the preserved 'Butler––Henderson' compounded also by the wrong size 'GREAT CENTRAL'.

Ash ejectors, a favourite Robinson device of this period, were fitted to the six engines of the 1922 batch and, retrospectively, to the preceding five built in 1919. The original version of the ejector, which did its stuff near the smokebox tubeplate, was fitted at first; this was subsequently replaced by the later, longer, pattern which moved the blast of highly abrasive cinders

and ash away from the tubeplates. The ash ejectors were removed from the class in the 1940s, though some pictures exist of engines with a rivetted smokebox wrapper and an ash ejector.

Though not visible, both Director classes suffered from cracked mainframes. This was in no way uncommon on steam locomotives which suffered more than their fair share of racking strains, inherent in a machine with a continuously reciprocating action. To remedy this defect all eleven engines had an additional strengthening stay fitted behind the firebox in 1931–32. As a further contingency seven were given completely new rear frame sections, one ('Prince Albert') as late as 1956. A modification applied on the 11Fs was the provision of semi-circular cut outs in the mainframes to clear the sideways movement of the bogie wheels. On the earlier Directors this side clearance was achieved by bending the frame plate inwards a distance of 3″ ahead of the motion plate. Though the frames in this area were well braced by the cylinder block, a slightly different profile for the mainframe was introduced on the later engines. To compensate for the missing metal the frame of the 11F behind the cylinder block was cut as a longer 'S' shaped section; comparison of the photographs of class 11E with 11F and also the 9N 4–6–2 tank, which had a similar frame profile, should make this clear.

As with the 11E class there were a number of detail alterations carried out to the later engines in LNER days. Sight screens were fitted between the two side cab windows in the early 1930s. Sanding arrangements were altered around this time: the steam assistance being removed (which would seem to have been a retrograde

A King's Cross view with No.5506 getting under way with one of the Pullman trains over the GN main line. The picture provides a good illustration of a number of features established under LNER auspices: snifting valves either side of the smokebox, replaced eventually by a single valve behind the chimney, long-pattern ash ejector and 'flowerpot' chimney. Oil-feed pipes appear, signifying the presence of replacement hydrostatic lubrication, whilst the tender is of the later pattern with wider body and self-trimming coal space. Most significantly appearance-wise, the post-1928 black livery is borne and the deep valance over the coupled wheels has been cut away.

*GERARD POWYS DEWHURST*, No.507, was the second Great Central director whose name was carried on the 11F class 4–4–0. Though the title 'Director' was appropriate enough for what was, essentially, a refinement of an earlier engine of the same class title, only the first two of these succeeding engines actually carried directors' names proper. This picture, with the engine at the head of a down express, was taken at the west (Manchester) end of Guide Bridge station. Showing well are the ample, solid proportions of this most successful of Robinson classes. The picture also gives us the opportunity to comment on livery style for the class. Whereas the Atlantics had introduced the practice of painting the driving wheel splashers a beautiful shade of crimson lake, a practice perpetuated on *SIR SAM FAY*, the scheme was altered with the Directors. The rich green body colour was extended to cover the splasher panel below the nameplate where, as before, the company's coat of arms was placed, edged in black and white. Crimson lake was extended to the raised mainframe underneath the smokebox where it was edged black, lined yellow and to the valance under the footplate. As with the Atlantics this beautiful colour was also applied to the outside tender frames and axleboxes. Worthy of comment here is the black applied to the smokebox. No.507 looks to have had a spot of bother in this area, with paint badly blistered on the door and wrapper plate below the chimney.

Now numbered as LNER 5507, *GERARD POWYS DEWHURST* stands outside Guide Bridge circa mid-1920s. This was the first of the later 'Directors' to receive the replacement Gresley-pattern chimney, though it should be noted that this is not the actual design that was used on the rest of the class, but something of a hybrid and akin to that fitted to the D11/2s – the 'Scottish Directors'. The engine has lost its 'Intensifore' lubrication system but retains its short-pattern ash ejector. Wearing the LNER lined green livery, No.5507 carries the oval cast numberplate on the cabside, bearing resemblance to previous Great Central practice: these were carried by a few former GC engines in this period.

*GERARD POWYS DEWHURST* appearing as BR No.62661 at Trafford Park shed on May 31st 1953 when the Manchester based D11s were working Manchester – Chester stopping trains via Northwich. Overall condition can only be described as 'workaday' with smokebox char deposited on the front running plate and a generally dirty condition (Trafford Park was never well-off for cleaners) apparent. All the alterations carried out to the class in their final years can be observed : smokebox with snaphead rivets and twin handles to the door, lowered top lamp iron and boiler with low dome cover. Notice the shallow curve to the tank top, indicating the last pattern of GC tender with the self-trimming coal bunker. This engine received the tender previously coupled to No.5505 in May 1927 and retained it until withdrawal in November 1960.

*B.K.B.Green*

No.508 was named *PRINCE OF WALES,* after the eldest son of King George V and Queen Mary who later became, albeit uncrowned, Edward VIII. Despite the abdicated monarch's retreat into exile, the name was left after the momentous events of 1936. In GC days No.508 gets away from Rugby with an up stopping train.

This picture, taken at Gorton, presents a good, strong view of the 'Improved Director' with livery details showing up particularly well. The balance of daylight reveals the raised front mainframe has the same hue as the coupling rod valance. Likewise, the splasher panel shows the rich Brunswick green used on the cab, boiler clothing and tender tank. The fitting on the smokebox side is the superheater header discharge valve, a Robinson-patented device installed as part of superheater element protection in conjunction with the combined blower and steam circulating valve. It was introduced on the original 'Directors' after the earlier arrangement of the steam jet draught retarder had been removed; it was incorporated into the later class from new. The cup lubricators appearing at the bottom of the front mainframe were applied to the first five of the class only.

'Magnificent' can easily become a cliche when applied to Robinson's engines, but little other than words like this are left when confronted by a view such as we see here. No.508 has backed alongside the coaling stage at Leicester and stands with all its pre-1923 glory oozing in abundance. What more is there to add? On the embankment running into the stage are some of the Great Central's 30-ton steel bogie loco coal wagons. Vacuum-braked, they were built in 1902 by the Birmingham Carriage & Wagon Company at a cost of £255 10/- each.

step) and a reliance on gravity sanding retained. Sand for tender first running was, as standard on the Great Central, by means of a vertical pipe from the front of the tender (q.v.) A feature which altered the front 'face' of the class was the fitting of twin handles to the smokebox doors in lieu of the Robinson wheel and single handle. Prior to the outbreak of World War II the top lamp iron was dropped down on to the smokebox door as part of safety considerations in readiness for the Manchester – Sheffield – Wath electrification scheme.

## ALLOCATION & WORK

The 11Fs were built in two batches: five in 1919/1920 and a further six in 1922. Like their predecessors, the 11Es, the Improved Directors were put to work straight away on express work on the London Extension. To this end, Neasden was allocated the first five engines, Nos. 506 – 510 as well as the second six, Nos. 501 – 505 and 511 (yes, the reversed batch numbers are confusing!) The arrival of the new machines displaced the earlier Directors.

1924 saw movement of the class to the opposite end of the line when No. 507 and No. 510 were sent to Gorton, to be followed, the year after, by a further four: Nos. 506/8/9 and 511. To sum up, the total Director allocation in 1925 (i.e. both 11E and 11F series) was split broadly between north and south – Gorton and Neasden.

From 1927 to 1933 several 11Fs (by now classed LNER D11) were transferred to former Great Northern sheds, principally for duties between Kings Cross and Leeds. The prime mover behind this scheme was W.G.P.Maclure, former G.C. Running Superintendent who was given a similar post for the LNER's Southern Area and had engineered the transfer of the 9P 4–6–0s to G.N. territory in 1924. The engines worked, chiefly, 'The West Riding Pullman' between King's Cross/Leeds/Harrogate and 'The Edinburgh Pullman' (later 'The Queen of Scots' and running between Kings Cross and Glasgow). All told, seven members of the class found a home at one time or another at Copley Hill shed (Leeds) between 1927 and early 1933.

1933 saw them split between the two major north and south sheds, as before. The arrival in 1933 of Gresley B17s for top link duties at Gorton displaced four D11s to Sheffield: these were Nos. 5501, 5508, 5509 and 5511. Other sources recount graphically the stories of Gorton men being more than reluctant to be parted from their beloved Directors. But, with more of the big 4–6–0s coming on stream, the days of 4–4–0 power on the most important services over the former Great Central main line were, obviously, numbered. Further moves took place, to Sheffield, Retford and Lincoln.

With the Second War in progress further movement of D11s took place: to Immingham, Langwith and Mexborough. Immingham received more of the 4–4–0s in 1943 and 1944 – Nos. 5508, 5509 and 5511. By the end of the War Neasden and Mexborough had four engines each with three based over at Immingham. Just before Nationalisation the latter shed hosted all eleven engines. Duties at that time included 'The North Country Continental' between Lincoln and Sheffield. 'The Continental' was one of the first long distance cross country workings in the north of England. It was also, incidentally, one of the first trains in the country to carry a restaurant car and had origins on the Great Eastern Railway going back to 1885. This situation pertained until the spring of 1950 when D11s began to be moved over the Pennines for duties over former C.L.C. routes.

Initially three engines were sent over; Trafford Park, Heaton Mersey and Walton (Liverpool) receiving D11s. Heaton Mersey's 'Prince Albert' and 'Mons' led active lives on both stopping and express trains to and from Liverpool and Manchester. One interesting working from Heaton Mersey was the through Liverpool coaches off the Marylebone to Manchester mail train from Godley Junction. This ran via Stockport (Tiviot Dale), Northenden and Skelton junctions to Glazebrook and thence to Liverpool (Central). Interestingly, G.N. large Atlantics had plied this route pre-War with Hull – Liverpool trains, by-passing Manchester. Another string to the Heaton Mersey Director bow were stopping trains from Manchester Central over the South District Line of the former Midland Railway.

By the spring of 1951 the rest of the class, other than the two at Heaton Mersey, were on the strength at Trafford Park, but only one, 'Princess Mary' now B.R. No. 62664 was in active use there, the rest being stored at the Manchester shed. Something of an awakening took place in 1952 when 'Ypres' moved west to Northwich to assist members of the earlier Director class, 11E. 1953 saw 62666 and 62667 embarking on something of a tour visiting Immingham, Boston, Mexborough and Lincoln.

*PRINCE OF WALES* **circa 1938, after the removal of the valances over the coupled wheels and the fitting of a long-pattern ash ejector. Livery is now lined black with large** *LNER* **on the tender and the engine number on the cab side. Though a boiler with the earlier, tall-pattern dome cover is fitted, the chimney is of the third variety, the pseudo-Robinson, post-'flowerpot' type. In this picture the engine is leaving Wilbraham Road station on the Manchester Central – Fairfield line with the mid-day slow train to Sheffield.**

*William Lees*

The final phase: looking back at our picture of a Class 11E inside Manchester Central, we take a step in time away from the station over the lines of the former M.S.J & A., part of the Manchester – Chester route. The date is May 24th 1952 when the D11/1s were working trains to Chester over the former C.L.C. route from Central station. *PRINCE OF WALES*, now No.62662, is at the head of a 5-coach stopping train, the 6.00 pm SO to Chester, and has just cleared Timperley station, heading towards Altrincham. To the left, out of sight, is the Bridgewater Canal ('The Duke of Bridgewater's Navigation') that paralleled this historic railway line for much of its length. The engine, exhibiting all the final features of the class, is coupled to a standard 4,000 gallon Robinson tender. This was one of the engines that did not receive a tender of the later self-trimming pattern.

*R.E.Gee*

*PRINCE ALBERT* was the second of the 11F Directors to receive a 'royal' name and was delivered on 27th March 1920, three weeks after its fraternal partner. It was photographed at Nottingham Victoria with an up express whilst having its tender tank topped up. Alone of all our LNER-period pictures this is the only one to show a green-liveried engine with the long-pattern ash ejector and 'flowerpot' chimney. Gresley snifting valve appears on either side of the chimney, an arrangement limited to a few engines only. Altogether, livery-style and boiler mountings, together with the cut-away valances conspire to make a fascinating case-study indeed.

*R.K.Blencowe collection*

In early 1958 *PRINCE ALBERT*, then B.R. No.62663, had been transferred to Staveley, a sub-shed of Sheffield's Darnall, for duties on stopping trains between Sheffield (Victoria) and Nottingham and on such a working is seen entering Sheffield Victoria. In the background a rake of Pullman coaches, used for the *MASTER CUTLER* stands in a siding evoking memories of long-distant Pullman workings to the city in the 1920s. The self-trimming tender was attached in August 1950 and remained with the engine until withdrawal in 1960. Particularly untidy features of the locomotive are the oil feed piping from the hydrostatic lubricator and the snap-head rivetting on the bufferbeam; protrusions, it is felt, of which Robinson would not have approved.

The 1950s were to prove the last decade in which the 'Directors' were to be seen at work in regular service. In this period the 11F class worked a number of railtours, the most notable of which was, possibly, Ian Allan's famous *PENNINE PULLMAN* which completed a round trip from Marylebone to King's Cross on May 12th 1956, consisting of ten coaches, eight of which were Pullmans, including the famous *DEVON BELLE* observation coach at the rear. The train was hauled by various locomotives throughout its journey. At Midland Junction Manchester, between Ashburys and Phillips Park, 'Directors' Nos.62664 *PRINCESS MARY* and 62662 *PRINCE OF WALES* took over from Class EM2 Co–Co electric No.27002. Running via Miles Platting, Rochdale and the Calder Valley line the two vintage engines completed their run at Rotherwood sidings outside Sheffield where they handed the train over to A4 Pacific No.60014 *SILVER LINK* for the final leg back to London. In this photograph, just one no doubt of many hundreds shot on the day, the two Great Central veterans are seen at Luddendenfoot, near Sowerby Bridge, heading east. The rugged beauty of the Pennines provides an appropriate backdrop.

*B.K.B.Green*

Looking dirty and down at heel, No.62664 waits at Nottingham Victoria on July 27th 1959 with a train of vans which, by the look of things, are to be backed onto a stopping passenger train. *PRINCESS MARY* was fitted with J39 cylinders and associated long-travel valves in September 1945. The view, showing the curved end to the reach rod and two horizontal rows of fixing bolts for the cylinders (supplanting the original 'U'-shaped pattern of bolts) should be compared with pictures taken in the Great Central/LNER era. 62664 was withdrawn from service a little over a year after this picture was taken, in August 1960 and cut up at Doncaster the same month.

*B.K.B.Green*

The 1922 series of Class 11F Directors broke with the previous naming theme and substituted instead six names belonging to conflicts of the First War. No.501 *MONS* was the first of this sextet, emerging from Gorton in September 1922. In early LNER days 501 hauls a 7-coach express out of Marylebone past the locomotive yard. From here the driver is given a cheery wave as 8B Atlantic No.358 is turned. Newly-liveried 9N tank No.30 is seen waiting at the back of the yard. *Collection of Brian Hilton*

11Fs were to be seen regularly at work over the lines of the former Great Northern Railway up until the early 1930s. In the somewhat austere lined black livery, instituted as part of the 1928 economies, *MONS* (still with tall domed boiler) makes an impressive start out of Retford with an express bound for Sheffield. Now LNER No.5501, *MONS* is coupled to a tender of the self-trimming pattern; in use with this locomotive from February 1928 until August 1950.

*P.Ransome–Wallis*

I felt that if only one picture of a 'Director' was to appear in this book then it would have to be this one of *ZEEBRUGGE* as BR No.62666 at Manchester Central. Taken in the early 1950s and looking in 'ex-works' condition, the picture summarizes for me all that I remember of GC engines during that decade. As a teenage train spotter at Central in 1956-57 I well remember 'Directors' simmering away, looking thoroughly unkempt and dirty, their job as station pilots keeping them in long periods of enforced idleness. 62666 will shortly be moving away from alongside platform 6 and along to Cornbrook carriage sidings with what looks like the stock of a St.Pancras – Manchester express. The crisp detail of the photograph makes the revelation of detail, especially rivets, an easy one. Notice the 'U' of fastenings on the smokebox door where the baffle plate is secured; small alterations such as this, along with the lowered top lamp iron and twin door handles all conspire to alter the latter-day front profile of the locomotive. Just visible is the curved end to the tender front bulkhead signifying the self-trimming tender acquired by 62666 in February 1938 and carried until withdrawal in December 1960. *ZEEBRUGGE* was the last 'Director' to go.

No.5503 *SOMME* making a brisk start from Guide Bridge with an up express. Lined black livery, 'flowerpot' chimney and long-pattern ash ejector all point to an early 1930s view. The boiler still carries the original tall dome cover; below footplate level the cut-away valances had by then become an established feature. Signalling enthusiasts receive something of a bonus here, the curious siting of the up platform home signal making for an interesting case study.

*R.K.Blencowe collection*

Two 'Directors' for the price of one. On the left, No.62666 *ZEE-BRUGGE* and on the right No.62667 *SOMME*, both thoroughly grimy and unkempt and a long way indeed from their Great Central prime. The location is the former GC station at Chesterfield Central, and the date, though unrecorded, is possibly sometime during the summer of 1959 when members of the class were being used on Sheffield – Nottingham stopping trains. The finials and brackets of the GC signals provide positive proof of the location, along with the famous crooked spire in the background – did the Devil really catch his tail to distort the famous structure?

*(below)* Well turned-out for an RCTS railtour, No.62667 *SOMME* pauses at Mexborough on June 7th 1953.

*N.E.Stead*

No.504 *JUTLAND* was outshopped from Gorton on November 18th 1922. The practice of running engines in before painting them in full livery would (as with No.511) have given rise to the application of the new owning company's initials being applied in lieu of the 'Great Central' applied universally hitherto. Despite the change of ownership, 504 parades at Neasden in impeccable condition. Indeed, the photograph must have been taken soon after painting, so immaculate is the finish. Not only is the early livery style worth noting (and comparing with *MARNE*) but we are also presented with an excellent example of the last pattern of Robinson tender: the wider-bodied self-trimming version. Observe the horizontal bulkhead compared to the curved shape of the earlier tenders. 504 was to exchange this tender in October 1923 for that off B3 No.6164.

To add another facet to our previous story we go forward in time to cast our eyes over a beautiful summer scene in 1924 on the London Extension. A Brackley to Leicester stopping train nears Woodford with No.504c *JUTLAND* at its head. Notice the plain L N E R initials on the tender, compared with the previous picture and the 'c' suffix, applied to some former GC engines (from late August 1923 to February 1924) to mark them out as Central division motive power. Close scrutiny reveals *JUTLAND* to have now received the tender with Iracier axleboxes off No.6164 (and, hence, the change of lettering style). A splendid elevated position gives a view of some details of the engine not readily seen from ground level. Though the GC had its industrial base in Manchester and its power base in London, the rolling English countryside as so beautifully portrayed here in Northamptonshire, was its heartland. The four coaches of the train are comprised of later Great Central 'Matchboard' stock and are bolstered by a 15 ton bogie fish van at the front and five cattle wagons at the rear. In the background are the splitting home signals for Culworth Junction, site of the branch running south-west to Banbury. 504c had its first trip into Gorton works on November 1st 1924. It emerged as LNER 5504 on December 20th.

Making a stark contrast to the earlier views is this shot of *JUTLAND* in her final years at the head of a stopping passenger train alongside platform 4 at Doncaster. Alas, the grubby veteran appears to hold no interest for the four young 'spotters' sat on the porter's trolley. Quite likely they will be waiting for an unusual A3 to appear, or better still, a 'Streak'!

*Collection of R.K.Blencowe*

In 1954 Heaton Mersey lost its two D11s – 'Prince Albert' going over to Lincoln, whilst 'Mons' went west to Northwich. Over the next two or three years only Lincoln and Northwich had D11s engaged in traffic.

Spring 1957 saw the movement of five engines from Lincoln over to Sheffield (Darnall). In the summer of that year the D11s were employed on stopping trains from Sheffield and were also observed as far apart as Leicester and York on express duty. Come the autumn of 1957 and all five of the Sheffield engines were put into store. By the beginning of 1958 six of Trafford Park's engines were likewise indisposed. The spring of that year saw an awakening though, and Trafford Park's Directors were trundled over the Pennines via the Dore and Chinley line to Sheffield

(Darnall). The only useful work done that summer by the itinerants was station pilot duties at Sheffield Victoria, with one loco, 62663, going to Staveley. The onset of winter saw the engines put back into store: 62660, 62661, 62665, 62666 and 62669 were laid up at Staveley and Nos. 62664, 62667, 62668 and 62670 were at Darnall. 62662 'Prince of Wales' kept itself busy, again as station pilot at Sheffield Victoria.

Come the summer of 1959 and the first withdrawal had taken place; 62665 'Mons' – taken out of service in May and scrapped at Gorton in July. The rest of the engines were stirred back into life yet again and were used largely on Sheffield to Nottingham stopping trains. That year another Director, 62661, was sent to Staveley to partner 62663. At the end of the summer the (now ten) D11s were rooted in a life-

style akin to certain animals and were promptly put back to rest for a winter's hibernation. Summer of 1960, however, saw them stirred from their slumbers and put back into traffic for what proved to be the last time.

In August 1960 four engines, 62662, 62664, 62667 and 62669 were withdrawn and all were cut up at Doncaster the same month. Extinction was complete by the end of 1960 when 62666 (Great Central No.502, 'Zeebrugge' of October 1922) had her fire dropped for the last time. Happily, No.62660 (GC No.506 'Butler–Henderson') survived the inevitable cutting–up. Today the engine has taken its rightful place on the lines of its former owner and could until recently be seen on the Great Central Railway at Loughborough, as part of the National Collection.

## SUMMARY OF CLASS 11F 4-4-0

### (LNER D11)
### (ENGINES BUILT 1919-1922)

| NUMBER | BUILDER | DATE BUILT | NAME | WITHDRAWN |
|---|---|---|---|---|
| 506 | Gorton | December 1919* | BUTLER–HENDERSON | October 1960 |
| 507 | – ' – | February 1920 | GERARD POWYS DEWHURST | November 1960 |
| 508 | – ' – | March 1920 | PRINCE OF WALES | August 1960 |
| 509 | – ' – | March 1920 | PRINCE ALBERT | May 1960 |
| 510 | – ' – | May 1920 | PRINCESS MARY | August 1960 |
| 501 | – ' – | September 1922 | MONS | May 1959 |
| 502 | – ' – | October 1922 | ZEEBRUGGE | December 1960 |
| 503 | – ' – | November 1922 | SOMME | August 1960 |
| 504 | – ' – | November 1922 | JUTLAND | November 1960 |
| 505 | – ' – | December 1922 | YPRES | August 1960 |
| 511 | – ' – | December 1922 | MARNE | November 1960 |

NOTES:–

a) All of class re-numbered by the LNER by the addition of 5000 to their original numbers.

b) The 1946 LNER re-numbering scheme began at 2660 (for 5506) and ran to 2670 (for 5511) without any breaks. British Railways added 60,000 to these numbers. Thus the class in their final days ran in the number range 62660 – 62670.

* No. 506 has been recorded as entering traffic on December 27th 1919.

Last of the line, at least as far as the GC's orders went was No.511 MARNE. Emerging from Gorton erecting shop on December 23rd 1922 it was the last engine built by or for the Great Central. Photographed at Gorton in 1926, the engine was undergoing trials. As with the previous three 11Fs the former company's legend was omitted from the tender side and plain L N E R substituted. 511 differed, however, in not receiving the company's crest on the splasher panel. LNER green, a lighter shade than that of the GC, was applied. It was GC policy not to apply the final body colour until engines were run-in, this being done wearing 'shop grey'. The LNER livery and number was, therefore, acquired before it was released to traffic on April 14th 1923. Notice the cabside has been edged with black and white and this treatment has also been applied to the tender side. Splasher panels and valance, along with tender underframes are painted black. The final pattern of tender with the wider body and self-trimming coal space is attached but this was surrendered to B3 No.6169 in August 1925, another later tender was acquired in 1927 (q.v.). *P.F.Cooke*

10 coaches are behind the tender of **62669** *YPRES* at Cleethorpes as the fireman trims the coal ready for departure with a service to Sheffield. Dirty, uncared-for, and minus shedplate, the engine looks very much as if it has reached the end of its life. Detail, however, is well depicted.

*N.E.Stead*

The 'Improved Directors' had been condemned to black as long ago as the late 1920s in the wake of the 1928 economy scheme. Notable exceptions were the Scottish variants, some of which were turned out after the War in green livery. As we have seen, the former LNWR livery style could look very presentable on the class, but exceptions to even this rule presented themselves from time to time. Here, at Manchester London Rd on March 5th 1959, *YPRES* backs with gusto into the main line platforms alongside the platforms of the former M.S.J.& A. system. Livery is now plain black with no lining at all, a nadir in the life of the class. Gorton works was, so it is recorded, prone to this aberration whereby their former beauties were dispatched in an unlined state. At least two other members of the class were treated in this manner. Perhaps overtones of the former competition 'next door' had something to do with it! 62669 was withdrawn in the August of the following year.

*B.K.B.Green*

The Great Central had only just over eighteen months left as a separate entity when No.72, the first 9Q, appeared from Gorton Works in May 1921. On the tender top can be seen the oil tank bearing witness to the existence of this locomotive as an oil-burner in the first few months of its life. At Guide Bridge and appearing in shop grey, the immediate similarity to the 'Lord Faringdon' design will be apparent. The steeper inclination of the outside cylinders shows well, as do some of the smaller details such as short pattern ash ejector, Ross 'pop' safety valves and top feed.

# Class 9Q 4–6–0

Enthusiasts fortunate enough to have observed most of Robinson's biggest engines at work have remarked that the class of 4–6–0 known as LNER B7, the last of the long line of Robinson locomotives of this wheel arrangement, were his best of that type. Self–assured, powerful, master of the job, these elegant and capable–looking machines appear to have been well received and highly esteemed.

Like many of Robinson's designs that preceded the 9Q, the engine evolved out of a previous locomotive. The 9P or Lord Faringdon had first emerged in the uncertain, dark days of the First War. On May 21st 1920 the Locomotive, Carriage and Wagon Committee discussed the construction of new engines. They decided to authorize building at Gorton of: '10 4–6–2 passenger tank engines, 10 Glenalmond (sic) with 4 cylinders, 6 Director class and also 20 8–wheels coupled engines and a further 10 Glenalmond type locomotives with 4 cylinders.'

The word Glenalmond is interesting of itself. Maybe it was a Boardroom hangover from before the First World War, relating to the 1A 4–6–0 design of the same name, which had first appeared in 1913.

In typical Robinson fashion, the earlier design was weighed up and subjected to subtle modifications. A 6′ 9″ express passenger locomotive became a 5′ 8″ mixed traffic design by the simple expedient of reducing the coupled wheel diameter and altering the wheelbase in two stages. Prior to any alterations, though, cylinder centre lines, bogie and centre coupled wheel position were maintained at the same spac-

ings as the parent engine. By working to these outlines Robinson was able to maintain a degree of standardisation – the same length of frame, type of bogie, pattern of cylinders and outside connecting rod (10′ 10″ long).

The boiler from the Lord Faringdon locomotive was used on the mixed traffic engine – a development of that on the Sir Sam Fay – Class 1. Pitched at 8′ 11″ above rail level, the boiler was in three rings, maximum diameter 5′ 6″ and rolled up from ⅝″ steel plate. A 28 element superheater of the front – cover type was fitted, the ends of the elements being expanded directly into the cast iron header in what was then time–honoured Robinson fashion.

Inside the frames, the crank axle (the design from the 9J 0–6–0 and doing duty as the front coupled axle) was set 6″ further back than on the Lord Faringdon design. This called for longer inside connecting rods (at 7′ 0″) and enabled an associated improvement to be made in the layout of the Stephenson valve gear. A difference to the parent design was the inclination of the cylinders, angled equally on the 9P but inclined at 1 in 11¼ for the inside pair and 1 in 14½ for the outside. As with the Lord Faringdon engines, rocking shafts were employed to drive the valve spindles of the outside cylinders, the curious arrangement of inside admission of steam for inside cylinders and outside admission for the two outside cylinders being retained as a consequence of adjacent cranks moving at 180 degrees to one another. A reduction of 13″ in the coupled wheel

diameter brought about scope to deepen the ashpan. By bringing forward the rear coupled axle by seven inches Robinson was able to incorporate a damper at the back of the ashpan with a consequent improvement in air supply.

May 1921 saw the arrival of the first 9Q, Gorton works then turned out a further two engines, one per month in the succeeding May and June. Vulcan Foundry, at Newton-le-Willows in Lancashire, were then engaged to build a further ten locomotives and these appeared between September and November in that year. In the meantime, Gorton began a third batch of ten engines, in August 1921. The company's old friends 'over the way' at Beyer, Peacock continued construction with a further five. Both the Gorton and Beyer, Peacock batches were completed by August 1922, making twenty eight of the class in total to date.

Construction then continued under LNER auspices. A final batch of ten was built at Gorton between August 1923 and March 1924. These last locomotives differed from their Great Central antecedents in several respects: four of them were equipped with a different pattern of outside cylinder. This had a straight, slab side with squared ends to enlarged steam chests and marked the quartet out from the earlier engines which, like their 9P counterparts, had an almost Great Western sloping outside cylinder casing. These later cylinders carried snifting (vacuum relief) valves at the end of their steam chests, although these were later removed. Wider spaced piston valves were used in these

No.72 became LNER 5072 in November 1925. Taken at Gorton on June 27th 1933, this picture shows the locomotive wearing the final pre-War LNER livery style of black, lined red with yellow numerals and figures shaded red and brown. The Great Central had adopted the black goods livery for these mixed-traffic 4–6–0s from the outset, the LNER's colour scheme being a mere variation of this, although lacking the more elaborate lining details favoured by the parent company and, of course, the superb cast oval number plates. No.5072 is still fitted with the 'Intensifore' lubrication system but lacks the superheater header discharge valve on the smokebox side, its duty now done by a Gresley snifting valve situated behind the chimney – this one, the second pattern to be carried by the class, is the famous 'flowerpot'.

*Collection of Brian Hilton*

cylinders and straighter, more direct steam passages were incorporated. In the later life of the class the improved cylinders were fitted to certain other members of the class when renewal became necessary. This appears to have been carried out to some thirteen of the twenty eight Great Central engines.

As stated previously, the 9Q was a mixed traffic version of the Lord Faringdon and very much a 'lookalike'; nowadays we might use the term 'clone'. The comfortable and commodious Robinson cab with its two side windows had made its appearance on the second series of Directors and had then been used on the later 8Ms and 9P engines. On the post–Grouping 9Q series this cab, given generous height in accordance with the generous Great Central loading gauge, was reduced in height. This difference is very noticeable in photographs, as is the alteration applied to the cab spectacles – reduced from an outline that followed the sloping contours of the Belpaire casing to a single, elongated oval shape. To conform to the LNER composite loading gauge, the 1923 locomotives were fitted with a reduced height dome cover to the new standard, with both whistle and safety valves cut down to suit. Chimneys were reduced in height from 15″ to 11″ and, as post–Grouping practice encroached, the remainder of the class had the Doncaster–inspired chimneys of the 'flowerpot' variety fitted. These were later exchanged (in the 1930s) for a single cast pattern which resembled somewhat the original Robinson type. Engine No. 472 seems to have suffered more than most of the class in respect of the variety of

chimneys received. These varied from an experimental pattern of 10¼″ in height in 1923 (applied to the last batch) through a type fitted to the Scottish Director 4–4–0s, then to a 'flowerpot' and, finally, back to one of the single cast patterns in the manner of the rest of the engines. A further deviant was No. 463 which acquired a chimney of the 04 (8K) pattern towards the end of its life around Nationalisation.

These last 4–6–0s carried all or most of the varying pieces of apparatus which Robinson had introduced (but not always perfected) over the years. Principal amongst these and applied to the 9Qs were: top feed for the boiler (an obviously Great Western–inspired device, but seemingly disliked by the LNER), header discharge and combined blower and steam circulating valves to look after the superheater, and his well known Intensifore hydrostatic pressure–fed lubrication system. The horizontal intensifier was placed on the left hand side of the cab. Two six-feed oil distributors were sited on the upper part of the firebox front, one on either side. These each provided two feeds to the driving axleboxes, two feeds to the steam chests and two feeds to the cylinders. Ross 'pop' safety valves, which had first appeared on the R.O.D. 2–8–0s, were applied and retained. Possibly, the header discharge valve and its associated combined blower and circulating valve were over–complicated for the purpose they served and were early casualties. They were replaced by Gresley's simple snifting valve which took up its position behind the chimney, although some sitings were noted with a side

mounting on the smokebox. Robinson's ash ejector, something of a precursor of the self–cleaning smokebox, had been fitted to the whole of the class from new.

The LNER series (then classed B7/2) were equipped with the long pattern ash ejector, identified by the long pipe above the vacuum ejector on the right hand side of the locomotive. Though the earlier engines had been built with the short pattern ash ejector, these, too, were later equipped with the longer variety (it was noted that the steam blast of the short ejector was found to be corroding the smokebox tubeplates). Although useful the ash ejectors were removed from all the class before withdrawal.

Another Robinson–inspired device fitted to the class from new was a pyrometer, identified by a loop of pipework emerging from the top of the left hand side of the smokebox. Used for measuring the high temperature in the 'dry' side of the superheater header, a report has suggested that enginemen did not understand the working of the device and this led to its removal. Certainly it was taken out of use in very early LNE days, if not during the Great Central regime itself.

In the 1932–36 period the LNER removed the 'Intensifore' lubrication system which appeared prone to air locks, and substituted Eureka or Detroit systems with sight feeds. These lubricators were characterized by the long oil feed pipes straggling the side of the boiler casing which looked remarkably unworkmanlike in some cases. A Wakefield mechanical lubricator was fitted to cope with driving axlebox lubrication and was applied as standard towards the end of the 1930s.

The pioneer engine, No.72, was fitted with Robinson's patented 'Unolco' system of oil firing when it was built in May 1921. This would only appear to have lasted some three months before it was removed. As with other Robinson oil conversions, the tank (holding 1,215 gallons of fuel) was mounted in the coal space, extending well above the coal plates.

In keeping with near-universal Great Central locomotive practice, all the class were equipped with steam brake for the engine and vacuum ejector for the train. Tenders for the class fell into two broad types: Engines up to and including No. 466, the second locomotive of the third batch, were equipped with the standard G.C.R. 4,000 gallon pattern. Tenders of Robinson's final design holding 4,000 gallons of water and possessing a self-trimming coal bunker with a nominal six tons of coal were coupled to the remainder of the engines. (Nos.467 – 474, 31 – 35, 475 – 480 and 5481 – 5484). Some later swaps concerning tenders were made in LNER days with engines acquiring the standard tender (i.e. with original bunker) and these have

**No.73 followed the pioneer of the class one month later, in June 1921. Gorton Works records show the building costs for the trio to be £9,633 per engine, a huge increase over pre-First War prices, even allowing for the extra two cylinders. In original condition and displaying something of the mixed-traffic nature of the class, No.73 pauses at Guide Bridge at the head of an up express.**

been recorded as :–

5470* August 1929 until withdrawal.
5474   March 1929 until October 1940.
5477   January 1938 until withdrawal.
5478   January 1948 until withdrawal.
5481   July 1929 until withdrawal.

*Recorded as having had a direct exchange of tenders with No. 5037.*

The allocation of the 9Q engines in the short run up to Grouping was fairly widespread. Gorton had the biggest number with ten engines, Neasden had six, Woodford four, Immingham and Leicester three each. At the head of the Great Central system, so to speak, Sheffield had an allocation of just two. The LNER engines (the final batch of ten in 1923/24) were split between Gorton, with seven, and Neas-

den, with three. Shortly after, two of the Manchester engines were transferred eastward to Immingham. The three Leicester 9Qs (now B7) were moved away in 1924 with Annesley later acquiring two.

As befitted their designation, the B7s (the LNER classification is more appropriate as so little of their work was actually done in Great Central days) covered a wide sphere of duty. At the northern end of the erstwhile G.C. system the Gorton engines were deployed on both semi and fully fitted goods trains to both the east coast ports and Liverpool, the Midlands and Marylebone. A peculiarity of workings out of Liverpool was the running of light engines from Gorton to the Huskisson goods depot, to take early evening fitted meat trains of up to fifty refrigerated vans over to York. Excursion workings of both ordinary and special nature were under-

taken on both the lines of the C.L.C. and the former parent system.

Similar duties were performed by those engines which were allocated to Neasden – fitted (or 'piped') goods trains and passenger duties in the form of excursion work, deputising even for B3s (9P) when the occasion arose. Fish traffic had long been something of a Great Central speciality and a number of B7s allocated to Woodford shed in the 1920s were deployed on these and other fitted goods trains. At Woodford, the new arrivals had displaced Robinson's other 5′ 8″ mixed traffic engines, the three 8N 4–6–0s (B6s), on West of England expresses between Banbury and Sheffield.

Gorton lost four B7s in the mid 1930s when more modern motive power, in the shape of Gresley K3s, arrived. One of the displaced 4–6–0s was transferred over to

A close-up of the motion bracket of an anonymous member of the 9Q class, taking in such often missed details as bogie, sandbox, cylinder and valve cover details. A peculiarity of both Robinson's 4-cylinder 4–6–0 classes was the drive, via rocking levers, from inside to outside cylinders with attendant transposition of steam admission. Here, the rocking lever can just be glimpsed above the piston rod support of the motion bracket with the projecting forward arm to drive the valve spindle visible under the footplate framing. Robinson's bogies on his 4–6–0s were all of the Adams pattern as devised by the Locomotive Engineer on the London & South Western Rly. With this design the bogie axleboxes were equally sprung by means of an equalising beam split about its centre into two halves. The beam carried an inverted leaf spring and both this and the beam itself were held in a pin bolted through and secured by a bracket rivetted to the bottom of the bogie frame. Side-play, to a total of 6½″, was controlled by a pair of link connected leaf springs. Modellers will have a tough time incorporating all the detail shown here into a working locomotive.

G.H.Platt

A second batch of 9Qs, ten in number, were commenced immediately at Gorton after the initial three locomotives had been completed. Almost parallel with this, Vulcan Foundry began work on a third batch, again, of ten. To complicate matters, different number sequences were selected for both these batches, the two-digit numbers in the 70's series having been taken up by the early Robinson 0–6–0 goods engines of the 9H class. No.472 had been built at Gorton in July 1922; she is seen here on that shed yard in early LNER days in what appear to be very unsalubrious surroundings. 472 displays the altered chimney profile adopted for this one engine in the later part of 1923; this had a

height of only 10¼" and resembled that carried later by the B17 class. Though we have entered the LNER period the locomotive still carries the full Great Central black goods livery with cylinder covers, oil boxes, works plate and tender axleboxes all well polished with paintwork gleaming all over in the best GC tradition. Notice the hole to the rear of the superheater header discharge valve on the side of the smokebox; this carried the pipe arrangement from the pyrometer, a device then abandoned. The engine received LNER number 5472 in May 1924 and was one of the class to be fitted with the later pattern of cylinders, in June 1941. She was withdrawn in August 1948.

No.468 emerged from Gorton in March 1922. She was still a relatively new engine when photographed at Guide Bridge on Saturday, July 8th 1922 at the head of a down express.

In LNER days the mixed-traffic 4–6–0s found their way on to the former Great Northern line in company with the bigger-wheeled 'Lord Faringdons'. In the early years of the LNER we see No.5469 storming down the line past Greenwood signalbox and heading towards Hadley Wood Tunnel. Conditions for the engine crew inside the tunnel are best left to the imagination.

*B.K.B. Green collection*

No.469 was completed at Gorton in April 1922 and received her LNER number, 5469, in May 1924. Back on home territory and still appearing in the first numbering style, but now with 'flowerpot' chimney, the locomotive is seen at a brisk pace heading along over Charwelton troughs. This lovely rural summer view, with trees in full leaf and wild flowers in ample profusion at the trackside, epitomises the heart of England that the Great Central's London Extension penetrated en route to the Metropolis. 5469 became 1377 in November 1946 and was withdrawn in February 1950 as British Railways No.61705.

*(opposite top)* Though the LNER took control of the Great Central as and from January 1st 1923 there was bound to be an interim period before all the locomotive stock could receive one new, corporate, identity. Here, then at Stalybridge, we have a Great Central locomotive No.470 of May 1922 in 'as built' condition mechanically but displaying ownership details relating to both companies. On the tender can be seen the later L N E R (no ampersand or full stops) with painted numbers underneath, a style that lasted until 1929. The cabside has received the LNER number (acquired in February 1924) but this is still in the form of a cast oval plate, N.E.R. style with building date and place added.

*(opposit lower)* No.5473 makes a brave sight as it sweeps through Dunford past a splendid array of Great Central semaphores with a down mixed freight train.

*(right)* Just one month after No.465 had emerged from Gorton Works, in August 1921, Vulcan Foundry completed the first of their batch of ten 9Qs. Delivery took only three months and was completed by the end of November 1921. Vulcan gave the engines the works numbers 3478 – 3487 and running numbers 36 – 38 and 458 – 464 were allotted by the GC. The company's literature under the heading of 'service' describes the locomotives as *fast goods* engines and shows a boiler pressure of 200 lb. p.s.i.; this was at odds with Gorton records and contemporary literature which showed a lower pressure of 180 lb. With this head-on shot of No.38, the third of the Vulcan batch, the massive frontal proportions of the class can be surveyed. Gleaming from head to toe, the engine was photographed new under the loading gauge outside Vulcan works, Newton-le-Willows, Lancashire, in October 1921.

*J.P.Richards/Author's collection*

*(below)* With this view taken inside Vulcan's works, we have a rare opportunity to study one of the company's batch of engines under construction. The massive, solid design, with the front end of the locomotive strongly braced by the inside cylinders is instantly grasped. The offset of the valve chests towards the centreline of the engine is very noticeable, though both valves and pistons have yet to be installed. A layer of insulating material is sandwiched between the inside cylinder block and the mainframes, the whole ensemble resting on stands and jacks.

*J.P.Richards/Author's collection*

The following locomotives from the 1921 & 1922 batches are known to have received cylinders of the later pattern (identified by the straight sides to the casing and longer steam chests) as fitted to Nos.481/482 & 5483/5484.

| GC NO. | NEW CYLS. FITTED |
|---|---|
| 36 | May 1940 |
| 38 | December 1940 |
| 461 | September 1946 |
| 462 | March 1937 |
| 464 | January 1943 |
| 465 | September 1945 |
| 466 | November 1941 |
| 467 | December 1947 |
| 468 | March 1936 |
| 469 | January 1941 |
| 471 | November 1943 |
| 472 | June 1941 |
| 33 | September 1937 |

Liverpool Brunswick to work trans–Pennine freights.

Over at the East Coast port of Immingham, B7s were used on what were termed 'Butter' trains between there and Manchester – a reminder of the once huge amount of freight traffic that was conveyed by rail in those far off days. These trains would appear to have had a smart turn–around, the crews lodging overnight in Manchester and returning the next day with the empty stock. Boat trains from Immingham to Marylebone were also worked by B7s, as were the celebrated and popular Eason's excursion trains which ran from Grimsby to Kings Cross over the former Great Northern line (see also 9P section).

Traditional work for the B7s in the form of fitted freights was slipping away from the class by the start of the Second War. It was this conflict, however, that was to give the engines some of their most notable work. America had entered the War in December 1941, providing regular B7 haulage of troop specials from Edge Hill

and on to C.L.C. tracks at Allerton. By 1943 all twenty eight locomotives were based at Gorton covering all eventualities of working and including loans to local sheds at Trafford Park and Heaton Mersey as well as further afield to Liverpool. 1945 saw a migration of nine B7s eastwards to Sheffield, followed by a further nine the following year, four returning to Manchester in 1947.

This aftermath of war, when the railways were in a very run–down state, saw the sun beginning to set on the career of these, the last of Robinson's numerous 4–6–0 classes. Goods work of a varied nature seems to have been normal duty for the class in post–war years, though their use even on express passenger trains has been recorded. Edward Thompson's B1 engines were now finding their feet, to the detriment of many former Great Central engines.

History has been far from kind to this Robinson mixed traffic engine. Throughout the many and varied writings on Ro-

binson's locomotives that have appeared, the B7s have been repeatedly marked down for what has always been reported as a high coal consumption. 'Miners' friends' and 'Black Pigs' are two common epithets that the class has been tagged with over the years. These seem to have been added by outside observers; two former Gorton drivers I have spoken to refer to the engines as 'Four Cylinders'. Though the truth may be somewhat inescapable, the business of fuel economy needs putting in perspective. High the coal consumption may have been, but perhaps not as high as some other company's engines of a similar pedigree. Gresley's original Pacifics were, doubtless, better engines after acquiring long travel valves, but the necessary changes were begun well into the LNER era and long after Robinson had departed the scene. Looking at the B7 design, it needs to be regarded as a very solid, sturdy and workmanlike engine. It served its purpose well, was fast and equally at home on passenger and freight duties; positive values indeed!

In the early 1940s reports were received from Gorton Works of bent frame plates in the region ahead of the inside cylinders. The reported treatment for this malaise was to heat the plate up and hammer it back into shape. A more permanent remedy was applied to several locomotives and this took the form of convex-shaped extensions to the front frames as seen here on No.1378 (470) at Gorton. Livery is now the plain black with the truncated wartime 'N E' on the tender, the ash ejector is the later, long pattern and a low dome cover is fitted. Snap-head rivets adorn the smokebox wrapper and twin fastening handles have replaced the very characteristic Great Central spoked wheel and single handle arrangement. A curiosity is the existence of a second lamp iron at the top of the smokebox door, the bulk of the class receiving a single, lower lamp bracket in lieu of the upper one. 1378 was allocated B.R. No.61378 but this was never carried, withdrawal taking place in August 1948.

On April 19th 1947 with No.1374 enters Lincoln Central with an up stopping passenger train, the coaling tower belonging to the adjacent former Great Northern engine shed can be clearly seen on the left hand side of the picture. From Lincoln the ex-GC line turned north via Barnetby and Brocklesby to reach New Holland, Barton-on-Humber, Immingham, Grimsby and Cleethorpes. 1374 was one of the earlier locomotives to be fitted with the improved cylinders with longer steam chests, a modification carried out in November 1941. These cylinders were characterised by their slab-sided appearance and engines fitted with them had a small dimple in their front framings, required to house the end of the gland of the longer steam chest. Notice, again, the curved front frame extensions. 1374 was withdrawn in November 1948 having never carried its B.R. number.

*H.C.Casserley*

To study the full glory of this class in their Great Central prime we move eastwards to the GC main line at Guide Bridge on May 20th 1922 to observe No.38 in traffic. The engine is waiting at the up platform on the south side of the station at the head of a local train, the first vehicle of which is an ex-M.S.& L 6-wheel coach.

An interesting contrast with the previous picture is this shot of the same engine just over a quarter a century later. Taken at Retford in June 1947 we see the former No.38 pausing to take water while on express passenger duty and carrying its final LNER number of 1365; something of a rather sorry look abounds compared to that of its earlier years. As No.5038 the engine had received the improved pattern of cylinders in December 1940. Other changes in the meantime have conspired to alter the profile of this member of the class: twin handles for fastening the smokebox door, oil-feed pipes alongside the boiler casing, third pattern of chimney with snifting valve behind and lowered top lamp bracket. Rather less obvious is the appearance of snap-head rivets on the buffer plank and smokebox wrapper with patch plates on the front framing where the dimples had been sited for the valve chest extensions. Livery, if that is not too fine a term, is plain unlined black, albeit without the foreshortened 'NE' applied during wartime because it had LNER restored in April 1947. No.1365 was withdrawn in June 1949 having carried the number 61702 of its new owners BR for just about one month but still with LNER on the tender.

*W.Potter*

9Q No.32 was the second of the quintet completed by Beyer, Peacock in the summer of 1922 which were allocated the running numbers 31 – 35 by their owners. Tenders apart, this penultimate batch did not differ in any significant respect from their predecessors except that some engines of both this and the subsequent Gorton batch carried buffers with a more pronounced oval shape, the remainder conforming to a rather more pointed pattern. On Saturday, 24th March 1923 we call at Aintree on Grand National Day to look at No.32, the second Beyer, Peacock locomotive, completed by the company in July the previous year. Pausing in the siding before returning over the lines of the CLC, No.32 has its coal trimmed by the fireman; the GC clerestory composite coach and CLC signal provide finishing touches to this period view. Although the GC was by then part of the LNER, the engine still wears the livery of its former company and did not actually receive its new number 5032 until February 1925. Becoming 1384 in December 1946, the locomotive was withdrawn in August 1948 having never received its British Railways number.

*A.A.Torrance/cty Martin Ashworth*

Plans had been made to rebuild the B7 class as two cylinder locomotives in the same manner as the one, solitary, B3 locomotive – No. 6166 which had appeared in 1943. These plans bore no fruit and, though all thirty eight locomotives were carried into British Railways' stock in 1948, withdrawal began in April of that year. The slaughter was well under way by the end of 1948 and no less than twenty of the class were seen off by the end of December. A further fourteen engines succumbed the following year, leaving just four to soldier on into 1950. 61709, Beyer, Peacock No.35 of August 1922 departed in January with 61705, (No. 469) and 61710 (475) followed a month later. Summer 1950 saw the last B7 leave the stage: No. 61711 – formerly No. 478, one of Gorton's third batch from October 1923, was withdrawn from traffic in July.

Of all Robinson's 4–6–0s built over the years from 1903 to 1924, only 'Immingham' now remained in traffic, and she had only a short time left before being withdrawn, in the November of 1950. Displaced by Thompson's numerous B1 4–6–0s in the post–War wake of motive power building, the B7s had had only a short life. It was left to Robinson's last 4–4–0s and his celebrated 2–8–0s to carry the torch that had been kindled in the dawn of the twentieth century, into the last decade of steam operation on British Railways.

The B7s were well established in the Manchester area with Gorton shed possessing the lion's share of the allocations, a situation that lasted up to the outbreak of war. Excursion traffic and special workings out of Manchester appear to have been the prerogative of the class during this period. The line from Chorlton Junction to Fairfield carried a variety of traffic to and from Manchester Central and Liverpool and saw all the various classes of Great Central locomotives over the years. Coming up the 1 in 340 bank from Chorlton Junction towards Wilbraham Road and Fallowfield is No.5458, notched well forward, with an 8-coach express. The first two vehicles are comprised of ex-GN 12-wheeled clerestory stock, a corridor composite behind the tender and a corridor 3rd. brake following. Working books for the period list this stock on Cleethorpes – Liverpool trains, returning on 2.20 pm departures Tue/Wed/Thu and 2.30 pm Mon/Fri/Sat. Livery style of the engine is the post-1929 black with 12″ LNER on the tender, the long-pattern ash ejector is carried and top feed still appears behind the later LNER pattern of chimney.

*G.M.Shoults*

The LNER maintained the black livery of the 9Q class, simplifying the lining to red only. Until 1929 the company initials were displayed in 7½″ high numerals above the engine number. An early designation for former Great Central locomotives was the use of a 'C' suffix after the number which was increased by 5,000 from February 1924. While still maintaining the oval GC cabside plate, No.458c pauses in strong sunshine before backing down to head a local train out of Nottingham Victoria.

*Collection of Brian Hilton*

No.5459 outside Gorton shed in the 1930s in spanking condition and providing an excellent example of the post-1929 livery style. The shed staff seem to have taken the class's reputation for heavy coal consumption a trifle too seriously! On shed with 5459 that day were former 11F 4–4–0 'Director' No.5504 *JUTLAND* and 9N tank No.5373.

*G.H.Platt*

No.5035, the last of the Beyer, Peacock engines, photographed by G.H.Platt at Gorton in 1936. Fully coaled-up, the engine appears to be ready for excursion duty. Post 1929 livery, long pattern ash ejector with no top-feed and the third type of chimney contrive to form a second deviation of style from the Great Central era.

*G.H.Platt*

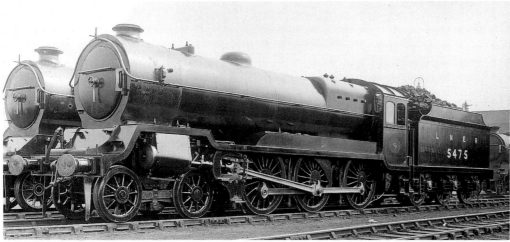

A fine shot of the erstwhile No.475 at Neasden in its earlier LNER guise, still in lined black livery and with the outline of the GC numberplate still discernible on the cabside. The tender is the final pattern of the Robinson 4000 gallon design; fitted with self-trimming coal bunker, these were recognisable by the shallower outward curve to the tank top and the flat shape of the bulkhead across the front of the coal space, both features which can be seen here.

*Collection of Brian Hilton*

The rather decrepit surroundings of Liverpool's Brunswick shed, from where the M.S.& L. had maintained a presence since 1872, are the backdrop for this picture of No.5476 in 1938. The view depicts well the atmosphere of steam shed working, with a Gresley K3 peering from behind under the sheerlegs as a bonus. In this period the B7s were frequent visitors to the city on both passenger and freight workings. By the late 1930s the B7s had had their original 'Intensifore' lubrication system removed and replaced variously by Eureka and Detroit sight-feed systems. Witness again, the drooping oil-feed pipes along the boiler clothing; standard now, too, was a Wakefield mechanical lubricator in front of the long splasher to look after the driving axle-boxes. 5476 became No.1389 in October 1946 and was withdrawn as such in February 1949 before being allocated a new BR number.

*G.H.Platt*

No.479 was one the last of the class (with No.481) to be built with the original design of outside cylinders. In this late 1930s view at Neasden the squatter proportions of these post-Grouping engines stand out well, along with such minutia as the later lubrication system and snifting valve. Livery style is the third version of the 'LNER' house style instituted in the post-1928 period. Over a body colour of gloss black, this used 12″ high yellow letters and numerals which were shaded in red and brown and picked out with white. Tender tank and coalplate, splashers, cab sides and front, framing and boiler bands were lined, as seen here, in red. The front buffer beam (or 'plank') was red, edged with black with a white line around. Bufferbeam numerals were gold, shaded brown and black.

A post-1928 view of 5482 at Lincoln GN shed. This was the second engine to be built with the improved cylinders and the last to be put into traffic with its Great Central number. Subtle differences from the earlier engines were the raised dimples in the front framing. These were covers to give easy access to the steam chest air valves. Each steam chest had two, one at each end. They were removed in later years, their place occupied by square patches. Note that the boiler top-feed survives and 'Intensifore' lubrication is still carried.

*T.G.Hepburn/Rail Archive Stephenson*

B7 No.5458 hard at work near Denham on the GW&GC Joint line between Northolt Junction and Ashendon Junction.

5484, the last of the class, hard at work on the London Extension in the vicinity of East Leake with a fitted van train. Both this and No.5483 were outshopped with their LNER numbers, still in the GC style with oval cast plates attached to the cabsides. 5484 was withdrawn in June 1948 never having carried its B.R. number.

The last one. With the withdrawal of BR No.61711, GC No.478 of October 1923, class B7 became extinct. There is little glamour apparent in this picture at Sheffield's Darnall shed of this same locomotive appearing in the temporary guise of E1391 (1946 number with regional prefix). Filthy, with not a hint of polish anywhere, this was life in the raw. Observe also the monstrous pile of coal on the tender! July 1950 saw the disappearance of this locomotive from traffic. With it, all bar one member of Robinson's nine 4–6–0 classes had gone from the scene.

Viewed by a lone observer, the former No.483, now a much-sullied LNER specimen numbered 1396 stands, dead and out of steam, in a siding at York in 1948. Well illustrated are the detail changes marking the class out in the last few years of their life: curved front extensions to the mainframes, twin smokebox door handles, no ash ejector, lowered front lamp bracket and patch plates covering the dimpled spaces ahead of the outside cylinder valve chests. The shallow curved profile of the later tender sides is well represented in this narrow view. Snap-head rivets adorn the smokebox and, a little less obtrusively, the same fittings are used to secure the front bufferbeam. No.1396 would survive just about another year, she received her first BR number, 61396, in February 1949, became 61713 in April and was withdrawn in the September.

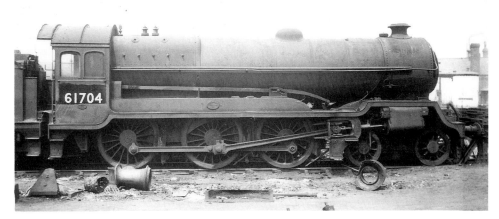

Only eleven locomotives lasted long enough to actually carry their allotted British Railways number. Cold, lifeless and far removed from her Great Central days as No.467, 61704 stands in a line at Gorton on May 7th 1949; she had received her new number just eight days earlier. This engine received cylinders of the later pattern in December 1947, these look surprisingly pristine in this view. 61704 was officially withdrawn one month after this picture was taken.

*J.Duncan*

A sad sight at Darlington early in 1949 showing No.470 (then 1378) in the process of being cut up for scrap, one other member of the class, 1360, can be glimpsed in the background. Though a trifle melancholy, these pictures are an invaluable source of detail, showing parts of the locomotive not normally visible. The various pieces of platework that made up the platform or running plate have been cut away and litter the foreground now revealing the top of the mainframe profile as a straight line; this should be compared with the picture in Gorton Works.

## BUILDING LIST 9Q ENGINES

| NUMBER | BUILDER | WORKS NO. | DATE BUILT | WITHDRAWN |
|---|---|---|---|---|
| 72 | Gorton | n/a | May 1921 | September 1948 |
| 73 | –'– | n/a | June 1921 | March 1949 |
| 78 | –'– | n/a | July 1921 | April 1949 |
| 36 | Vulcan Foundry | 3478 | September 1921 | June 1948 |
| 37 | —'— | 3479 | October 1921 | June 1948 |
| 38 | —'— | 3480 | October 1921 | June 1949 |
| 458 | —'— | 3481 | October 1921 | December 1948 |
| 459 | —'–– | 3482 | October 1921 | September 1949 |
| 460 | —'— | 3483 | October 1921 | October 1948 |
| 461 | —'— | 3484 | November 1921 | August 1948 |
| 462 | —'— | 3485 | November 1921 | November 1948 |
| 463 | —'— | 3486 | November 1921 | January 1949 |
| 464 | —'— | 3487 | November 1921 | September 1948 |
| 465 | Gorton | n/a | August 1921 | August 1948 |
| 466 | –'– | n/a | October 1921 | September 1948 |
| 467 | –'– | n/a | February 1922 | June 1949 |
| 468 | –'– | n/a | March 1922 | October 1948 |
| 469 | –'– | n/a | April 1922 | February 1950 |
| 470 | –'– | n/a | May 1922 | October 1948 |
| 471 | –'– | n/a | June 1922 | February 1949 |
| 472 | –'– | n/a | June 1922 | August 1948 |
| 473 | –'– | n/a | July 1922 | December 1949 |
| 474 | –'– | n/a | August 1922 | June 1949 |
| 31 | Beyer, Peacock & Co. | 6107 | July 1922 | May 1948 |
| 32 | —'— | 6108 | July 1922 | August 1948 |
| 33 | —'— | 6109 | August 1922 | January 1949 |
| 34 | —'— | 6110 | August 1922 | June 1949 |
| 35 | —'— | 6111 | August 1922 | January 1950 |
| 475 | Gorton | n/a | August 1923 | February 1950 |
| 476 | –'– | n/a | August 1923 | February 1949 |
| 477 | –'– | n/a | September 1923 | November 1948 |
| 478 | –'– | n/a | October 1923 | July 1950 |
| 479 | –'– | n/a | November 1923 | June 1949 |
| 480 | –'– | n/a | November 1923 | August 1948 |
| 481 | –'– | n/a | December 1923 | April 1948 |
| 482 | –'– | n/a | December 1923 | November 1948 |
| 5483 | –'– | n/a | February 1924 | September 1949 |
| 5484 | –'– | n/a | March 1924 | June 1948 |

NOTES:–

a) All the class, except the last two into traffic, had 5000 added to their numbers after Grouping.

b) Under the LNER re-numbering scheme, devised in 1943 and implemented in 1946, the B7 class were allotted the numbers 1360 – 1397. This was a strictly consecutive scheme and did not take into account the slightly overlapping batches of engines turned out from Vulcan Foundry and Gorton Works in 1921. The first BR re-numbering scheme added 60000 to all numbers but only two engines, 1391 (formerly 478) and 1396 (formerly 5483) actually carried these.

c) Twelve locos had a further British Railways number allotted, but a strictly consecutive block of numbers for the whole class could not be applied, as interim numbers in the series were needed for Thompson's new B1 4–6–0s then coming into traffic. The post-1948 survivors were thus encompassed within the number block 61702 – 61713.

Locos that received the new British Railways number were:–

| GC NO. | 1946 NO. | 2nd BR NO. | | GC NO. | 1946 NO. | 2nd BR NO. |
|---|---|---|---|---|---|---|
| 38 | 1365 | 61702 | | 34 | 1386 | 61708* |
| 459 | 1367 | 61703 | | 35 | 1387 | 61709 |
| 467 | 1375 | 61704 | | 475 | 1388 | 61710 |
| 469 | 1377 | 61705 | | 478 | 1391 | 61711 |
| 473 | 1381 | 61706 | | 479 | 1392 | 61712 |
| 474 | 1382 | 61707 | | 5483 | 1396 | 61713 |

* Allotted but not carried.

The first of the Scottish Directors appeared in July 1924, just about eight months after the order was placed. The Kitson engines were delivered to Gorton and run-in on the Chorlton Junction to Fairfield line. At Fallowfield, we see the engine that was to become No.6383 (later named *JONATHAN OLDBUCK*) in its shop grey paint with its running number roughly chalked on the cabside. Notice the oval shape below the cab windows where the traditional GC pattern numberplate had been fixed in time honoured Gorton tradition.

*William Lees*

A scene in Gorton works with No.6389 (later *HAYSTOUN OF BUCKLAW*) looking freshly delivered from Kitsons. With grey paintwork and minus bogie wheels, coupling rods and tender, 6389 has the GC style numberplate attached to the cabside.

*William Lees*

# The Scottish Directors

Something of a myth has grown up surrounding the origins of these engines. Gresley, so the story goes, was so pleased to have been given the post of C.M.E. at the recommendation of Robinson, that he effectively repaid Robinson by ordering two batches of twelve 'Improved Directors' for service over former North British routes in Scotland. As with many stories bordering on the apocryphal, the reality may be somewhat dissimilar.

That Robinson was offered the post is well established. What has not been said too often in print is that Robinson's services were retained at Gorton in the form of Locomotive Consultant for a year after Grouping to help smooth the transition of the smaller company into the larger whole. North of the border, on the lines of former North British company, the motive power situation was in something of a desperate state. No new engines had been built for some time; one suspects the North British management, well aware of the impending amalgamation, had staved off the introduction of new locomotives until someone else could foot the bill!

At the risk of stating the obvious, Gresley was a shrewd and talented engineer and knew a good engine when he saw one. Thus, 'horses for courses' saw the Director design taken for what it was: a sound, well engineered, free steaming, medium duty express passenger locomotive. It had only one drawback. The generous Great Central loading gauge was incompatible with that pertaining over North British lines. It was a simple job, nonetheless, to look at the Director outline and simply cut down the cab and boiler mountings. $3^{15}/_{16}''$ was lopped off the height of the cab, $5^{7}/_{8}''$ off the dome and $3''$ off the chimney. With these simple criteria applied and the necessary drawings to hand, the third batch of Directors, known ever after as 'The Scottish Directors', was born.

Outside contractors were engaged to build the engines. Initially entitled 11F Altered, the official LNER classification became D11/2, with the Great Central 11Fs becoming D11/1. Kitson & Company, of Leeds, and Armstrong Whitworth, at their Scotswood, Newcastle upon Tyne works, shared the construction; orders for the twenty four locomotives were placed in December 1923 and delivery was expedited thus over the period from July to November 1924 (see table 1).

Drawings were, quite logically, prepared at Gorton for issue to the two manufacturers. One curious difference between the two batches was the emergence of the Kitson engines in shop grey and the Armstrong Whitworth engines in LNER green. Gorton undertook the painting of the Leeds engines, seemingly after running–in which would appear to have been standard practice. Armstrong Whitworth dispatched their locomotives to Gateshead after an initial steaming before the engines went north to Scotland.

The loss of the higher profile of the cab roof was one obvious detail difference between the Great Central engines and these later derivatives. Because of the shallower spectacle plate the front cab windows were altered; the curved portion over the Belpaire shoulders was done away with, the front window now assuming a simple oval shape. A chimney just $1'\ 0''$ high eschewed Robinson practice and anticipated somewhat the Gresley versions later applied to the erstwhile 11Es and 11Fs, complete with snifting valve behind. So too did the dome covers, similarly reduced in height. Though at first the Great Central Directors had had the raised portions of the footplate over the coupled wheels exposed and then promptly filled in, the 1924 locomotives were duly turned out with valances. It is appropriate to relate at this point that these Scottish Directors were the first of the series to have their valances cut away, the English engines being so–treated slightly later on.

A detail development which anticipated later LNER practice was the abandonment of Robinson's arrangement of a single piston ring on the valve heads in favour of four narrow rings, in order to improve steam tightness. No Intensifore lubrication was applied to the D11/2s, the LNER–favoured Detroit and Eureka systems of the hydrostatic type were built in from new. One other Robinson device was retained,

*BAILIE MACWHEEBLE* was the first of the Kitson built engines to appear. Numbered initially 6378 the locomotive became LNER 2671 in September 1946 and British Railways 62671 in April 1948. Showing the early form of post Nationalisation insignia, the engine stands on Thornton Junction shed on August 2nd 1953. 62671 was withdrawn from service in May 1961 and stored at Inverurie Works. She was cut up there just over a month later in the June.

*B.K.B.Green*

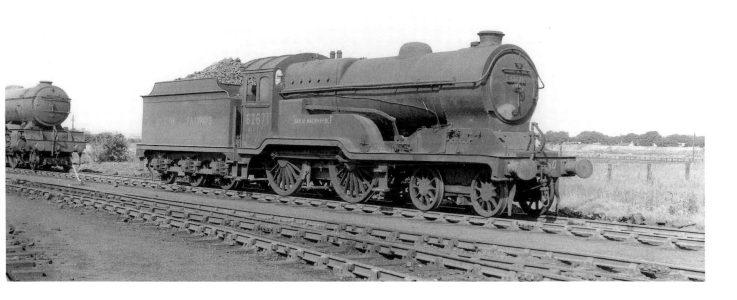

| ORDER NO. | BUILDER | WORKS NOS. | RUNNING NOS. | DELIVERED |
|-----------|---------|------------|--------------|-----------|
| 504G | Kitson & Co | 5379 – 5390 | 6378 – 6389 | July – October 1924 |
| E41 | Armstrong Whitworth & Co | 605 – 616 | 6390 – 6401 | October – November 1924 |

No.62676 ex-Cowlairs works but still sporting what appears to be a well battered dome cover. Lining on the engine has only been applied to the cab side sheet and the running plate valance; boiler bands, it seems, were never painted anything other than black in BR days.

*R.K.Blencowe*

(below) Eastfield, Sunday August 3rd 1952. Piles of ash and clinker in the foreground make for something of typical engine shed scenery as No.62672 *BARON OF BRADWARDINE* parades in a line of engines sandwiched between another class member and an unidentified V2.

*B.K.B.Green*

The former No.6381 *FLORA MACIVOR* was definitely not looking her best when she was photographed in front of the picturesque stone built engine shed at Anstruther, a fishing port on the northern shore of the Firth of Forth. Now the property of British Railways and numbered 62674, the engine represents something of a nadir in our views of this magnificent Great Central design: with smokebox drawing air, oil feed piping all awry and generally filthy condition; the shed cleaners have managed, however, to reveal Flora's identity! Just discernible is the curved row of cylinder fixing bolts, conversion to long-travel valves with new cylinders was made in 1953.

*Collection of R.K.Blencowe*

From Carlisle, running due north and west to Edinburgh was the North British company's splendid 98 mile 'Waverley' route. It is very fitting to include a picture of a Scottish Director at work on this line in view of the names given to the class. These were titles taken from Sir Walter Scott's novels, associated with this wild and beautiful part of the British Isles, the famed Border country between England and Scotland. Hawick, 45 miles north of Carlisle, was an important centre on the Waverley route possessing its own engine shed as well as being the starting and finishing point for some local trains to Carlisle and Edinburgh. On August 3rd 1953 No.62677 *EDIE OCHILTREE* leaves Hawick with a Bank Holiday Monday relief train, 7.55 a.m. to Edinburgh Waverley. Bonus points are provided by the lofty North British signalbox with lattice post signals and the sight of B1 No.61398, with express headlamps up front, standing in the station yard.

*B.K.B.Green*

this was the long pattern of ash ejector, something which the Scottish drivers took some getting used to, so it is stated. Ross 'pop' safety valves of the short pattern were fitted, mounted on a shallow base.

A feature retained, perhaps rather perversely, was the right hand drive of the Great Central design. North British locomotives had been driven from the left for long enough and this imported feature must have presented drivers with problems in signal sighting and braking which, perhaps, had not been fully anticipated. Firemen were able to shovel right–handed and, moreover, could use both hands. Single handed firing was the norm on the N.B.R. 'Scott' 4–4–0s and the problems of getting to grips (literally) with this technique were graphically illustrated in the wonderful writings of Norman Mc Killop ('Toram Beg').

In this third series of Directors the brass beading over the splasher tops, a feature beloved of Gorton, was done away with and both series of engines were turned out without names. Indeed, it was not until April 1925 that names were applied at all. When these appeared, the Gaelic tags, with a deep attachment to the characters abiding in the novels of Sir Walter Scott made a fascinating contrast to the starkly English forms of their Great Central predecessors; 'Walter Burgh Gair' and 'The Earl of Kerry' excepted of course! Unlike their counterparts though, no brass nameplates were ever carried by the Scottish engines. Gilt transfers were used for the names originally, giving way to hand–painting with some fairly elaborate shading later on. Plain, unshaded Gill Sans lettering, favoured in the latter days of the LNER, was the norm in latter days. A point worth mentioning was the use, in all periods, of upper case letters.

Standard Great Central pattern tenders were attached to the D11/2s with 4,000 gallon water and a nominal 6 ton coal capacity. As the North British lines had no

water troughs, water pick–up was, logically, done away with, a feature shared by the tenders supplied to the R.O.D. 2–8–0s. All but four of the class were given J39 pattern cylinders with extended valve travel and 8″ piston valves between 1939 and, surprisingly, as late as 1956. Sundry details such as the fitting of sight screens to the cab sides paralleled their English contemporaries along with the alterations mentioned to the sanding gear. One other modification, carried out in the mid–30s was the fitting of a lowered top lamp iron to accommodate destination board brackets.

*REBUILDING WITH J39–PATTERN CYLINDERS AND L.T. VALVES*
*All except four, 6382, 6395, 6396 and 6397, of the D11/2s were rebuilt:–*

NO.    L.T. VALVES FITTED

6378 — April 1945
6379 — October 1943
6380 — May 1943
6381 — May 1953
6383 — November 1946
6384 — April 1948
6385 — June 1945
6386 — June 1956
6387 — June 1940
6388 — March 1943
6389 — July 1940
6390 — May 1946
6391 — May 1943
6392 — March 1941
6393 — April 1939
6394 — July 1943
6398 — June 1945
6399 — July 1949
6400 — July 1941
6401 — May 1942

An immediate difference that marked the Scottish class out from their Sassenach sisters in their final years was the retention of the Great Central smokebox door fastening on the majority of the class with the characteristic Robinson wheel and

single handle. Something of a medley of frontal differences occurred when smokebox doors were swapped about with those from former N.B.R. Atlantics. These had handrails of a shorter length which were set somewhat higher than the ex–Great Central pattern. Curved handrails (in ex–NBR fashion) appeared on a number of engines; these caused vagaries in the siting of the B.R. smokebox door numberplates.

In the 1930s eight of the D11/2s were equipped with drop firegrates to enable them to use wet ashpits that had been installed at Glasgow's Eastfield shed. Engines so altered between 1933 and 1935 were Nos. 6378, 6379, 6380, 6387, 6388, 6389, 6397 and 6398. The remainder of the class would appear to have been given this modification after the end of the War. A change that had begun in the War itself was the alteration of the position of the pipework for the front vacuum brake. This pipe had originally been concealed within the front casing below the smokebox and tucked away behind the front buffer beam as with the Great Central series. The modified arrangement was unmistakable and gives an immediate clue to pictures in pre and postwar time spans. Steam brakes were supplied for the engine and tender, the vacuum ejector providing braking power for the train. Beginning in 1934 the steam brake controls were modified to give a more gentle application than hitherto with the so–called 'trigger' type of control fitted originally. Post–War, eight of the class were given LNER standard buffers with round heads in place of the characteristic G.C. pattern.

Following the awful collision at Castlecary in 1937 the Edinburgh to Glasgow line was equipped with the Strowger–Hudd pattern of automatic train control. From mid–1939 eleven of the Scottish Directors were equipped with this pattern of A.T.C. The fitting was carried out over a period of two years. The engines involved were Nos. 6379, 6381, 6382, 6383, 6384, 6385, 6387,

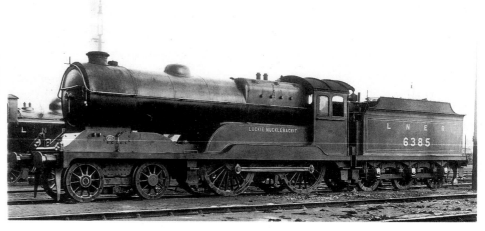

**No.6385 was named *LUCKIE MUCKLEBACKIT* in May 1925, an incredible-sounding name and making this class of engines, for one enthusiast at any rate, one of the most fascinating series of named locomotives ever. 6385 had its valances removed in March 1926 making it relatively easy to pinpoint the time span in which this picture was taken.**

*WIZARD OF THE MOOR*, No.6391, the second of the Armstrong Whitworth engines heads towards Edinburgh Waverley on August 4th 1938 with a seven-coach up stopping train. The class had now long been relegated to the doldrums of the black livery along with their English sisters. A distinguishing feature applied by Cowlairs works to the Scottish engines in the pre–War period was the LNER on the tender which appeared in letters only 7½″ high instead of the normal 12″, but still applied by shaded transfers. Cowlairs were still using up stock of 7½″ LNER from the 1923-29 years, and which they also used on tank engines in all the 25 years of the LNER.

*L.Hanson*

This view of 'Wizard' at Eastfield shed in December 1947 after re-numbering makes an interesting comparison with the previous picture. Now No.2684, the engine sports the restored LNER green livery with black and white lining. In the interim it has also received a new smokebox with a curved hand-rail to the door, lost its ash ejector and acquired new cylinders with longer-travel valves. 2684 was one of several Scottish Directors to receive LNER Group-standard buffers around this time, the round heads looking somewhat out of place compared to the GC oval variety.

A fine study of No.6392 *MALCOLM GRAEME* in its pre-War condition, notice the enclosed vacuum pipe at the front of the engine and the curved row of cylinder fixing bolts indicating the existence of the original cylinders and valves. The small LNER initials on the tender side in 7½″ letters look a decided mis-match against the 12″ engine numbers. The oval plate on the smokebox was a small numberplate, displaced from the cab side when the second version of the LNER livery arrived with the need for a clear space for the 12″ numerals.

*MALCOLM GRAEME* as No.62685 at Haymarket on May 20th 1956. In the 1950s Inverurie works undertook repairs to the class and adopted the practice of painting a simple lined rectangle around the cabside number. This was at odds with painting practice at Cowlairs and Gorton who copied LNER practice in following the outline of the upswept valance. Notice too, the use of the smaller BR 'lion and wheel' emblem on the tender side, another Inverurie vagary in this period.

*B.K.B.Green*

*(left)* Like their English counterparts, the D11/2s endured periods of storage late in their lives when summer traffic demands abated. Here at Haymarket, on September 6th 1959, No.62685 suffers the ignominy of being used as a stationary boiler. Withdrawn from traffic at the end of 1961, the engine eked out an existence alongside the Caledonian Hotel in Edinburgh on further stationary boiler duty before being cut up by T.W.Ward's at Inverkeithing in July 1963.

*(below)* Journey's end. *LORD JAMES OF DOUGLAS* now carrying its BR number of 62687, simmers in front of the buffer stops at Glasgow Queen Street at 8.25 on the morning of Friday, May 24th 1957. Its next duty will be to 'bank' the train hemming it in up the incline towards Cowlairs.

*Raymond Keeley*

A splendid study of No.62686 *THE FIERY CROSS* (ex-6393) taken on June 7th 1953 at Eastfield. Quite apart from the imposing view as such, there is much to comment on. The vacuum pipe has now been moved to the more usual position outside of the buffer beam, compare this to the pictures of the GC Directors in BR days. The smokebox door retains the GC handwheel, the top lamp iron is lowered and the destination board brackets can just be made out either side of the central handrail knob. Snap-head rivets appear on the front of the smokebox and around the outer part of the door. These details were not standard throughout the British Railways period; modellers please note! Group standard buffers have been fitted and the shed name and class designation appear on the beam itself. The perspective of the picture shows the tender front bulkhead clearly, denoting the later GC pattern tender with widened body. No D11/2 tender was fitted with water pick-up apparatus, because there were no track troughs in the Scottish Area. Two bonus points for good measure are the Eastfield breakdown crane and a glimpse of sister (or should it be brother?) engine *EVAN DHU* – 62673.

*A.C.Gilbert*

High above the waters of the Firth of Forth and emerging from that cathedral of steel, the Forth Bridge, is No.6394 *LORD JAMES OF DOUGLAS* at the head of a southbound stopping train.

*Collection of R.K.Blencowe*

An almost broadside view of 6395 as built i.e: without name and with valance over the coupling rods still intact. The engine became *ELLEN DOUGLAS* in October 1925 concurrent with removal of the valances. Some running repairs to the front right-hand of the engine are going to be needed, a rough shunt having pushed the buffer beam downwards. Notice the numberplate still attached to the cab side and the rectangular makers plate on the front mainframe. These plates appear to have been removed when Wakefield mechanical lubricators were fitted during the war.

6390, 6392, 6400 and 6401. Wartime restrictions, unfortunately, caused the scheme to be abandoned from around 1942.

In the prewar years after 1928 the D11/2s suffered the black livery style with red lining which had likewise afflicted their Great Central forbears. A considerable improvement in the livery situation arose after the end of hostilities in 1945. Cowlairs managed to reapply the lovely LNER green livery to no less than sixteen of the twenty four locomotives. The works succeeded in getting several D11/2s (62671, 62677, 62683 and 62690) painted green with the BRITISH RAILWAYS legend on the tender sides. Such verdant glories did not last, however, and the all–pervading black with the LNWR lining chosen as the British Railways standard eventually became the norm, both north and south of the Border.

The new 4–4–0s were apparently popular with their Scottish crews which says a lot for a class which was completely foreign to them hitherto. Reports state that enginemen found their new charges a trifle slow off the mark, particularly when ascending the notorious 1 in 46/41 of Cowlairs incline.

When built, the D11/2s were split between Eastfield (Glasgow) which housed Nos. 6378, 6379, 6380, 6397, 6398 and 6400. Haymarket had Nos. 6381 – 6385 and 6401. St.Margaret's was allocated Nos. 6389 – 6392 and 6399. Further north, Dundee was given 6386 and 6393 – 6396, while Perth absorbed just two Directors – Nos. 6387 and 6388. Perth lost these two (replaced by new D49's) in 1928 to St.Margaret's with allocations fairly steady until during the Second War.

History repeated itself for former Great Central types when, in November 1926, No. 6399 'Allan-Bane' was sent to Stratford at the behest of W.G.P.Maclure for trials on the lines to Colchester and Cambridge. In the event, Gresley K2s (which had a lighter axle loading) were used, with the Director being sent, in January, to work trials from Leeds to Kings Cross. One other foray south is worth mentioning; No. 6401 'James Fitzjames' (the last of the class) was sent to Neville Hill shed from August to November 1943 while one of Gresley's 'Hunt' 4–4–0s was working in Scotland.

In the postwar era the Scottish Directors were finding themselves deployed on a very wide variety of duties. The Edinburgh district seemed a case in point where some twenty–two of the engines had been recorded as working a variety of trains all around the city.

Withdrawal of the D11/2s began in September 1958 with No. 62679 'Lord Glenallan' and No. 62683 'Hobbie Elliot', cut up at Kilmarnock Works. The demise of the class was completed in the November of 1961 when No. 62691 'Laird of Balmawhapple' and No. 62693 'Roderick Dhu' were taken out of service. Like their southern sisters, the Scottish engines had spent long periods in and out of store according to demand. However, no reprieve came for these final two, and after lingering at Bo'ness until February 1963 they were cut up by Connells at Calder the following month.

Thus was completed the life–cycle of a class which had seen service over much of the English and Scottish railway system; a rather unique distinction for the 4–4–0 type, shared only, perhaps, by the equally famous LMS Compounds.

**6397 was named** *THE LADY OF THE LAKE* **in May 1925 and had its valances cut away at the same time. In this picture, at Haymarket, it is worth pointing out the white lining applied to the cab windows and the oval number plate on the cab side. Subtle differences like this make the subject of locomotive histories ever fascinating, marking small landmarks in the development of a particular class history.**

A magnificent spectacle, packed with period atmosphere, at Inverkeithing with No.6401 *JAMES FITZJAMES* leading an ex-GN D1 4—4—0 (number not known) on a down (northbound) express. No.6401 presents something of a difference with its name applied yet still running with the deep valance over the coupling rods. Records show the name was applied in May 1925 and the valances cut away the following March.

## CLASS D11/2 THE SCOTTISH DIRECTORS

### Part 1 – engines built by Messrs. Kitson & Co. July – October 1924
(Works Nos.5379 – 5390)

| NUMBER | 1946 NUMBER | NAME | WITHDRAWN |
|---|---|---|---|
| 6378 | 2671 | BAILIE MACWHEEBLE | May 1961 |
| 6379 | 2672 | BARON OF BRADWARDINE | September 1961 |
| 6380 | 2673 | EVAN DHU | July 1959 |
| 6381 | 2674 | FLORA MACIVOR | July 1961 |
| 6382 | 2675 | COLONEL GARDINER | October 1959 |
| 6383 | 2676 | JONATHAN OLDBUCK | October 1959 |
| 6384 | 2677 | EDIE OCHILTREE | August 1959 |
| 6385 | 2678 | LUCKIE MUCKLEBACKIT | March 1959 |
| 6386 | 2679 | LORD GLENALLAN | September 1958 |
| 6387 | 2680 | LUCY ASHTON | September 1961 |
| 6388 | 2681 | CAPTAIN CRAIGENGELT | July 1961 |
| 6389 | 2682 | HAYSTOUN OF BUCKLAW | July 1961 |

### Part 2 – engines built by Messrs. Armstrong Whitworth & Co. October & November 1924
(Works Nos.605 – 616)

| NUMBER | 1946 NUMBER | NAME | WITHDRAWN |
|---|---|---|---|
| 6390 | 2683 | HOBBIE ELLIOT | September 1958 |
| 6391 | 2684 | WIZARD OF THE MOOR | October 1959 |
| 6392 | 2685 | MALCOLM GRAEME | January 1962 |
| 6393 | 2686 | THE FIERY CROSS | July 1961 |
| 6394 | 2687 | LORD JAMES OF DOUGLAS | August 1961 |
| 6395 | 2688 | ELLEN DOUGLAS | July 1961 |
| 6396 | 2689 | MAID OF LORN | July 1961 |
| 6397 | 2690 | THE LADY OF THE LAKE | July 1961 |
| 6398 | 2691 | LAIRD OF BALMAWHAPPLE | November 1961 |
| 6399 | 2692 | ALLAN–BANE | November 1959 |
| 6400 | 2693 | RODERICK DHU | November 1961 |
| 6401 | 2694 | JAMES FITZJAMES | November 1959 |

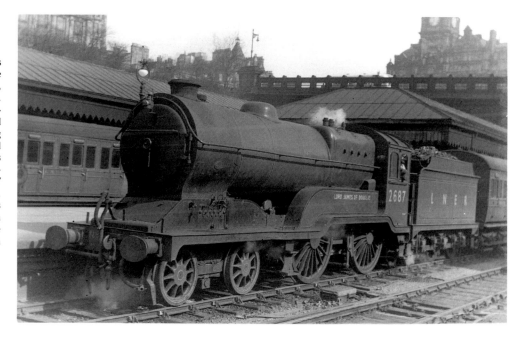

A sight to gladden the hearts of enthusiasts in the post-War period must have been the re-appearance, after such a long absence, of the splendid LNER lined green livery. The return of green paintwork was particularly welcome on this ex-Great Central design, deprived for so long of something approaching its ancestral livery. On April 9th 1948, the unmistakable surroundings of Edinburgh Waverley station are the setting for this picture of LORD JAMES OF DOUGLAS, with its post-War number, 2687, at the head of a local working. This was one of the class to be fitted with a drop grate in the post-war period; the small cover over the operating mechanism can be seen just in front of the cab.

As if to prove that no two members of a class were quite alike in any given period, we look at *LAIRD OF BALMAWHAPPLE,* now BR No.62691, at Haymarket on May 20th 1956. A short lining panel around the cab side is immediately obvious with the small 'lion and wheel' emblem on the tender side. By the time the British Railways era had begun all the class had received Wakefield mechanical lubricators, the drive for this was taken from a small return crank attached to the front right-hand crank pin. The smokebox numberplate stands above the curved handrail, the door having received twin handles; most engines having retained their GC pattern wheel and handle. B1 No.61024 *ADDAX* can be seen in the background.

*B.K.B.Green*

62692 *ALLAN BANE* is coaled to the limits of the loading gauge outside Haymarket shed on May 20th 1956. Withdrawn in November 1959, the engine was one of seven taken out of service in that year.

*B.K.B.Green*

*RODERICK DHU* with the first British Railways insignia on the tender, BR lined black livery with full lining panel on the cabside and numbered 62693. Frontal differences exist between this and the LNER period shot: the handwheel on the smokebox door having given way to twin handles and the straight handrail substituted by one of a curved pattern. 62693 was withdrawn in November 1961 and stored at Bo'ness until February 1963. Finally she was cut up by Connells at Calder in the March of that year.

*Collection of R.K.Blencowe*

*JAMES FITZJAMES* at Haymarket shed on May 21st. 1957 showing well the differences that evolved in the class over a period of around a quarter of a century. Wakefield lubricators, long-travel valves and a rivetted smokebox have all appeared and a buckled front running plate (to which the class seemed curiously prone) gives the engine something of a down-at-heel appearance. It was the last of the Armstrong Whitworth engines and the last Scottish Director to enter traffic and was amongst the first to be withdrawn, in November 1959. In the background a K3 undergoes some attention to its driving axleboxes giving a rare glimpse of the exposed mainframe.

*Raymond Keeley*

No.1712 the first of the thirteen post-Grouping engines from Hawthorn Leslie & Co. (works No.3616 of September 1925) based on the Robinson 9N 'Coronation Tank', seen working from Gateshead shed in 1926. With side windows replacing the previous large open aspect and now with an even lower roof, the cab had a somewhat extra long appearance compared with the Great Central built engines. The LNER modifications to the Robinson design saw these locomotives good for 30 years service.

# Class A5 4–6–2 Tank

Aside from the Scottish Directors, a second Robinson design was perpetuated under LNER auspices. This was the 9N 4–6–2 tank of 1911, classified A5 by the LNER. Twenty one 9Ns had appeared under Great Central ownership, with a further ten turned out from Gorton in the first half of 1923. Hawthorn, Leslie & Co. built a further thirteen for the LNER at their Forth Bank Works, Newcastle, between September 1925 and March 1926. These post–Grouping engines differed from the parent design in some significant respects.

Visually, the principal difference was the provision of side–window cabs, a feature lacking on the original Robinson engines, although the 1923 batch had been thus fitted and the originals were eventually altered to match. As with the LNER B7s, these post–1923 A5s were brought within the LNER loading gauge. This was achieved by reducing the height of the cab, fitting a Gresley pattern of (built–up) chimney with a lower dome and reducing the width of the cab, bunker and side tanks by two inches. The overall wheelbase of the engine was increased by four inches with the movement forward of the front bogie, away from the leading coupled axle.

Another, later, visual difference was the alteration to the front raised mainframe profile after complaints by ex–N.E.R. enginemen of difficulties encountered when 'oiling–up' between the frames.

Mechanically, the cylinder block was redesigned; long travel piston valves were fitted, these were reduced down from 10″ diameter to 8″. This same cylinder block was used in the Gresley J38 and J39 0–6–0s, the re–cylindered Directors and one rebuilt D49 4–4–0 No. 365 'The Morpeth.' Westinghouse brakes (eventually removed in 1932–1934) were provided for the engine and train with vacuum ejector also provided for train use. After removal of the Westinghouse gear, the locomotives were provided with a steam brake, thus bringing them into line with their Great Central cousins. The driving position was from the left as opposed to the universal right hand of Great Central engines. Another small visual difference was the alteration of the cab spectacles to a one-–piece design which did not follow the outline of the Belpaire firebox. A Gresley snifting valve appeared behind the chimney with muffled Ross 'pop' safety valves. Like Robinson, Raven of the North Eastern had devised his own form of lineside

train control, his fog signalling apparatus, and this was fitted to all thirteen A5s soon after they went into traffic. This system was abandoned towards the end of 1933 and the apparatus removed from the engines.

Later LNER modifications included the alteration of the front sandbox above the platform and the drilling of lifting holes in the front mainframes. Unlike their Great Central counterparts the caged–in bunker top was not removed, although one engine, No. 1712, had its coal bunker enclosed by steel sheeting in 1937, an experiment to prevent coal dust blowing into the cab. One small detail difference noted on one of the engines in its later life was the provision of a Gorton chimney on the former No. 1766 (B.R. No. 69836).

The alterations wrought on the erstwhile Great Central design brought about an increase of weight in working order of 4 tons, 11cwt. This was despite a decrease in capacity of 180 gallons of water and 3 cwt. coal. The LNER A5s lasted intact until 1957 when withdrawal commenced with No. 69833. The remaining twelve were all seen off the following year, the last to go No. 69837, taken out of service in the December.

**For comparison, No.5168 of the 1911 build seen at Neasden in August 1924 from where these A5's performed well on the local workings for many years.**

*W.L.Good courtesy W.T.Stubbs*

## PRINCIPAL DIMENSIONS OF GC CLASSES COVERED IN THIS VOLUME

Key:– A *Class.*
B *Number in class.*
C *Type.*
D *Cylinder size (number)*
E *Boiler type.*
F *Working pressure sq. ins.*
G *Boiler barrel diameter.*
H *Boiler barrel length.*
I *Number of tubes large/small.*
J *Total heating surface sq. ft.*

K *Grate area sq. ft.*
L *Tractive effort at 85% boiler pressure pounds/tons.*
M *Tender/tank water capacity gallons.*
N *Tender/bunker coal capacity tons.*
O *Driving wheel diameter.*
P *Total weight of locomotive empty/loaded.*
Q *Total weight of tender empty/loaded.*
R *Total length of locomotive and tender.*
S *Total wheelbase of locomotive and tender.*

*Note:* All dimensions and figures extracted from Great Central Rly Locomotive Diagram book.

| A | B | C | D | E | F | G | H | I | J | K | L | M | N | O | P | Q | R | S |
|---|---|---|---|---|---|---|---|---|---|---|---|---|---|---|---|---|---|---|
| 1B | 20 | 2–6–4T | 21x26 (2) | No.5S | 180 | 5′ 3″ | 12′ 3″ | 24/157 | 1752 | 26 | 28759/12·8 | 3000 | 5 | 5′ 1″ | 74·15/97·45 | — | 46′ 4¾″ | 37′ 6″ |
| 8K | 129 | 2–8–0 | 21x26 (2) | No.6S | 180 | 5′ 0″ | 15′ 0″ | 22/110 | 1745 | 26 | 30813/13·75 | 4000 | 6 | 4′ 8″ | 67·5/73·4 | 24·3/48·3 | 61′ 8½″ | 51′ 2½″ |
| 8M | 19 | 2–8–0 | 21x26 (2) | No.8S | 180 | 5′ 6″ | 15′ 0″ | 28/116 | 2123 | 26 | 30813/13·75 | 4000 | 6 | 4′ 8″ | 68·2/75·2 | 24·3/48·3 | 61′ 8½″ | 51′ 2½″ |
| 8N | 3 | 4–6–0 | 21x26 (2) | No.8S | 180 | 5′ 6″ | 15′ 0″ | 28/116 | 2123 | 26 | 25375/11·32 | 4000 | 6 | 5′ 8″ | 65·9/72·9 | 24·3/48·3 | 61′ 2½″ | 50′ 8½″ |
| 9P | 6 | 4–6–0 | 16x26 (4) | No.7S | 180 | 5′ 6″ | 17′ 3″ | 28/116 | 2387 | 26 | 24772/11·03 | 4000 | 6 | 6′ 9″ | 71·75/79·1 | 24·3/48·3 | 63′ 0⅜″ | 52′ 9½″ |
| 9Q | 28 | 4–6–0 | 16x26 (4) | No.7S | 180 | 5′ 6″ | 17′ 3″ | 28/116 | 2387 | 26 | 29952/13·37 | 4000 | 6 | 5′ 8″ | 72·15/79·5 | 24·3/48·3 | 63′ 0⅜″ | 52′ 9½″ |
| 11E | 10 | 4–4–0 | 20x26 (2) | No.5S | 180 | 5′ 3″ | 12′ 3″ | 24/157 | 1752 | 26 | 19700/8·8 | 4000 | 6 | 6′ 9″ | 55·51/61·0 | 24·3/48·3 | 58′ 11½″ | 48′ 8½″ |
| 11F | 11 | 4–4–0 | 20x26 (2) | No.5S | 180 | 5′ 3″ | 12′ 3″ | 24/157 | 1752 | 26 | 19700/8·8 | 4000 | 6 | 6′ 9″ | 55·8/61·15 | 24·3/48·3 | 58′ 11½″ | 48′ 8½″ |

CLASS 1B 2–6–4

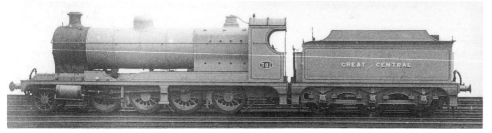

CLASS 8K 2–8–0 REBUILD

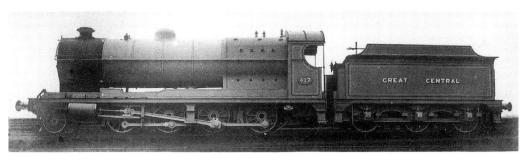

CLASS 8M 2–8–0

CLASS 8N 4–6–0

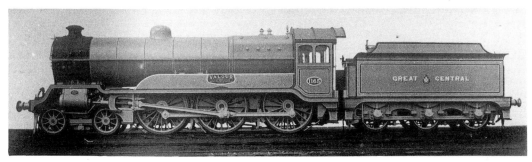

CLASS 9P 4–6–0

CLASS 9Q 4–6–0

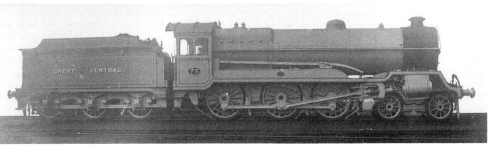

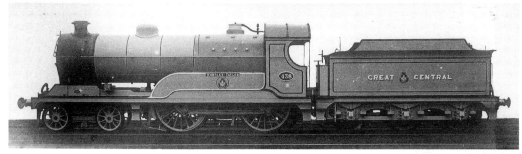

CLASS 11E 4–4–0

CLASS 11F 4–4–0

4-6-0 GOODS ENGINES TYPE B-3

Class 1A 4-6-0. Scale: 7 mm/ft approx.

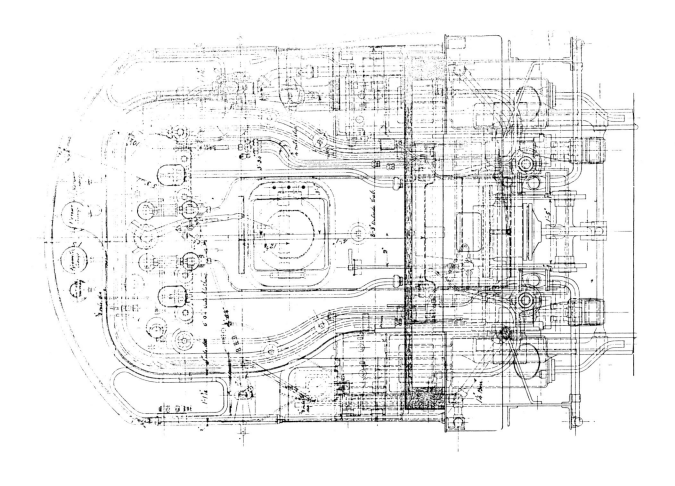

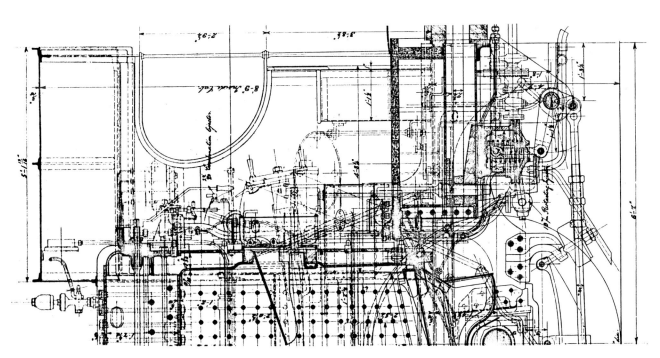

*Class 1A 4–6–0. Cab detail. Scale: 12 mm/ft approx.*

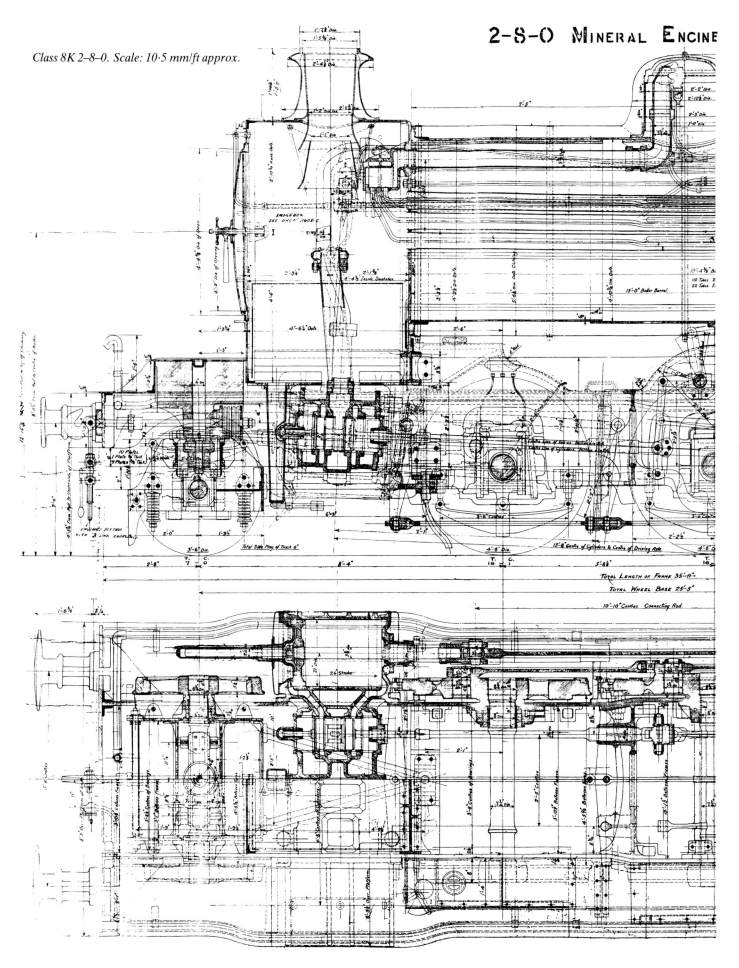

*Class 8K 2–8–0. Scale: 10·5 mm/ft approx.*

2-8-0 MINERAL ENGINE

es **SK** CLASS (O-4 TYPE)

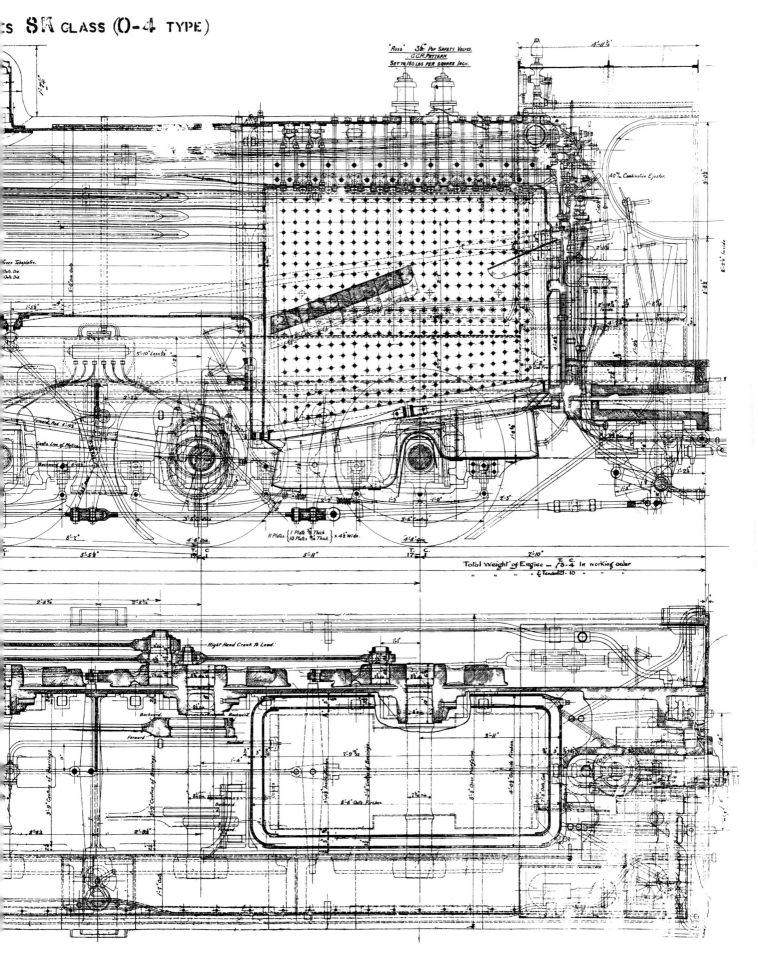

**GREAT CENTRAL RAILWAY**

ATLANTIC TYPE ENGINES Nos 192 & 194

*Class 8B 4–4–2. Scale: 5 mm/ft approx.*

**DRAWINGS:** *Although the quality of the original drawing is somewhat variable, we felt that to leave some of them out purely on the grounds of inferior quality would be something of a minor crime in the eyes of some readers so, herewith are included a selection to complement those in Volume 1. Please note that all the drawings are reproduced to approximate scales only.*

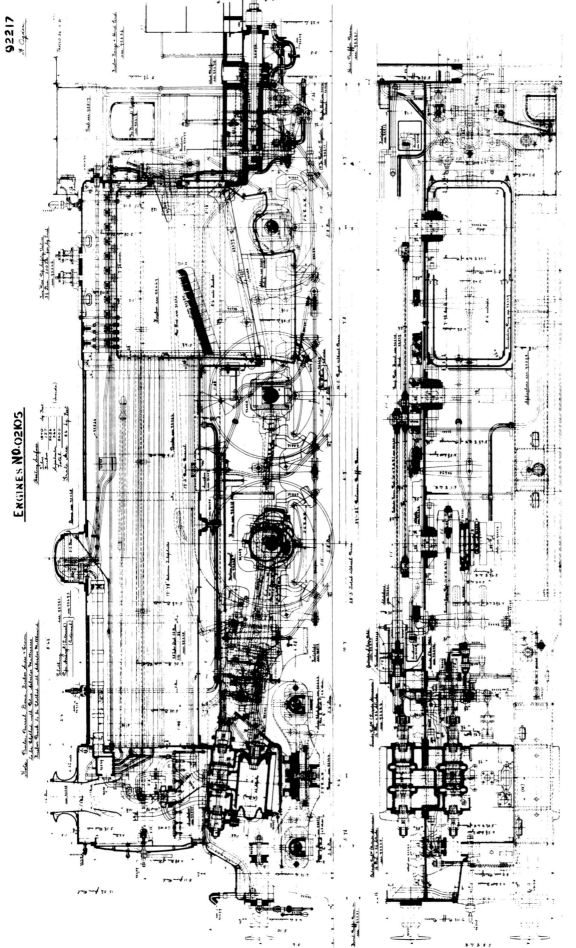

*Class 9Q 4-6-0. Scale: 6 mm/ft approx.*

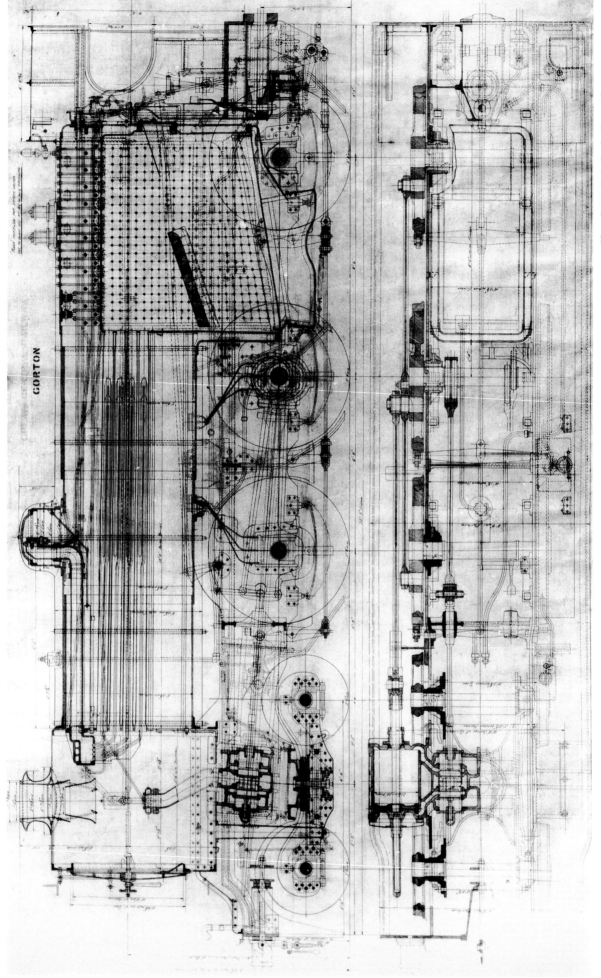

GORTON

*Class 8N 4–6–0. Scale: 7 mm/ft*

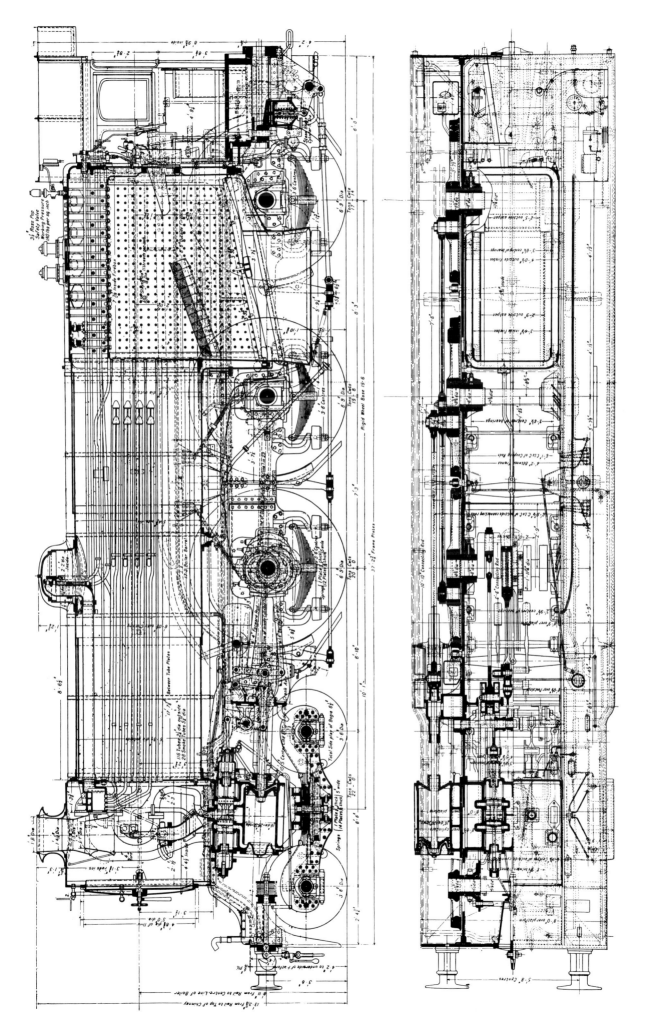

*Class 9P 4-6-0. Scale: 6·4 mm/ft approx.*

*Cty of Museum of Science & Industry in Manchester*

# GREAT CENTRAL LOCOMOTIVES

*Class 11E 4–4–0. Scale: 17 mm/ft approx.*

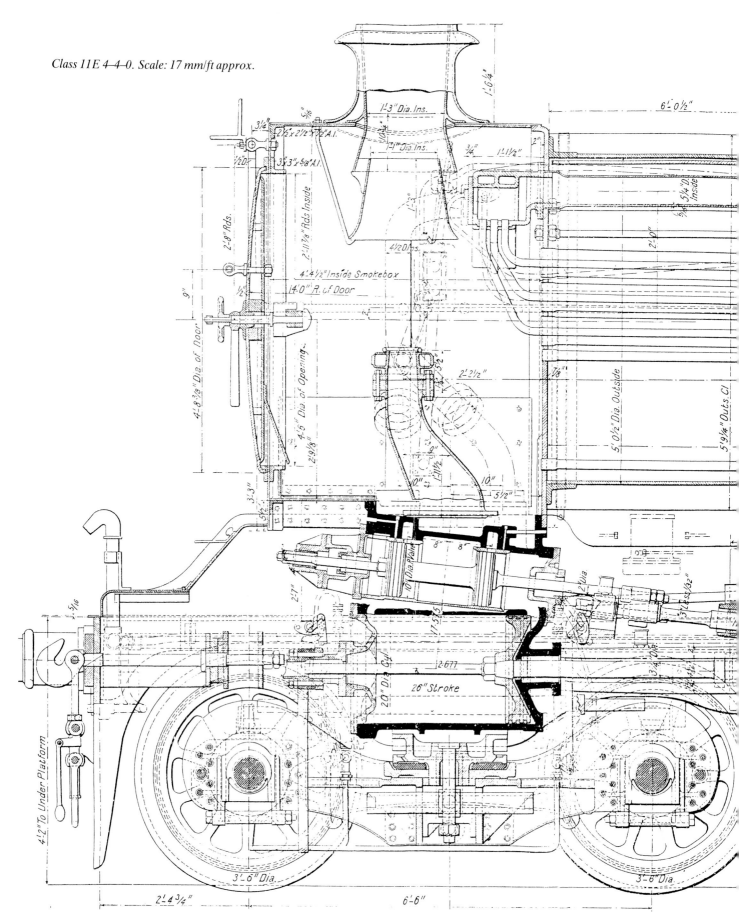

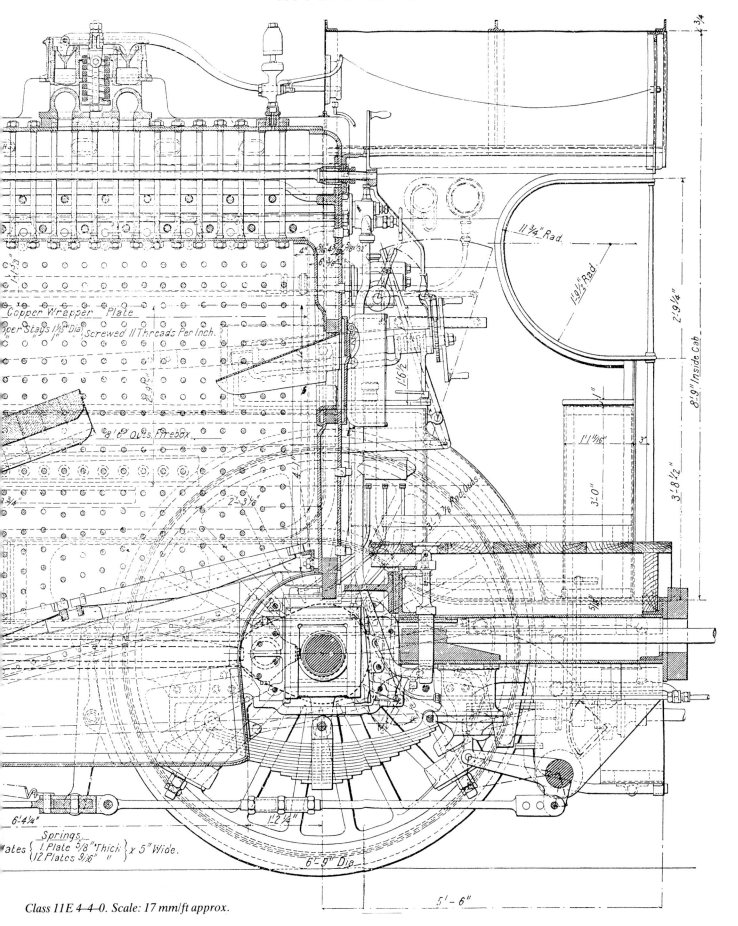

Copper Wrapper Plate

8'6" Outs. Firebox

11 3/4" Rad.

1 9 1/2" Rad.

8'9" Inside Cab

2'-9 1/4"

3'-8 1/2"

3'-0"

6'- 9" Dia.

6'-4 1/4"

5'- 6"

*Springs*
Plates { 1 Plate 5/8" Thick } x 5" Wide.
{ 12 Plates 9/16"    "   }

*Class 11E 4–4–0. Scale: 17 mm/ft approx.*

N° 622.

4-4-0 PASSENGER ENGINES N° D-10 TYPE

L.N.E.R
DRAWING
622-C

*Class 11E 4-4-0. Scale: 7 mm/ft approx.*

*Class 11F 4-4-0. Scale: 7 mm/ft approx.*

L. N. E. R.

4-4-0 PASSENGER ENGINES TYPE D11.

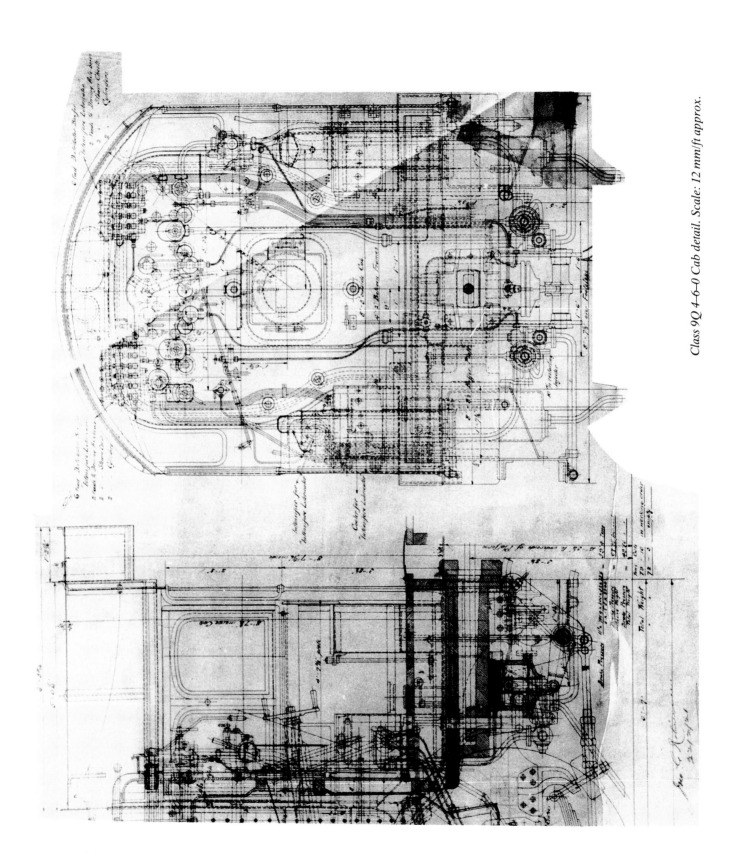

*Class 9Q 4–6–0 Cab detail. Scale: 12 mm/ft approx.*

APPENDIX 2.

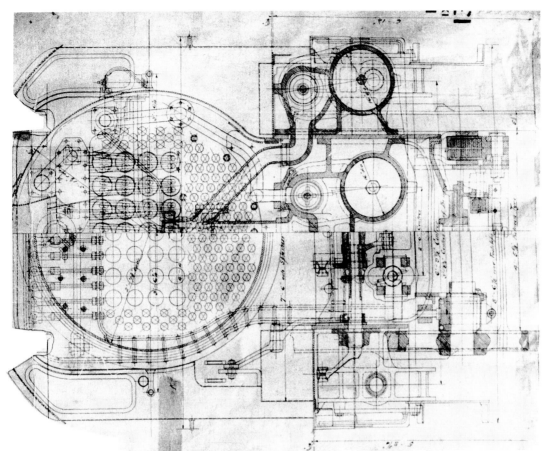

*Class 9Q 4–6–0 (cross section). Scale: 12 mm/ft approx.*

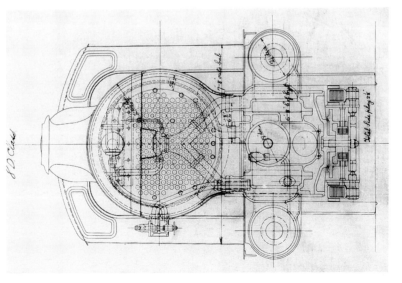

*Class 8D 3-cylinder 4–4–2 (cylinder section). Scale: 7 mm/ft approx.*

*Class 11F Valve Gear. Scale: 15 mm/ft approx.*

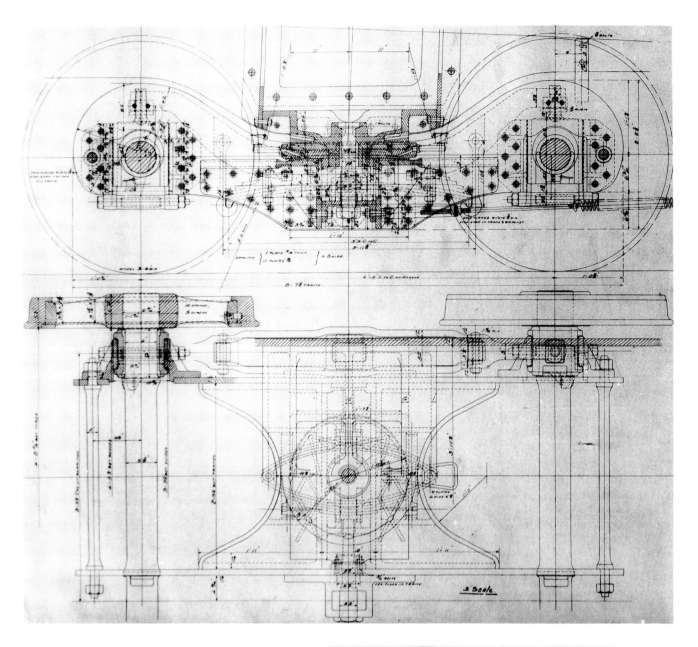

*Class 8G 4–6–0. (Bogie arrangement). Scale 18 mm/ft approx.*

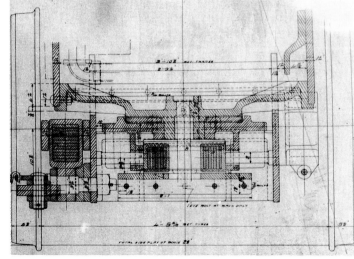

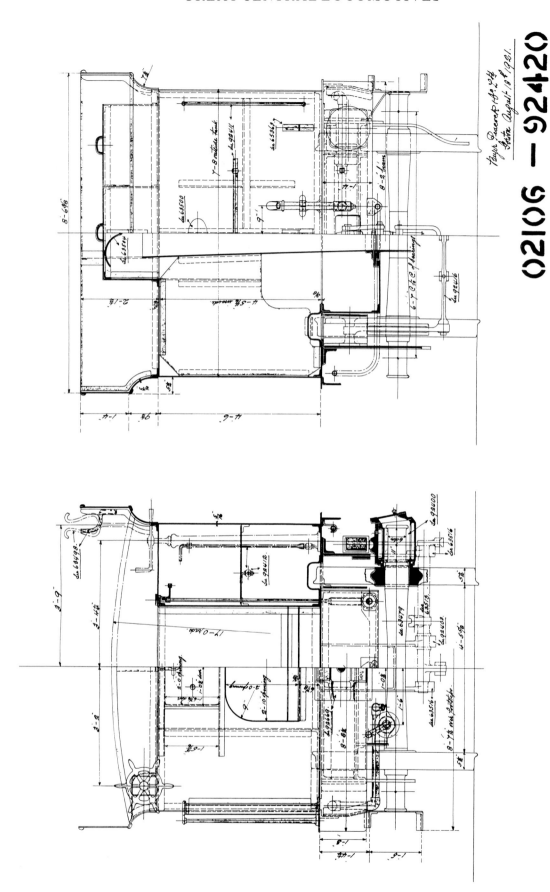

*Standard 4000 Gallon Robinson Tender (end elevations). Scale: 10 mm/ft approx.*

# Tenders

The original Directors, GC class 11E, were equipped with the standard Robinson 4,000 gallon tender holding a nominal 6 tons of coal. This design was carried over to the second series, the Class 11F machine which appeared in 1919. The final six 11Fs, of 1922, received the wider bodied tenders with self–trimming coal bunkers. This could be identified by the reduced flare apparent between the tank side and the coal guard. These were later swapped (q.v.) for the tenders carried by the (then) B3 (9P) class when these engines went into service on the G.N. main line, in 1923–24. This last Robinson tender could also be identified by the flat top to the bulkhead ahead of the coal space. Photographs used throughout the book show this quite readily in many cases.

The LNER Directors for the North British lines (D11/2) carried the later pattern of tender but minus the water pick–up apparatus. Throughout the building of the classes Gorton practice of allocating the tender the same number as the locomotive, was followed. Photographic evidence suggests that, apart from the well–documented changes, no Directors were ever paired with tenders of any other pattern.

Our drawing shows the tenders built by Beyer Peacock and Co. for the five 1922 9Q 4–6–0s (B7s). These, again, were of the standard 4,000 gallon/6 tons of coal pattern; they were built to order No. 02106.

The standard tenders weighed 24 tons 6 cwt. empty. An interesting point is that this weight almost exactly doubled when full to 48 tons 6cwt.

*(upper)* **The working end of tender No.5432 detached from 62653 *SIR ED-WARD FRASER* and showing plenty of detail. The numberplate is prominent above the open tool cupboard, notice also the broken handles on the 'ships wheel'.** *(right)* **The rear of 551 at Gorton shed in 1936. Yet another view offering plenty of detail.**

*Standard 4000 Gallon Robinson Tender (side elevation). Scale: 10 mm/ft approx.*

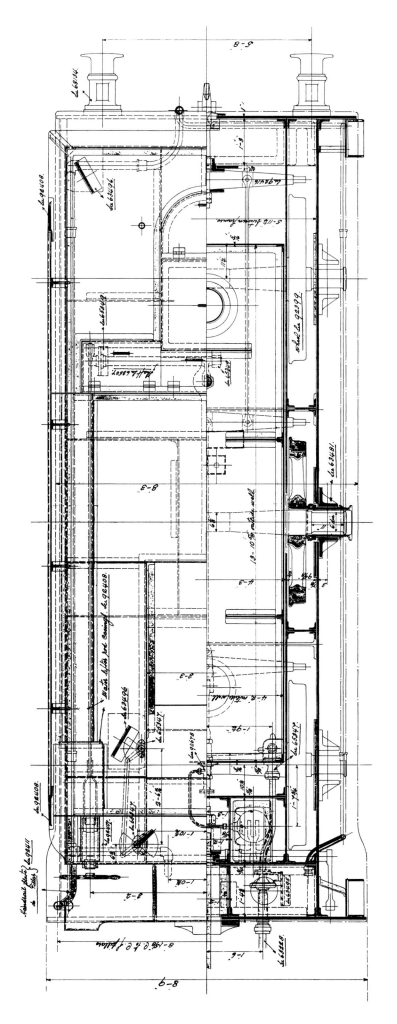

*Standard 4000 Gallon Robinson Tender (plan). Scale: 10 mm/ft approx.*

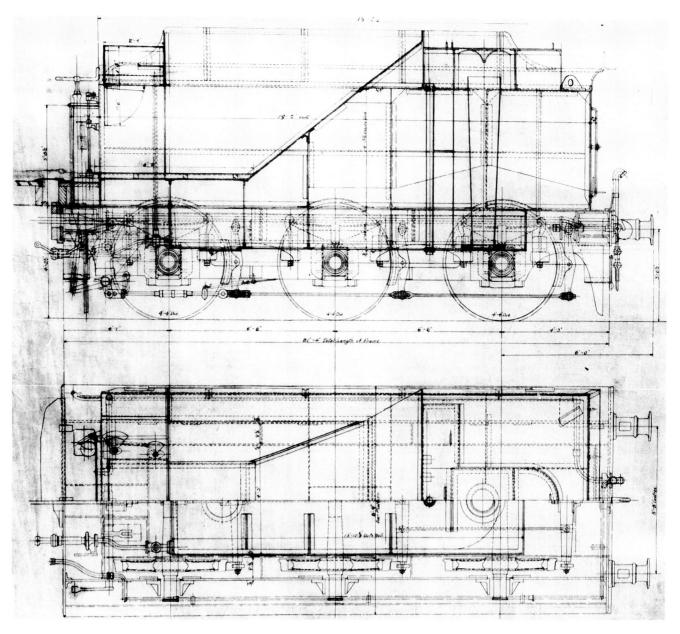

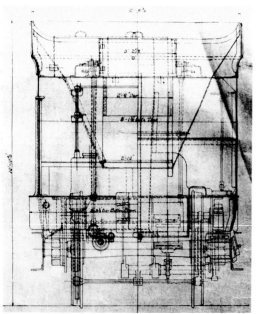

*Self Trimming 4000 Gallon Tender. Scale: 7 mm/ft approx.*

# Name & Numberplates

Drawing of a typical cabside numberplate. *(below)* **A selection of the robust but nevertheless decorative nameplates from the Robinson era.**

DRAWING №7600

3½" LETTERS FOR ENGINE NAMEPLATES

NOTE:- THE LETTERS C.G.O.Q.4 S. TO BE MADE ⅛" HIGHER THAN THE OTHERS

*PURDON VICCARS* showing the long side strips which were an integral part of the plate and joined up perfectly with the splasher beading. Sadly, at the time of the photograph, the engine was awaiting scrapping at Gorton – 22nd March 1953. *B.K.B.Green. (right)* Gorton driver Butterworth, left, and his fireman at Aintree, having brought a race special with *CITY OF LIVERPOOL* to the Grand National – 24th March 1923.

*(right)* Privately preserved LNER works plate off *EARL BEATTY*. *(above)* Drawing to show position of compant crest in relation to nameplate.

# Allocations

GREAT CENTRAL LOCOMOTIVE ALLOCATIONS AS AT 31st December 1922

## SHED LIST

ANNESLEY
BARNSLEY
BIDSTON
BRUNSWICK (Liverpool)
CHESTER
GORTON (Manchester)
IMMINGHAM
KEADBY
LANGWITH

LEICESTER
LINCOLN
MEXBOROUGH
NEASDEN
NEW HOLLAND
NORTHWICH
RETFORD
SHEFFIELD (Neepsend)
STAVELEY

STOCKPORT (Heaton Mersey)
TRAFFORD PARK (Manchester)
TUXFORD
WALTON (Liverpool)
WIGAN
WOODFORD
WREXHAM

| | | | | | | |
|---|---|---|---|---|---|---|
| 1 Gorton | 62 Mexborough | 123 Walton | 184 Immingham | 245 Gorton | 306 Annesley |
| 2 Chester | 63 Keadby | 124 Stockport | 185 Gorton | 246 Langwith | 307 Brunswick |
| 3 Wigan | 64 Mexborough | 125 Walton | 186 Mexborough | 247 Gorton | 308 Lincoln |
| 4 Annesley | 65 Mexborough | 126 Stockport | 187 Lincoln | 248 Lincoln | 309 Mexborough |
| 5 Gorton | 66 Tuxford | 127 Barnsley | 188 Wrexham | 249 Retford | 310 Chester |
| 6 Wigan | 67 Mexborough | 128 Neasden | 189 Barnsley | 250 Neasden | 311 Lincoln |
| 7 Mexborough | 68 Barnsley | 129 Neasden | 190 Wrexham | 251 Barnsley | 312 Langwith |
| 8 Gorton | 69 Mexborough | 130 Stockport | 191 Trafford Park | 252 Woodford | 313 Gorton |
| 9 Chester | 70 Sheffield | 131 Stockport | 192 Leicester | 253 Lincoln | 314 Lincoln |
| 10 Mexborough | 71 Staveley | 132 Stockport | 193 Chester | 254 Retford | 315 Lincoln |
| 11 Mexborough | 72 Gorton | 133 Mexborough | 194 Woodford | 255 Gorton | 316 Gorton |
| 12 Mexborough | 73 Gorton | 134 Gorton | 195 Gorton | 256 Langwith | 317 Langwith |
| 13 Mexborough | 74 Mexborough | 135 Mexborough | 196 Immingham | 257 Langwith | 318 Langwith |
| 14 Sheffield | 75 Mexborough | 136 Mexborough | 197 Woodford | 258 Leicester | 319 Gorton |
| 15 Sheffield | 76 Walton | 137 Barnsley | 198 Woodford | 259 Leicester | 320 Woodford |
| 16 Sheffield | 77 Mexborough | 138 Staveley | 199 Mexborough | 260 Woodford | 321 Immingham |
| 17 Sheffield | 78 Gorton | 139 Keadby | 200 Barnsley | 261 Woodford | 322 Lincoln |
| 18 Trafford Park | 79 Walton | 140 Keadby | 201 Woodford | 262 Woodford | 323 Woodford |
| 19 Sheffield | 80 Walton | 141 Brunswick | 202 Gorton | 263 Woodford | 324 Retford |
| 20 Stockport | 81 Walton | 142 Barnsley | 203 Leicester | 264 Leicester | 325 Woodford |
| 21 Barnsley | 82 Walton | 143 Keadby | 204 Langwith | 265 Leicester | 326 Annesley |
| 22 Sheffield | 83 Walton | 144 Immingham | 205 Leicester | 266 Leicester | 327 Annesley |
| 23 Neasden | 84 Walton | 145 Mexborough | 206 Mexborough | 267 Leicester | 328 Annesley |
| 24 Neasden | 85 Keadby | 146 Mexborough | 207 Woodford | 268 Brunswick | 329 Annesley |
| 25 Barnsley | 86 Staveley | 147 Keadby | 208 Gorton | 269 Trafford Park | 330 Sheffield |
| 26 Gorton | 87 Barnsley | 148 Mexborough | 209 Woodford | 270 Brunswick | 331 Mexborough |
| 27 Trafford Park | 88 Lincoln | 149 Mexborough | 210 Gorton | 271 Annesley | 332 Mexborough |
| 28 Wrexham | 89 New Holland | 150 Keadby | 211 Gorton | 272 Immingham | 333 Mexborough |
| 29 Trafford Park | 90 Brunswick | 151 Mexborough | 212 Staveley | 273 Annesley | 334 Gorton |
| 30 Mexborough | 91 Barnsley | 152 Mexborough | 213 Sheffield | 274 Annesley | 335 Mexborough |
| 31 Leicester | 92 Gorton | 153 Keadby | 214 Woodford | 275 Gorton | 336 Neasden |
| 32 Leicester | 93 Gorton | 154 Lincoln | 215 Woodford | 276 Neasden | 337 Annesley |
| 33 Leicester | 94 Brunswick | 155 Gorton | 216 Woodford | 277 Immingham | 338 Woodford |
| 34 Gorton | 95 Brunswick | 156 Langwith | 217 Langwith | 278 Immingham | 339 Neasden |
| 35 Gorton | 96 Brunswick | 157 Brunswick | 218 Langwith | 279 Annesley | 340 Langwith |
| 36 Immingham | 97 Brunswick | 158 Neasden | 219 Woodford | 280 Gorton | 341 Neasden |
| 37 Immingham | 98 Stockport | 159 Mexborough | 220 Lincoln | 281 Woodford | 342 Neasden |
| 38 Immingham | 99 Walton | 160 Keadby | 221 Neasden | 282 Neasden | 343 Annesley |
| 39 Keadby | 100 Walton | 161 Staveley | 222 Langwith | 283 Retford | 344 Woodford |
| 40 Langwith | 101 Brunswick | 162 Keadby | 223 Langwith | 284 Retford | 345 Annesley |
| 41 Tuxford | 102 Gorton | 163 Mexborough | 224 Gorton | 285 Neasden | 346 Mexborough |
| 42 Langwith | 103 Walton | 164 Mexborough | 225 Gorton | 286 Retford | 347 Mexborough |
| 43 Langwith | 104 Retford | 165 Neasden | 226 Gorton | 287 Retford | 348 Mexborough |
| 44 Mexborough | 105 Retford | 166 Neasden | 227 Annesley | 288 Gorton | 349 Mexborough |
| 45 Trafford Park | 106 Sheffield | 167 Neasden | 228 Woodford | 289 Gorton | 350 Mexborough |
| 46 Wigan | 107 Retford | 168 Neasden | 229 Langwith | 290 Gorton | 351 Annesley |
| 47 Chester | 108 Sheffield | 169 Neasden | 230 Retford | 291 Gorton | 352 Gorton |
| 48 Mexborough | 109 Sheffield | 170 Neasden | 231 Retford | 292 Annesley | 353 Gorton |
| 49 Mexborough | 110 Brunswick | 171 Wrexham | 232 Gorton | 293 Lincoln | 354 Gorton |
| 50 Trafford Park | 111 Sheffield | 172 Brunswick | 233 Woodford | 294 Annesley | 355 Gorton |
| 51 Mexborough | 112 Mexborough | 173 Mexborough | 234 Gorton | 295 Retford | 356 Mexborough |
| 52 Gorton | 113 Lincoln | 174 Brunswick | 235 Gorton | 296 Retford | 357 Trafford Park |
| 53 Gorton | 114 Trafford Park | 175 Brunswick | 236 Gorton | 297 Woodford | 358 Leicester |
| 54 Barnsley | 115 Wrexham | 176 Brunswick | 237 Gorton | 298 Neasden | 359 Wrexham |
| 55 Chester | 116 Stockport | 177 Lincoln | 238 Woodford | 299 Lincoln | 360 Leicester |
| 56 Barnsley | 117 Stockport | 178 Wrexham | 239 Langwith | 300 Lincoln | 361 Leicester |
| 57 Keadby | 118 Brunswick | 179 Trafford Park | 240 Langwith | 301 Sheffield | 362 Woodford |
| 58 Mexborough | 119 Stockport | 180 Immingham | 241 Woodford | 302 Annesley | 363 Leicester |
| 59 Barnsley | 120 Stockport | 181 Immingham | 242 Gorton | 303 Gorton | 364 Leicester |
| 60 Immingham | 121 Stockport | 182 Immingham | 243 Annesley | 304 Retford | 365 Leicester |
| 61 Immingham | 122 Stockport | 183 Immingham | 244 Annesley | 305 Sheffield | 366 Langwith |

**Gorton, variety and quantity. The biggest of the GC engine sheds, which was only natural as it was at the heart of the empire.**

| | | | | | | | | | |
|---|---|---|---|---|---|---|---|---|---|
| 367 | Neasden | 418 | Retford | 469 | Woodford | 520 | Gorton | 571 | Mexborough |
| 368 | Woodford | 419 | Retford | 470 | Gorton | 521 | Barnsley | 572 | Mexborough |
| 369 | Woodford | 420 | Gorton | 471 | Gorton | 522 | Gorton | 573 | Mexborough |
| 370 | Annesley | 421 | Mexborough | 472 | Gorton | 523 | Gorton | 574 | Gorton |
| 371 | Neasden | 422 | Gorton | 473 | Gorton | 524 | Gorton | 575 | Gorton |
| 372 | Neasden | 423 | Gorton | 474 | Gorton | 525 | Gorton | 576 | Gorton |
| 373 | Neasden | 424 | Gorton | 475 | Mexborough | 526 | Gorton | 577 | Gorton |
| 374 | Neasden | 425 | Gorton | 476 | Mexborough | 527 | Gorton | 578 | Stockport |
| 375 | Annesley | 426 | Gorton | 477 | Mexborough | 528 | Gorton | 579 | Stockport |
| 376 | Mexborough | 427 | Gorton | 478 | Trafford Park | 529 | Gorton | 580 | Gorton |
| 377 | Gorton | 428 | Gorton | 479 | Trafford Park | 530 | Wrexham | 581 | Stockport |
| 378 | Gorton | 429 | Neasden | 480 | Wigan | 531 | Wrexham | 582 | Gorton |
| 379 | Gorton | 430 | Gorton | 481 | Wigan | 532 | Gorton | 583 | Gorton |
| 380 | Annesley | 431 | Gorton | 482 | Wigan | 533 | Barnsley | 584 | Gorton |
| 381 | Sheffield | 432 | Neasden | 483 | Wigan | 534 | Gorton | 585 | Gorton |
| 382 | Sheffield | 433 | Gorton | 484 | Trafford Park | 535 | Gorton | 586 | Gorton |
| 383 | Sheffield | 434 | Gorton | 485 | Mexborough | 536 | Gorton | 587 | Gorton |
| 384 | Mexborough | 435 | Gorton | 486 | Mexborough | 537 | Gorton | 588 | Gorton |
| 385 | Sheffield | 436 | Gorton | 487 | Mexborough | 538 | Brunswick | 589 | Gorton |
| 386 | Mexborough | 437 | Neasden | 488 | Mexborough | 539 | Wrexham | 590 | Stockport |
| 387 | Annesley | 438 | Gorton | 489 | Mexborough | 540 | Gorton | 591 | Stockport |
| 388 | Mexborough | 439 | Gorton | 490 | Mexborough | 541 | Gorton | 592 | Stockport |
| 389 | Annesley | 440 | Annesley | 491 | Mexborough | 542 | Gorton | 593 | Stockport |
| 390 | Mexborough | 441 | Annesley | 492 | Mexborough | 543 | Gorton | 594 | Gorton |
| 391 | Mexborough | 442 | Gorton | 493 | Trafford Park | 544 | Barnsley | 595 | Gorton |
| 392 | Mexborough | 443 | Gorton | 494 | Mexborough | 545 | Mexborough | 596 | Gorton |
| 393 | Gorton | 444 | Gorton | 495 | Wigan | 546 | Barnsley | 597 | Stockport |
| 394 | Gorton | 445 | Gorton | 496 | Wigan | 547 | Mexborough | 598 | Stockport |
| 395 | Gorton | 446 | Annesley | 497 | Trafford Park | 548 | Gorton | 599 | Stockport |
| 396 | Gorton | 447 | Neasden | 498 | Trafford Park | 549 | Staveley | 600 | Stockport |
| 397 | Mexborough | 448 | Neasden | 499 | Trafford Park | 550 | Staveley | 601 | Sheffield |
| 398 | Mexborough | 449 | Neasden | 500 | Trafford Park | 551 | Staveley | 602 | Sheffield |
| 399 | Sheffield | 450 | Neasden | 501 | Neasden | 552 | Staveley | 603 | Staveley |
| 400 | Mexborough | 451 | Neasden | 502 | Neasden | 553 | Staveley | 604 | Sheffield |
| 401 | Mexborough | 452 | Neasden | 503 | Neasden | 554 | Staveley | 605 | Sheffield |
| 402 | Mexborough | 453 | Wrexham | 504 | Neasden | 555 | Staveley | 606 | Sheffield |
| 403 | Immingham | 454 | Wrexham | 505 | Neasden | 556 | Staveley | 607 | Sheffield |
| 404 | Mexborough | 455 | Wrexham | 506 | Neasden | 557 | Staveley | 608 | Sheffield |
| 405 | Mexborough | 456 | Trafford Park | 507 | Neasden | 558 | Staveley | 609 | Staveley |
| 406 | Mexborough | 457 | Chester | 508 | Neasden | 559 | Staveley | 610 | Staveley |
| 407 | Mexborough | 458 | Neasden | 509 | Neasden | 560 | Staveley | 611 | Sheffield |
| 408 | Annesley | 459 | Neasden | 510 | Neasden | 561 | Immingham | 612 | Sheffield |
| 409 | Bidston | 460 | Neasden | 511 | Neasden | 562 | Lincoln | 613 | Barnsley |
| 410 | Wrexham | 461 | Neasden | 512 | Staveley | 563 | Mexborough | 614 | Staveley |
| 411 | Neasden | 462 | Woodford | 513 | Staveley | 564 | Lincoln | 615 | Staveley |
| 412 | Gorton | 463 | Neasden | 514 | Barnsley | 565 | Sheffield | 616 | Staveley |
| 413 | Gorton | 464 | Neasden | 515 | Barnsley | 566 | Immingham | 617 | Sheffield |
| 414 | Retford | 465 | Sheffield | 516 | Mexborough | 567 | Immingham | 618 | Staveley |
| 415 | Retford | 466 | Sheffield | 517 | Mexborough | 568 | Mexborough | 619 | Sheffield |
| 416 | Gorton | 467 | Woodford | 518 | Gorton | 569 | Mexborough | 620 | Lincoln |
| 417 | Mexborough | 468 | Woodford | 519 | Gorton | 570 | Barnsley | 621 | Staveley |

| | |
|---|---|
| 622 | Sheffield |
| 623 | Barnsley |
| 624 | Langwith |
| 625 | Staveley |
| 626 | Sheffield |
| 627 | Sheffield |
| 628 | Sheffield |
| 629 | Barnsley |
| 630 | Barnsley |
| 631 | Sheffield |
| 632 | Sheffield |
| 633 | Sheffield |
| 634 | Barnsley |
| 635 | Staveley |
| 636 | Staveley |
| 637 | Staveley |
| 638 | Sheffield |
| 639 | Sheffield |
| 640 | Sheffield |
| 641 | Northwich |
| 642 | Sheffield |
| 643 | Sheffield |
| 644 | Northwich |
| 645 | Northwich |
| 646 | Northwich |
| 647 | Northwich |
| 648 | Gorton |
| 649 | Northwich |
| 650 | Northwich |
| 651 | Gorton |
| 652 | Northwich |
| 653 | Northwich |
| 654 | Northwich |
| 655 | Northwich |
| 656 | Northwich |
| 657 | Northwich |
| 658 | Northwich |
| 659 | Gorton |
| 660 | Northwich |
| 661 | Northwich |
| 662 | Northwich |
| 663 | Northwich |
| 664 | Gorton |
| 665 | Northwich |
| 666 | Northwich |
| 667 | Northwich |
| 668 | Northwich |
| 669 | Northwich |
| 670 | Sheffield |
| 671 | Barnsley |
| 672 | Sheffield |

| No. | Depot | No. | Depot | No. | Depot | No. | Depot | No. | Depot | No. | Depot |
|---|---|---|---|---|---|---|---|---|---|---|---|
| 673 | Sheffield | 757 | Mexborough | 841 | Immingham | 925 | Brunswick | 1009 | Lincoln | 1093 | Woodford |
| 674 | Sheffield | 758 | Barnsley | 842 | Wrexham | 926 | Leicester | 1010 | Immingham | 1094 | Woodford |
| 675 | Sheffield | 759 | Mexborough | 843 | Stockport | 927 | Annesley | 1011 | Immingham | 1095 | Sheffield |
| 676 | Sheffield | 760 | Barnsley | 844 | Immingham | 928 | Wrexham | 1012 | Immingham | 1096 | Sheffield |
| 677 | Sheffield | 761 | Barnsley | 845 | Retford | 929 | Wrexham | 1013 | Lincoln | 1097 | Sheffield |
| 678 | Sheffield | 762 | Mexborough | 846 | Immingham | 930 | Annesley | 1014 | Sheffield | 1098 | Sheffield |
| 679 | Sheffield | 763 | Barnsley | 847 | Retford | 931 | Stockport | 1015 | Sheffield | 1099 | Sheffield |
| 680 | Sheffield | 764 | Annesley | 848 | Gorton | 932 | Gorton | 1016 | Annesley | 1100 | Sheffield |
| 681 | Sheffield | 765 | Annesley | 849 | Annesley | 933 | Chester | 1017 | Brunswick | 1101 | Sheffield |
| 682 | Immingham | 766 | Barnsley | 850 | Annesley | 934 | Neasden | 1018 | Immingham | 1102 | Sheffield |
| 683 | Sheffield | 767 | Retford | 851 | Retford | 935 | Wrexham | 1019 | Sheffield | 1103 | Sheffield |
| 684 | New Holland | 768 | Trafford Park | 852 | Trafford Park | 936 | Walton | 1020 | Sheffield | 1104 | Sheffield |
| 685 | Immingham | 769 | Mexborough | 853 | Trafford Park | 937 | Annesley | 1021 | Lincoln | 1105 | Lincoln |
| 686 | Immingham | 770 | Annesley | 854 | Trafford Park | 938 | Wrexham | 1022 | Annesley | 1106 | Gorton |
| 687 | Immingham | 771 | Woodford | 855 | Trafford Park | 939 | Annesley | 1023 | Annesley | 1107 | Lincoln |
| 688 | Mexborough | 772 | Neasden | 856 | Trafford Park | 940 | Gorton | 1024 | Lincoln | 1108 | Lincoln |
| 689 | Mexborough | 773 | Neasden | 857 | Trafford Park | 941 | Walton | 1025 | Annesley | 1109 | Lincoln |
| 690 | Mexborough | 774 | Annesley | 858 | Trafford Park | 942 | Neasden | 1026 | Sheffield | 1110 | Gorton |
| 691 | Mexborough | 775 | Annesley | 859 | Brunswick | 943 | Gorton | 1027 | Sheffield | 1111 | Lincoln |
| 692 | Mexborough | 776 | Gorton | 860 | Trafford Park | 944 | Chester | 1028 | Annesley | 1112 | Lincoln |
| 693 | Sheffield | 777 | Brunswick | 861 | Trafford Park | 945 | Neasden | 1029 | Sheffield | 1113 | Gorton |
| 694 | Walton | 778 | Brunswick | 862 | Brunswick | 946 | Gorton | 1030 | Sheffield | 1114 | Gorton |
| 695 | Walton | 779 | Brunswick | 863 | Brunswick | 947 | Sheffield | 1031 | Sheffield | 1115 | Lincoln |
| 696 | Walton | 780 | Brunswick | 864 | Brunswick | 948 | Langwith | 1032 | Sheffield | 1116 | Lincoln |
| 697 | Walton | 781 | Brunswick | 865 | Trafford Park | 949 | Sheffield | 1033 | Annesley | 1117 | Retford |
| 698 | Walton | 782 | Brunswick | 866 | Trafford Park | 950 | Sheffield | 1034 | Sheffield | 1118 | Lincoln |
| 699 | Walton | 783 | Walton | 867 | Trafford Park | 951 | Gorton | 1035 | Annesley | 1119 | Retford |
| 700 | Lincoln | 784 | Gorton | 868 | Trafford Park | 952 | Trafford Park | 1036 | Lincoln | 1120 | Langwith |
| 701 | Northwich | 785 | Brunswick | 869 | Brunswick | 953 | Sheffield | 1037 | Sheffield | 1121 | Langwith |
| 702 | Northwich | 786 | Immingham | 870 | Trafford Park | 954 | Sheffield | 1038 | Annesley | 1122 | Annesley |
| 703 | Northwich | 787 | Retford | 871 | Brunswick | 955 | Gorton | 1039 | Annesley | 1123 | Langwith |
| 704 | Northwich | 788 | Trafford Park | 872 | Trafford Park | 956 | Keadby | 1040 | Sheffield | 1124 | Annesley |
| 705 | Lincoln | 789 | Retford | 873 | Trafford Park | 957 | Langwith | 1041 | Sheffield | 1125 | Neasden |
| 706 | New Holland | 790 | Retford | 874 | Trafford Park | 958 | Mexborough | 1042 | Sheffield | 1126 | Woodford |
| 707 | Northwich | 791 | Retford | 875 | Trafford Park | 959 | Langwith | 1043 | Woodford | 1127 | Annesley |
| 708 | Immingham | 792 | Retford | 876 | Trafford Park | 960 | Mexborough | 1044 | Woodford | 1128 | Annesley |
| 709 | Northwich | 793 | Retford | 877 | Brunswick | 961 | Mexborough | 1045 | Trafford Park | 1129 | Annesley |
| 710 | Barnsley | 794 | Retford | 878 | Brunswick | 962 | Mexborough | 1046 | Woodford | 1130 | Stockport |
| 711 | New Holland | 795 | Retford | 879 | Brunswick | 963 | Mexborough | 1047 | Woodford | 1131 | Stockport |
| 712 | Staveley | 796 | Annesley | 880 | Brunswick | 964 | Immingham | 1048 | Woodford | 1132 | Langwith |
| 713 | Staveley | 797 | Immingham | 881 | Brunswick | 965 | Mexborough | 1049 | Woodford | 1133 | Langwith |
| 714 | Barnsley | 798 | Trafford Park | 882 | Wrexham | 966 | Gorton | 1050 | Woodford | 1134 | Gorton |
| 715 | Staveley | 799 | Retford | 883 | Wrexham | 967 | Trafford Park | 1051 | Woodford | 1135 | Langwith |
| 716 | Sheffield | 800 | Immingham | 884 | Bidston | 968 | Brunswick | 1052 | Gorton | 1136 | Langwith |
| 717 | Staveley | 801 | Trafford Park | 885 | Immingham | 969 | Trafford Park | 1053 | Mexborough | 1137 | Langwith |
| 718 | Barnsley | 802 | Retford | 886 | Bidston | 970 | Brunswick | 1054 | Mexborough | 1138 | Langwith |
| 719 | Barnsley | 803 | Trafford Park | 887 | Immingham | 971 | Trafford Park | 1055 | Sheffield | 1139 | Langwith |
| 720 | Staveley | 804 | Trafford Park | 888 | Wrexham | 972 | Brunswick | 1056 | Sheffield | 1140 | Langwith |
| 721 | Sheffield | 805 | Immingham | 889 | Immingham | 973 | Immingham | 1057 | Sheffield | 1141 | Langwith |
| 722 | Sheffield | 806 | Immingham | 890 | Staveley | 974 | Immingham | 1058 | Retford | 1142 | Langwith |
| 723 | Mexborough | 807 | Brunswick | 891 | Wrexham | 975 | Immingham | 1059 | Sheffield | 1143 | Langwith |
| 724 | Barnsley | 808 | New Holland | 892 | Bidston | 976 | Immingham | 1060 | Sheffield | 1144 | Keadby |
| 725 | Barnsley | 809 | New Holland | 893 | Wrexham | 977 | Immingham | 1061 | Sheffield | 1145 | Tuxford |
| 726 | Gorton | 810 | Brunswick | 894 | Neasden | 978 | Immingham | 1062 | Sheffield | 1146 | Langwith |
| 727 | Gorton | 811 | Trafford Park | 895 | Brunswick | 979 | Immingham | 1063 | Sheffield | 1147 | Tuxford |
| 728 | Gorton | 812 | Trafford Park | 896 | Gorton | 980 | Immingham | 1064 | Mexborough | 1148 | Tuxford |
| 729 | Gorton | 813 | Retford | 897 | Neasden | 981 | Immingham | 1065 | Sheffield | 1149 | Tuxford |
| 730 | Gorton | 814 | Sheffield | 898 | Wrexham | 982 | Immingham | 1066 | Sheffield | 1150 | Tuxford |
| 731 | Gorton | 815 | Trafford Park | 899 | Wrexham | 983 | Immingham | 1067 | Mexborough | 1151 | Tuxford |
| 732 | Gorton | 816 | Annesley | 900 | Gorton | 984 | Immingham | 1068 | Mexborough | 1152 | Tuxford |
| 733 | Gorton | 817 | Immingham | 901 | Wrexham | 985 | Immingham | 1069 | Mexborough | 1153 | Tuxford |
| 734 | Gorton | 818 | Retford | 902 | Wrexham | 986 | Immingham | 1070 | Mexborough | 1154 | Langwith |
| 735 | Gorton | 819 | Immingham | 903 | Wrexham | 987 | Immingham | 1071 | Mexborough | 1155 | Langwith |
| 736 | Gorton | 820 | Stockport | 904 | Brunswick | 988 | Immingham | 1072 | Mexborough | 1156 | Langwith |
| 737 | Gorton | 821 | Retford | 905 | Gorton | 989 | Immingham | 1073 | Mexborough | 1157 | Tuxford |
| 738 | Northwich | 822 | Retford | 906 | Wrexham | 990 | Immingham | 1074 | Keadby | 1158 | Langwith |
| 739 | Northwich | 823 | New Holland | 907 | Stockport | 991 | Gorton | 1075 | Mexborough | 1159 | Langwith |
| 740 | Northwich | 824 | Stockport | 908 | Walton | 992 | Immingham | 1076 | Keadby | 1160 | Tuxford |
| 741 | Northwich | 825 | Stockport | 909 | Stockport | 993 | Gorton | 1077 | Langwith | 1161 | Tuxford |
| 742 | Northwich | 826 | Stockport | 910 | Stockport | 994 | Immingham | 1078 | Gorton | 1162 | Tuxford |
| 743 | Northwich | 827 | New Holland | 911 | Brunswick | 995 | Immingham | 1079 | Retford | 1163 | Tuxford |
| 744 | Mexborough | 828 | Retford | 912 | Stockport | 996 | Immingham | 1080 | Langwith | 1164 | Gorton |
| 745 | Neasden | 829 | Stockport | 913 | Neasden | 997 | Immingham | 1081 | Neasden | 1165 | Gorton |
| 746 | Mexborough | 830 | Stockport | 914 | Chester | 998 | Immingham | 1082 | Neasden | 1166 | Gorton |
| 747 | Barnsley | 831 | Retford | 915 | Stockport | 999 | Immingham | 1083 | Leicester | 1167 | Gorton |
| 748 | Barnsley | 832 | Retford | 916 | Wrexham | 1000 | Immingham | 1084 | Woodford | 1168 | Gorton |
| 749 | Barnsley | 833 | Stockport | 917 | Neasden | 1001 | Immingham | 1085 | Walton | 1169 | Gorton |
| 750 | Mexborough | 834 | Stockport | 918 | Walton | 1002 | Immingham | 1086 | Leicester | 1170 | Mexborough |
| 751 | Chester | 835 | Annesley | 919 | Trafford Park | 1003 | Gorton | 1087 | Leicester | 1171 | Mexborough |
| 752 | Barnsley | 836 | Stockport | 920 | Wrexham | 1004 | Gorton | 1088 | Woodford | 1172 | Mexborough |
| 753 | Mexborough | 837 | Immingham | 921 | Walton | 1005 | Immingham | 1089 | Leicester | 1173 | Mexborough |
| 754 | Barnsley | 838 | Immingham | 922 | Brunswick | 1006 | Immingham | 1090 | Leicester | 1174 | Mexborough |
| 755 | Mexborough | 839 | Stockport | 923 | Leicester | 1007 | Immingham | 1091 | Woodford | 1175 | Mexborough |
| 756 | Chester | 840 | Immingham | 924 | Brunswick | 1008 | Immingham | 1092 | Leicester | 1176 | Langwith |

| | | | |
|---|---|---|---|
| 1177 Mexborough | 1222 Mexborough | | |
| 1178 Keadby | 1223 Annesley | | |
| 1179 Langwith | 1224 Annesley | | |
| 1180 Mexborough | 1225 Annesley | | |
| 1181 Immingham | 1226 Annesley | | |
| 1182 Mexborough | 1227 Annesley | | |
| 1183 Gorton | 1228 Annesley | | |
| 1184 Mexborough | 1229 Staveley | | |
| 1185 Mexborough | 1230 Staveley | | |
| 1186 Mexborough | 1231 Staveley | | |
| 1187 Mexborough | 1232 Staveley | | |
| 1188 Mexborough | 1233 Staveley | | |
| 1189 Mexborough | 1234 Gorton | | |
| 1190 Mexborough | 1235 Staveley | | |
| 1191 Mexborough | 1236 Staveley | | |
| 1192 Mexborough | 1237 Mexborough | | |
| 1193 Mexborough | 1238 Annesley | | |
| 1194 Mexborough | 1239 Gorton | | |
| 1195 Mexborough | 1240 Keadby | | |
| 1196 Mexborough | 1241 Mexborough | | |
| 1197 Mexborough | 1242 Immingham | | |
| 1198 Mexborough | 1243 Mexborough | | |
| 1199 Mexborough | 1244 Immingham | | |
| 1200 Mexborough | 1245 Immingham | | |
| 1201 Mexborough | 1246 Sheffield | | |
| 1202 Mexborough | 1247 Sheffield | | |
| 1203 Immingham | 1248 Mexborough | | |
| 1204 Immingham | 1249 Mexborough | | |
| 1205 Sheffield | 1250 Mexborough | | |
| 1206 Keadby | 1251 Staveley | | |
| 1207 Mexborough | 1252 Mexborough | | |

**Trafford Park at the turn of the century.**

| | | | | | |
|---|---|---|---|---|---|
| 1208 Mexborough | | | | | |
| 1209 Mexborough | 5B Trafford Park | 52B Gorton | 367B Immingham | 443B Annesley | 504B Wigan |
| 1210 Mexborough | 8B Bidston | 53B Gorton | 368B Walton | 446B Brunswick | 505B Walton |
| 1211 Staveley | 10B Wrexham | 62B Immingham | 370B Sheffield | 449B Neasden | 506B Walton |
| 1212 Annesley | 11B Wrexham | 63B Immingham | 371B Brunswick | 450B Neasden | 507B Lincoln |
| 1213 Annesley | 22B Gorton | 66B Langwith | 372B Neasden | 458B Mexborough | 508B Walton |
| 1214 Annesley | 31B Mexborough | 72B Bidston | 374B Walton | 459B Trafford Park | 509B Lincoln |
| 1215 Annesley | 32B Mexborough | 73B Retford | 400B Wrexham | 460B Mexborough | 510B Walton |
| 1216 Annesley | 34B Mexborough | 78B Wrexham | 407B Immingham | 461B Trafford Park | 511B Walton |
| 1217 Annesley | 35B Mexborough | 128B New Holland | 413B Mexborough | 462B Mexborough | 1145B Langwith |
| 1218 Annesley | 36B Trafford Park | 169B Annesley | 414B Immingham | 463B Mexborough | 1146B Tuxford |
| 1219 Annesley | 37B Trafford Park | 272B Immingham | 415B Immingham | 464B Trafford Park | 1147B Langwith |
| 1220 Annesley | 38B Mexborough | 273B Immingham | 417B Mexborough | 465B Mexborough | 1148B Langwith |
| 1221 Annesley | 41B Immingham | 274B Mexborough | 418B Brunswick | 466B Trafford Park | 1149B Langwith |
| | | 275B Gorton | 420B Gorton | 467B Mexborough | 1150B Langwith |
| | | 276B Gorton | 421B Annesley | 468B Mexborough | 1151B Langwith |
| | | 277B Mexborough | 423B Brunswick | 469B Trafford Park | 1152B Langwith |
| | | 279B Immingham | 425B Gorton | 470B Trafford Park | 1153B Langwith |
| | | 280B Immingham | 428B Annesley | 471B Wigan | 1154B Langwith |
| | | 309B Gorton | 430B Brunswick | 472B Wigan | 1155B Langwith |
| | | 336B Brunswick | 434B Gorton | 473B Wigan | 1156B Langwith |
| | | 338B Stockport | 439B New Holland | 474B Wigan | 1169B Langwith |
| | | 339B Stockport | 440B Staveley | 501B Wigan | |
| | | 340B Sheffield | 441B Trafford Park | 502B Wigan | |
| | | 342B Stockport | 442B Annesley | 503B Trafford Park | |

The operating staff of any company were the life blood of the railway and it is always a pleasure to come across pictures showing such personalities especially, as here, where men can be identified. Outside Leicester shed on Sunday, August 13th 1922, No.460, in original condition, was on display, cleaned and coaled-up. Fireman Percy Banyard is standing on the framing, Driver E.Johnson (no relation to the author!) stands, hand on cylinder cover whilst shed engineman H.Antill is sat on the front framing. An altogether very pleasing cameo, now, sadly, all passed away.

# BUTLER HENDERSON (The Survivor)

The pioneer of the 11F class, No. 506 'Butler–Henderson' was selected for preservation upon withdrawal in October 1960. At that point the locomotive had run over 1¼ million miles and still had the original cylinders and shorter–travel valves (i.e. not of the J39 pattern fitted to the rest of the class). Restoration was undertaken at Gorton to bring the engine back to its original condition, at least externally. The result, though not entirely faithful, was impressive. It has to be remembered that in those days there was nothing like the profusion of preserved locomotives on view as is the case today. Though steam was still very much in evidence, the sight of an engine in pre–1923 condition outside the (then) fairly stuffy museums was rare. I still remember the sensation 'Butler-Henderson' created when it went on view in the goods yard at Manchester Central in the March of 1962. Never mind if this beauty wasn't in steam, the mere sight of an almost pure Great Central locomotive in all its green and crimson lined glory was a thing to be wondered at.

In store at Darnall *(below)* in March 1958 with not a hint of what was to come. *(bottom)* A restored *BUTLER – HENDERSON* is unveiled to enjoy a life in preservation. School children of the 1960s *(opposite)* admire the paint job undertaken by Gorton Tank.

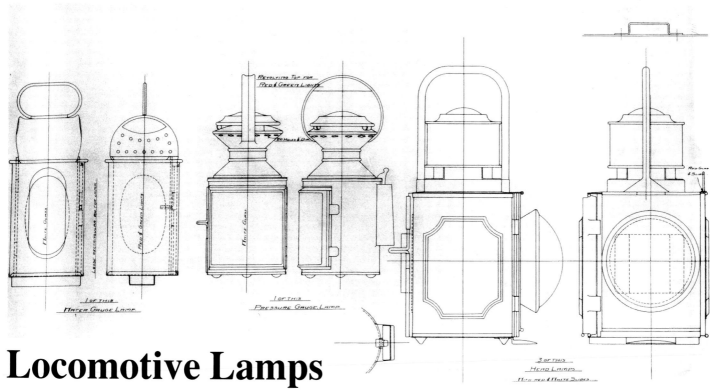

# Locomotive Lamps

# Addenda

The reception given to Volume 1 was very encouraging. Many readers troubled themselves to write and the overwhelming majority of those who did so voiced praise. Criticisms there were and these I fully acknowledge. It was good to hear that the main sources of dissatisfaction centred around what was left out of the book and not with the content per se. Biggest grumble, perhaps, was the omission of the weight diagrams which left some readers in the dark concerning some of the locomotives' principal dimensions. Though I was not able to include these, as such, in this volume either, I have, of course, included all the 'vital statistics' of the classes covered in a simple tabular format.

After the appearance of Volume 1 the following errors came to light:

*Page 9:* Lancashire, Derbyshire & East Coast Railway locomotives. The company was absorbed by the Great Central on January 1st. 1907. August 5th. 1891, was the date of the company's incorporation.

*Page 33:* Although No. 704 is correctly stated as having been broken up in April 1940 it has been brought to my attention that the engine had, in fact, been withdrawn on December 23rd. 1939.

*Page 52:* Parker 9H 0–6–0 became British Railways No. 65149 and not 65419 as stated.

*Page 55:* 9J (J11) 0–6–0 No. 1009 (LNER 6009) was rebuilt as described, becoming the prototype for Class J11/3. Thirty–one engines were so treated between 1943 and 1953.

*Page 59:* Information has come to light concerning the four–railed tender coupled to 11B No. 1042. The tender is from No. 285 (9J) to which No. 1042 was paired until its withdrawal in July 1939. 1042's original tender was coupled to No. 281 (another 9J) until January 1925. From here it was attached to 5087 (a Q4 – G.C. 8A) from March 1925 until October 1932. From that point it found its way behind No. 6077 (another Q4) until September 1943. On 6th. November 1943 the tender went to Woodford to do duty as a water carrier. Exactly how long this period at Woodford was is unknown

but it surfaced at Tuxford as water carrier No. 9930 until it was condemned on September 3rd. 1957. As a footnote, 1042 was the only small boilered member of the 11B series to receive an LNER number and paint style.

*Page 79:* Reference to the jacks on the footplate of No. 1120 should have made the point that the weight of 270lb. referred to was the total weight of the pair; i.e. each jack weighed 135lb.

*Page 89:* In the production of the block to print the photograph of Compound Atlantic No. 259, the NER coach referred to in the caption was in fact obliterated(!).

*Page 93:* Pollitt 11A 4–4–0 at the head of the train at Godley Junction is numbered 881 and not 681 as stated.

*Page 94:* Copley Hill is, of course, a district of Leeds.

*Page 96:* Class 5A 0–6–0 tank engines carried vacuum ejector as well as steam brakes.

*Page 104:* The caption relating to No. 1090 the Walschaerts Atlantic should have made reference to the eccentric rod instead of radius rod.

*Page 108:* Class 9N 4–6–2 tanks. I should have made a specific reference to the further eleven examples built in 1912 and 1917.

*Page 107 and 108:* Mea maxima culpa. It was very unfortunate that a repetition of the minuted report occurred. Dwindling supplies of sackcloth and ashes determine that such a thing will not manifest itself again!

*Page 120:* 8K 2–8–0 No. 1234. The historical information given is correct. Unfortunately, the photograph depicts No. 394 at Neasden on June 27th. 1914. This engine had been built at Gorton in April 1914 and was rebuilt to class O1 in March 1945. It was re–numbered 3619 in June 1946 and withdrawn as British Railways No. 63619 in October 1963.

*Page 126:* Class 1 4–6–0 'Sir Sam Fay'. History tells us there was one tender change. 5424 'City of Lincoln' received the tender from No. 5315 (a J11) from August 1929 until March 1930 whereupon it was paired again with its original.

# Acknowledgements

One very pleasant spin–off from researching and writing about the railway scene is the friendship and camaraderie that results. Over the last few years I have had the pleasure of corresponding with, meeting and talking to like–minded people, not only from all over Britain, but from other parts of the globe as well. Throughout all the effort that a work such as this demands I have been sustained by my wife, Mary, and to her first of all I offer my thanks for her unstinting support during my many hours away from the family scene. Ian and Sarah, too, have put in their 'pennorth answering the telephone and assisting in 'duties' whilst Dad has been otherwise engaged.

Particular thanks must go to Allan Brown who has shared his very wide knowledge of Great Central engines with me, has kindly loaned photographs and provided information from his collection of material. Through Allan's generosity I have been able to peruse the memoirs of the late Percy Banyard. Percy began work at Leicester G.C. shed in 1917 and handled every type of Great Central locomotive during his fifty one years of railway service. I must also thank David Jackson, Bryan Longbone and John Quick, three other G.C. experts, who have assisted me with some of the finer points of Robinson engines, especially liveries – always a tricky subject. Greg Fox, Ronnie Gee and Raymond Keeley have provided help in establishing locations and have enlightened me with their memories of former G.C. engines at work. Paul Dalton, one of J.G.Robinson's descendants, has also provided some splendid gems of information and has generously given help and photographs.

Reference sources in the shape of the Public Record Office at Kew, Manchester Central Library and The Greater Manchester Museum of Science and Technology have all played a most valuable part in my researches. A particular bouquet must go to Elizabeth Sprenger at G.M.Museum who was most helpful in sorting out

details from the Beyer, Peacock & Co. archives for me.

No serious Great Central enthusiast can afford to be without the incomparable 'Locomotives of the LNER' published by the RCTS and I acknowledge the value of these volumes in cross–checking my references.

Pictures provide the visual bulk of a work such as this and I am especially grateful to the following people for allowing me to use their valuable material: the late H.C.Casserley, Brian Green, Brian Hilton, Mrs.K.Platt (for permission to use photographs taken by her late husband, Geoffrey Platt), Bill Potter, Bill Rear, Charlie Shoults (for generously loaning me pictures taken by his late father, George Shoults), and to the family of the late V.R. Webster for their forebearance in allowing me to use pictures from Ray Webster's collection at a most difficult time. A thank–you too, to Jack Doyle for having provided the loan of weight diagrams and tables which assisted us in establishing accurate dimensions.

Some photographers must, by inevitable default, remain anonymous. One or two, whose whereabouts are unknown I cannot seem to contact. Others have passed on, cannot be thanked and the inevitable 'Author's collection' embraces the work of people who, though possessing the foresight to record the railway scene of the period, seem to have vanished into the mists of time.

The fount of locomotive knowledge goes ever deeper when one encounters Willie Yeadon. His expertise has been invaluable in reading the draft manuscript of this book and adding nuggets of information. He was a leading light in the RCTS series upon which parts of this text rests and has brought the knowledge won during that monumental exercise to bear without stint. My profound thanks to him also.

*E.M.Johnson, Burnage, Manchester, May 1992.*